The Woman Behind the
BLUE CURTAIN

The story of the "God Squad" Puppeteers
and Aletha Joice, the woman behind the scenes.

Pat Reddekopp

Pat Reddekopp

THE WOMAN BEHIND THE BLUE CURTAIN
The Story of the "God Squad" Puppeteers and Aletha Joice

Copyright © 2009 Patricia Reddekopp

Illustrations by Tara Epp.

ISBN-10: 1-926676-14-9
ISBN-13: 978-1-926676-14-2

Printed by Word Alive Press
131 Cordite Road, Winnipeg, MB R3W 1S1
www.wordalivepress.ca

WORD ALIVE PRESS
Just Write!

*To all the people who
have had a part in this story being written.*

ACKNOWLEDGEMENTS

Many hours of work reach completion before the curtain rises on scene one of a play. So also with the writing of *The Woman Behind the Blue Curtain*. I am deeply indebted to the family and friends of Aletha Joice. They told me about the person she was and the effect her touch had on their lives.

The story would not have come to fruition without the assistance of Aletha's husband. Glenn ate my cooking without bribery when he came to our house to answer questions, and willingly provided help in gathering information. He provided pictures and sorted through boxes of journals and puppet production materials for me. Reading the first rough draft to check the accuracy of facts I had included in the manuscript was not easy, yet Glenn also willingly consented to do that.

Aletha's daughter Bette-Jean[1] and her husband Don, Aletha's son Bob Joice[2] and his wife Shelley, along with their son Jake, spoke gladly of a woman who was a loving mother and grandmother. Though not a perfect woman, they told me of someone who was strong in her commitment to the Lord and her family. I extend a bouquet of thanks to them.

God Squad alumni, some now adults with children of their own, each had a part in bringing the memories of God Squad to life again. Contacting all of the former puppeteers was not possible, therefore I tried to speak to the earliest members, those who had been with God Squad longer lengths of time, and those who were part of the troop toward the end. I'm sure each of those who were unable to tell me about their memories, or did not respond, would have had their own unique stories to tell.

Often the response to my questions was "I'm not sure I have enough to tell." Nevertheless each person, whether it was one of Aletha's siblings, a friend from the past, or more recent friend and co-worker in various ministries, gave me a glimpse of the woman behind the blue curtain. Together it was enough for her story to unfold.

I owe great gratitude to Dawna Friesen, who, at the prompting of the Lord, volunteered to do proofreading. She became the answer to my prayer for someone who would be willing to proofread the manuscript with me. The time was right.

I wish as well to express my gratitude to Caroline Schmidt, publication consultant; Evan Braun, editor and formatter; Nicky Braun, cover designer; and Jen Jandays-Hedlin, events poster creator at Word Alive. Their hard work and willingness to share their expertise taught me much about what it takes to bring a finished book to you, the reader.

Thank you to future playwright Carolyn Gartke, who used her knowledge to go over *Martha's Folly* with an eye for how a skit should look. Your help despite your busy schedule was very special.

My thanks also to Leon & Janey Goertzen for their care and diligence in helping with the illustration photos.

My heartfelt thanks to my most stalwart encourager and supporter, my husband Dave. He never seemed to tire of listening when I vented ideas with him.

My thanks to our Heavenly Father, who provided this writer, usually introverted, with the courage to conduct interviews. Answers to questions made this book a possibility. During the process of determining who Aletha was, I also discovered more about the God she served and loved.

It is my prayer that in reading about this woman's life, a woman who wanted her Savior to be yours, you will come to understand that the heavenly Father she has gone to be with loves you just as deeply.

INTRODUCTION

The Woman Behind the Blue Curtain is a story about a woman dedicated to sharing her Lord Jesus with others. It was not intended to be a mystery story, yet I discovered I was trying to solve a mystery. Who was the woman behind the blue curtain? Who was Aletha Joice?

I interviewed dozens of people to help me find the answer. Each person had a unique comment or impression about the person they perceived Aletha to be. As I probed deeper, my questions and interest increased. I began to understand that the mystery, of the person Aletha was, would not be totally solved this side of heaven. I realized what an awesome job I had taken on to try and portray who Aletha was as a woman, wife, mother, grandmother, friend, and most of all, follower of God.

As I read the materials and journals Aletha's husband Glenn lent to me and spoke to people of all ages who had known and worked with Aletha, I found I could not write. Something painful inside me was resisting, preventing me from forming the words. Then I recognized the pain I was feeling. It was sorrow over the death of a woman I had been acquainted with before, but now knew in a way that caused me to grieve all over again. It wasn't until I accepted that the recording of her story would hurt at times that I could continue writing.

The Woman Behind the Blue Curtain is also about a troupe of young puppeteers, called God Squad, who were behind the curtain with Aletha, sharing in a puppet ministry. The God Squad story began long before the formation of the words to tell the tale in this book. It originated in the heart of a sixteen-year-old girl. After seeing some puppets in Winona Lake, Indiana come alive, she began to dream of using puppetry to tell about Jesus.

"I could use the puppets to teach health," a now mature Bette-Jean told me as we looked at the rows of puppet characters she had inherited, "or use puppetry as an art form in drama club. But if it stayed with that, it wouldn't be a ministry." Ministry was what her mother, Aletha Joice, wanted God Squad to be for the young people she loved.

This book is not a sequenced timeline or calendar of events. It is instead a collective event—the impact Aletha had before her Lord called her home, and the influence her life continues to have after she went to be with Him.

TABLE OF CONTENTS

THE CURTAIN IS ALMOST DOWN

BOOK ONE:

THE STORY OF
ALETHA JOICE BEGINS

The conversations and settings beginning the chapters in Book One are based on events that happened in the life of Aletha Joice. Although they employ actual names, the circumstances and conversations, apart from occasional phrases from Aletha's journals, are of the writer's imagination.

The essay style text appearing after the italicized narrative portions contain factual information.

"Lord, whatever is in my hand..."

Baby Born

"*It's a girl!*" *The wails of the infant the doctor handed to the midwife filled the tired mother with joy.*

Working quickly, the midwife wrapped the infant tightly in a warm, flannel blanket.

"Look at all that dark hair, mama," she said, gently placing the newborn daughter into the mother's waiting arms.

Elizabeth looked down into the little eyes. "I wonder what kind of person you will grow up to be, little one," she whispered.

Touching her infant's cheek tenderly, she continued. "Your father will be anxious to see you. You have brothers and a sister at home who want to meet you, too."

She looked up as the midwife reached out to take the baby. "We'll bring her to you again when you're settled in your room."

Elizabeth looked at the beautiful face of the baby in her arms. Leaning close, she kissed Aletha's soft cheek before handing her to the midwife.

As the midwife walked away with the new baby in her arms, Elizabeth marveled at the awesomeness of birth. A prayer for her daughter filled her heart. "May she love You, dear Father," she prayed. "May her life count for Your kingdom."

The jostling of the springless sleigh along the rutted road made Elizabeth want to groan, but her heart was joyful. As they came around the bend, she realized that despite all the work that lay ahead in raising her growing family, she was glad to be going home.

The tall hip roof on the barn came into view first, and then the house.

Walter stopped the horses and wrapped the reins around the post at the front of the sleigh box. He stepped down from the sleigh, then reached up for the baby so Elizabeth could climb down.

Elizabeth walked up to the front door of their small two-story house. She stopped on the step and took a deep breath. The non-antiseptic smells of the barnyard told her she was home.

Aletha Mary (Rogers) Joice was born on January 12, 1929 in Oungre, Saskatchewan.[i] Her parents, Walter and Elizabeth Rogers, lived on a farm near Oungre. The youngest of five siblings, Aletha had three older brothers—Franklin, Clifford, and Ken—and an older sister, Dorothy. At the time of this writing, Franklin and Dorothy have gone to be with the Lord. Franklin was killed during World War Two and Dorothy died in December 2001.

There were many babies born at that time and Dr. Brown, who delivered the babies, is reported to have remarked that the new town of Oungre, with such prolific births, should really be something.

"One of the benefits of being the baby is that you are not expected to be able to do anything. I made sure that was true just as long as I could." –ALETHA JOICE

---

[i] See Appendix I: More Information, Just for the Fun of It—"Oungre."

Brother

"Why would I want to hold her?" Eleven-year-old Franklin crossed his arms in front of his chest and glared at his mother.

"Son, you may not have any extra love for your baby sister, but you will speak respectfully to your mother." Franklin's father spoke sternly as he pushed his chair back from the dinner table. "Besides," he continued, "it wouldn't hurt you to be helpful with her."

Franklin opened his mouth to say more, then looked up at his father and decided to leave instead.

"Why would they want to have a baby at their age anyway?" Franklin muttered to himself as he went out the door. "They're too old to have a baby!"

The days sped by and before he knew it Franklin was watching his little sister totter across the floor to him. He had resisted at first, but it wasn't long before she had slipped into a place in his heart.

"Franklin," called his mother one day, "we're leaving. Come down so you're closer to Aletha. She's pretty fast on those little legs."

Franklin closed his magazine and, taking the stairs two at a time, plopped himself down on the living room floor where Aletha sat with some building blocks.

Aletha and her brother Franklin became closer as they grew up. When he was a teen, Franklin would take Aletha along when he was going out with his friends, as did her other brothers.

During the war, when Franklin went overseas, he gave Aletha a heart-shaped locket with the army insignia on the front. It contained space for pictures of the 'men' in Aletha's life, her three brothers Ken, Clifford, and Franklin.

"Time is precious but truth is more precious than time." –ALETHA JOICE

Granny's Quilt

A blue barrette holding her dark curls, Aletha sat quietly in front of her Granny's chair and observed carefully as Granny stitched. Granny looked up and smiled.

"See this red square?" Granny asked, pointing to the piece of flannel cloth on which she was working.

Aletha looked at the block Granny was touching.

"It's a piece from your father's shirt. There were still some good parts on the back, so I could get some nice red pieces. This one is from your Mama's old apron dress. It's pretty, don't you think?"

Aletha nodded and returned her grandmother's loving smile.

"Why do you call it a crazy quilt Grandma?"

"In days long ago, people began to put together pieces of clothes which weren't worn out yet. No two quilts were alike because the pieces were put together in whatever crazy way it worked. The shape of the pieces decided the pattern. Sometimes they would use fancy stitches on the seams of the pieces like I'm doing."

Aletha stood watching the needle going in and out of the fabric a little longer, then turned and went out of her Granny's room. She loved being with her Granny, but the outdoors called, too.

Her grandmother was a special person in Aletha's life. Granny Rogers, her father's mother, was widowed early in life and when Aletha was seven years old she came to live with the family. Aletha spent a lot of time in her grandmother's room, where she was introduced not only to crazy quilts,[i] but also to Jesus Christ, whose love she experienced through her grandmother.

Her grandmother was a frugal person, and at Christmas time when Aletha heard rustling sounds in her grandmother's room, she knew Granny was wrapping gifts with brown paper.

---

[i] See Appendix 1: More Information, Just for the Fun of It—"Crazy Quilts."

In a talk at a women's meeting one Christmas, referring to the special part her grandmother had in her life, Aletha described Granny Rogers as her "comfort and joy quilt patch."

"Granny made me my own crazy quilt, a comforter from the wool of my sheep, and a pillow from the feathers of my pet rooster. I still have my pillow. The crazy quilt has worn out. The comforter needs a new cover and the wool reworked." –ALETHA JOICE

Butt, Butt!

Aletha sat quietly so the kittens wouldn't be startled and run away. But the sunshine was so warm on the spot where the kittens curled up beside their mother that they just kept sleeping.

Aletha loved to climb up the long ladder along the wall in the barn to get to the hayloft. She had taken a downy chick along which, as usual, slept under her sleeve, in the crook of her arm.

Tiring of the kittens' inactivity today, Aletha moved the baby chick into her hands and went back down the ladder. When she came out the big barn door, Chubby rose and stretched. The collie sauntered along behind her, occasionally coming close for a rub behind his ears.

Aletha wandered around the yard, visiting the pigs, the roosters, and the new wooly lambs. When she approached the fence beside the barn, Fly, her favorite horse, stuck his head over the top rail. Aletha reached out to scratch his face. He nuzzled into her chest and then, satisfied at the attention, moved away to munch on more grass. He looked up briefly as the cows came past from the back of the barn.

Aletha leaned on the fence watching Fly and the cows until a jubilant shout came from behind the barn. "They're doing it again," Aletha muttered, dashing into the wide front door and through the dark interior of the barn.

"Come on you guys!" she shouted over the closed half of the split back door. "Stop tormenting Percy!" [i]

Her brothers looked up at her standing in the doorway and laughed.

"Aw, Aletha. He loves it. Watch!" they said, and swung the red cloth again. Percy gave a half-hearted run at it.

The snugly lamb she had brought home was no longer a lamb, and her brothers had taught Percy to butt. It was humorous to see Percy chasing unsuspecting visitors, but now they were bull fighting, with poor Percy as the bull.

"Enough," Aletha said, lifting the heavy metal latch on the door. She went to the panting sheep and began rubbing his neck. He leaned gratefully into her side.

---

[i] See Appendix 1: More Information, Just for the Fun of It—"Ewes, Lambs, and Percy."

When Aletha was seven, her parents moved to a farm near the village of Rapid City, Manitoba. The Little Saskatchewan River[ii] flowed through the ranch where the Rogers family lived, providing many hours of entertainment—including swimming and other river adventures. Aletha would float down the river, looking up at the clouds drifting overhead.

"I fell heir to the endless delights of the former horse ranch," Aletha said. She used the word *glorious* to describe horseback riding to her heart's content. She loved having pets—cats, dogs, roosters, pigs, horses, and sheep—particularly a lamb named Percy.

As an adult, when Aletha attended the local agricultural fair, she would go through the barns looking at the sheep. "She had a love for animals. She loved to tell stories about her pets." –ELAINE WALRATH[3]

[ii] See Appendix 1: More Information, Just for the Fun of It—"Little Sask."

The Shepherd's Care

"She's at it again," Granny sighed, watching Aletha's little pajama clad figure walk through her room. She called softly to her, but the little girl paid no attention. Not wanting to startle her awake, she let her go. Then, pushing the multi-colored quilt aside, she rose and went to the door, watching her granddaughter run quickly down the steps.

Going back to her bed, Granny lay down again and pulled the quilt around her shoulders. Tonight she would just have to wait. Last night, she had been able to stop her and tuck her in with her for the night, but tonight she hadn't noticed her coming in time.

Granny listened for the whistle she knew would come, then smiled as she heard the squeak of the back door closing. The click of the dog's toenails and patter of bare feet going through her room was followed by the creaking of the bed springs. Her little Aletha was once more settled in for the night.

"At times, I understand how the shepherd felt about lying at the door of the sheepfold," she said to herself. "I am aware of her wanderings and I'm watchful of her even though she doesn't know it."

"I (Aletha) did a lot of sleepwalking in my early years. To go downstairs, I had to go through my grandmother's room. If she couldn't stop me without waking me before I got to the head of the stairs, she'd let me go... because I just flew down those steps. Usually I'd go out the back door, whistle for my dog, and go back up to bed. But if she could stop me and talk me into bed with her,[i] I'd sleep safe and secure under her crazy quilt! And wake up in the morning wondering how I got there!" –Aletha Joice

"A shepherd... lies down at the entrance to the sheepfold to keep the enemy out. In my case, it was to keep this sheep in! And this sheep knew and trusted the 'shepherd's' voice, my Granny's!" –Aletha Joice

---

[i] The phrase "Talk me into bed" is Aletha's. It's a shortened way of saying, "Talk me into getting into bed."

Feather Tick

The feather tick folded around her as she landed in the middle of the cozy warmth. Aletha lay still for only a second, savoring the enjoyment of the billowy depths. Getting off the bed, she quickly fluffed the feather tick. Satisfied that it was again its original height, she went to the top of the stairs and listened for voices in the kitchen. Not hearing any, she went over to the window and glanced down into the garden. Her mother and grandmother were bent over the vegetable rows, pulling weeds.

"Oh, goody," she whispered, turning and taking another flying leap into the feathery mattress. She lay there, still savoring the sheer pleasure of it, then rose and fluffed away the traces of what she had been doing.

"Under her crazy quilt was a feather tick.[i] What a lot of down... it must have taken to fill that sheet-sized bag mattress. I'd eye her wondrously heaped-up bed, listen for Granny, then take a flying leap—into the middle of it, if I could! What a soft, cozy warm spot that was... Then I'd crawl out as quickly as I could [and] try to fluff it up to its original height so Granny wouldn't notice. I'm sure Granny always knew when I couldn't resist, but I can't remember her ever scolding me for it.

"The times of fun, leaping into Granny's feather tick, have long gone. Even then, the... joy was short lived—for fear Granny would catch me in the act!"
–Aletha Joice

Granny Rogers was still living when Glenn and Aletha got married, which provided Glenn the opportunity to become acquainted with Aletha's grandmother. He said she was a wiry, agile lady, and reminded him of Granny Clampet from the television show *The Beverly Hillbillies.*

---

[i] See Appendix 1: More Information, Just for the Fun of It—"Feather Tick."

School Days

The school bell clanged out its end of day message, and before the last tones faded over the hills, all that was left in the classroom was the dust settling on the recently occupied desks.

Aletha pedaled along the road, thinking about how much she loved going to school. The reading was the most fun. A song bird whistled and she stopped to look up at the trees to see if she could spot it. Maybe it would be a warbler like the one in the book today.

Aletha shivered and got back on her bicycle. In a short while, she would no longer be able to take her bike to school. The cool wind almost felt like winter would arrive tomorrow.

"How was school?" her mother asked as Aletha came in the door.

"Fine. We're getting parts for a play tomorrow. I hope I get something good."

Her mother smiled and turned back to peeling the potatoes. "Bring some carrots from the garden, would you?"

"Can I bring some popping corn, too?" Aletha leaned around the doorway, a garden basket in her hand. "Let's have a popcorn feast."[i]

"It's a little too early for the corn in the garden. It has to be dried first. But I suppose we could have a feast. I think there is still some popcorn left in the jar from last year. First we'll have to see if we have enough cream left to make the ice cream."

"Oh, goody," Aletha cheered, going out the door.

The Rogers' farm home was only one and a third miles away from the town of Rapid City, Manitoba, so most of the time in summer Aletha would ride her bike to school. On cold winter days, her father took her "in a wonderfully warm, covered sleigh." She describes how she hopped in and hopped out, not giving "any thought to his welfare; his cold fingers, his time there and back, his care of the horses... it was wonderful to be dependent." –ALETHA JOICE

---

[i] See Glossary for definition of popcorn feast.

Aletha compared her father's efforts to the time when their own children went to school. "It was I who scraped the miserable wind shields, heated the car, and drove there and back in all kinds of weather and on all kinds of streets!"
–ALETHA JOICE

Family Altar

The evening meal finished, Mother went to get the Bible.

As her mother began reading, Aletha listened with a part of her, but the other part was paying attention to what was happening around the table.

"...whatsoever things are lovely, whatsoever things are good, think on these things." [i]

Aletha's attention came back as Mother read the last words, then stopped and closed the Bible.

"Let's pray together," she said, kneeling down beside her chair. The rest of the family knelt, too, but it was like a signal that it was time to have a bit of fun. One brother playfully punched the other in the shoulder. The second one retaliated. Mother's glance stopped them for a short while, but as she bowed her head again, the teasing began anew. Aletha grinned at them and looked at her father, who was smiling at their antics.

Her mother asked God to bless each of them, to give them a personal knowledge of His love. Aletha listened to her mother's voice, wondering whether she would ever be able talk to God as though He were right there, the way her mother did. It was like she was talking to a close friend.

The family altar, or family devotions, were different in each of Aletha and Glenn's backgrounds.

Aletha described the family devotions in her background—fairly formal Bible reading and prayer—as the kind the family endured. In Aletha's childhood home, her mother led the Bible reading after supper. "Mother read—I think we were attentive then. We all knelt for prayer—Free Methodists did in those days. Mother prayed and I'm not proud of what happened then. We kids fooled around. Dad amused my brothers, pestered the cat, I rescued it. It was not a good scene."

For Glenn, evening devotions came sometime after supper, often—it seemed like always!—interrupting the fun of a great game of ball or tin can

---

[i] Philippians 4:8 (KJV).

cricket. Glenn's father would read Scripture, after which his mother or father prayed. He did not remember enjoying it, anxious to get back out to the game.

"While we didn't enjoy the kind we endured," Aletha continued, "we respected them in that our parents were doing what they felt was right for us... and were doing it out of love for us. What we both remember with appreciation is that our mothers always had private altar times, personal devotions, of Bible reading and prayer."

Aletha wanted family devotions in their home to be an enjoyable, fun, short time. "Glenn stuck to the more traditional type," she said, "especially *long* prayers! I'm sure my short prayers were not more meaningful than Glenn's—the kids always sensed his love for them and his forgiving spirit."

In a talk Aletha gave about the family altar, she concluded that "whether highly creative or not, participation of each family member is important. The kids will not always enjoy the family altar... but there will be memorable times that will make every effort worthwhile and special bonding will take place." –ALETHA JOICE

Weeds in the Trees?

Aletha set her lunch pail down on the kitchen cupboard and called to her mother. There was no answer, so she tiptoed to her parents' bedroom and peeked around the doorframe. She wasn't napping.

"Mother?" Aletha opened the door to the upper floor stairway and called again. No response there either.

The living room was quiet except for the ticking of the big grandfather clock. No point in checking Granny's room. She was away at Uncle Harold's for the day.

Her resources not used up, Aletha went out the back door and skipped across the grass to the barn. When she couldn't find her mother there either, she began to grow a bit worried.

Turning back toward the house, she spotted a dark blue patch among the trees at the far side of the garden. Relieved, Aletha went along the path between the rows of vegetables toward her mother. When she came closer, she opened her mouth to tease her mother about looking for weeds in the trees because she couldn't find enough in the garden, but what she saw stopped her. Her mother was kneeling with her head bowed. She had her hands tightly clasped in her lap, and her soft voice reached Aletha's ears. Although she was too far away to catch the words, Aletha knew her mother was praying.

Aletha turned quietly and went back to the house, the image of her mother kneeling among the trees firmly embedded in her mind

Aletha records in one of her journals that the memories of not finding her mother when she came home from school, and then "seeing her out in the trees praying, made a definite lasting impression." Other memories of Bible stories read, help in memorizing Scripture passages, and regular Sunday School and church attendance also impressed themselves on her mind.

Although her Father was not a Christian at that time, Aletha wrote that from her Dad she "learned the joy of living and the value of work." She recalled evenings "sitting on his knee, singing hymns, Irish songs, or roughing.[i] He worked hard and loved hard."

---

[i] See Glossary for the definition of roughing.

She felt that her mother's influence had left God's Word in her mind, but it was "truth without relationship." That truth, however, was not lost. Aletha later gave her life to God, the bud of truth her mother gave her from God's Word opening into the full blossom of her relationship with Him.

Although she never heard the words "I love you" from her parents, Aletha knew she was loved. But she promised herself that her children would hear those words along with God's Word.

Stranded!

"It's happened again!"

Father came into the kitchen in the middle of the hot August afternoon and reached for the tall tumbler on the ledge of the big kitchen sink.

"What's happened again?" Mother asked, lifting the last pork chop out of the flour and laying it in the hot frying pan.

Father dipped the blue metal dipper into the water bucket and filled the tumbler with water. He drank quickly. Mother wiped her forehead with her arm and set the empty plate onto the table. She waited while Father filled the tumbler again and began to drink more slowly.

"What's happened again?" Mother repeated, rubbing the sticky flour off her fingers.

Father leaned against the counter. "Someone got stranded in the cable chair. Sometimes I'm almost sorry I built the rotten thing."

"Now, Walter. You know that's not so. You need it to get to the pasture, not to mention the enormous pleasure you get watching the children sail across to the other side."

Father grinned. "You're right. I do love to hear their squeals. Well, I guess there's nothing else I can do except get the boat out and be the hero."

"No better way to cool off," Mother responded, smoothing her hair back from her forehead. She pushed her bottom lip out and blew against her face, a twinkle in her eye. "Supper will be ready by the time you get back."

What was the cable chair or cable swing?[i] It was a one-person chair hung on a pulley, which rolled along a cable stretched across the little river. On each side of the river was a pair of poles to which cables were attached. One cable was fastened at a high position on one pole and across on the other bank, at a low position on the pole opposite. A second cable was similarly fastened to the second set of poles, but the low and high positions were reversed. This way going across was always downhill.

---

[i] See Appendix 1: More Information, Just for the Fun of It—"Cable Chair," for a diagram of the cable chair setup.

On both sides, beside the pole to which the cable was fastened high up, was a platform with steps. The pulley was hooked onto the cable and the chair 'moored' at the pole. Once seated in the chair, the rider could loosen it from its moorings and scoot across the river along the cable.

Upon arrival on the other side, it was necessary to 'run' up the bank while still seated in the chair, stop, and unhook it from the cable. The rider would then climb the steps to the platform and 'moor' the chair on that side of the river, ready to go back.

If the rider did not run up far enough, the chair rolled back along the cable, but wouldn't have enough momentum to get all the way across the river and thus become stranded out over the water.

"I thought, 'Why must I get so down before I get so up?' God's humor came to me: 'If you didn't get down, you wouldn't get up. Foolish child!'" –ALETHA JOICE

War!

The radio crackled a little as the family sat listening in the living room.

"The Allied troops made several advances today..."

Aletha listened to the drone of the man's voice, wishing it would all go away.

"Mother..."

"Shhh. Not now. We're listening to the news."

She looked up at her mother, then once more leaned her head on the arm of the big living room chair. When her mother reached into her pocket for her handkerchief and wiped at her eyes, Aletha felt the familiar squeeze on her heart. How she missed her brothers. It seemed her mother's eyes would never be dry again. It was all so senseless.

When the news broadcast was over, Father reached over and switched the radio off. Sighing, he rose from his chair and went out the door.

Mother unfolded her handkerchief and wiped away more tears. How could she comfort her mother, Aletha wondered. She was sick and didn't need all this bad news every day. It all seemed so useless. Why fight a war? What did it accomplish? Maybe just brothers getting killed.

All three of Aletha's brothers were gone from home at the same time during the war.

Franklin was killed in a traffic accident after a party. Franklin had been the designated driver and was out of the vehicle when another vehicle hit him. It was hard for the family to accept because it could have been prevented.

Cliff was in the army, working in communications, and saw action on the continent following D-Day. He has only recently shared some of his experiences with Glenn.

Ken quit high school to join the army. This was toward the end of the war, so he did not see action.

Aletha experienced the difficulties brought on by the Second World War. "We inherit the social economic conditions of the world in which we grow up. I inherited the World War II years and the resulting traumas. We treasure peace." –ALETHA JOICE

Aletha's mother was ill with cancer and died during the war years. "Her illness [was] exacerbated by all the stress of losing a son in the war, and having the others in danger overseas, I'm sure," Aletha said in a presentation she made.

"Aletha wrote to Franklin when she became a Christian. She liked to believe he had become a Christian due to the pastor's and her letters." –BETTE-JEAN HAND

Romance and Reality

Aletha lifted the edge of the mattress and reached for the magazine she knew would be hidden there. Careful not to tear it, she pulled it out and slid down beside the bed. Leaning against the side, she opened the magazine to the Wild West romance story she had started reading and continued at the place she'd left the day before:

> *Tabitha reached up to brush the shiny mane on her tall gelding,*
> *her mind going back to Harper. So handsome! Tabitha's heart*
> *skipped a beat just thinking about meeting him.*

Settling herself more comfortably, Aletha sighed and turned the page. Soon she was absorbed in the tale of adventure and daring.

> *The creak of the barn door warned Tabitha...*

Turning the page quickly, Aletha felt like she really heard the creaking of the barn door. Just in time, she realized she'd heard the bottom step of the stairs outside her brother's bedroom squeaking. She jumped up and quickly put the magazine back under the mattress.

She reached the hallway just as her grandmother came around the corner of the stairs onto the top landing.

"Hi, Grandma," she said, hoping her guilty feelings didn't show on her face. She waited for her Grandmother to walk past, then skipped lightly down the stairs.

She was never sure why she would sneak up and read her brother's magazines at the risk of being caught. If her mother were still alive, she would not have approved of her behavior. It was just that she couldn't resist the interesting things words told her.

"I've loved the written word as long as I can remember. The Bible stories my mother read to me when I was too young to realize the concepts being instilled [still led me to believe] that God's written word is truth. The fairy tales my sister told me at bedtime took me into a world of fantasy where all the endings were happy ones. My brother's *True Life* magazines that I pulled from under his bed mattress—what romance; what adventure!

"I've become more discriminating, read more biographies, autobiographies, and books that help me in my Christian growth. But there are still times when I'm encouraged by the escape provided through the historic novel—wonderful descriptive and informative passages or hilarious happenings in the 'for fun' books!" –ALETHA JOICE

Aletha's sister Dorothy Evanowich's account in the area history book *Saga of the Souris Valley* indicated that the whole family loved to read. When the *Prairie Farmer*[i] paper arrived, there was a mad scramble to see who would get it first.

"She [Aletha] loved to read and felt there was value in reading. She always gave a book as a gift at a baby shower." –EILEEN REIMCHE[4]

---

[i] See Appendix 1: More Information, Just for the Fun of It—"Prairie Farmer."

Teen Homemaker

Aletha lay with her hands behind her head, looking up at the ceiling, trying not to cry anymore. Everything had changed. In spite of her resolve, the tears forced their way out of the corners of her eyes and joined the others on the tear-soaked pillow.

"Mother, why did you have to die?" she whispered. "It's so hard to do all the things you did so easily."

Death was becoming part of her life. She grieved the death of her mother, the death of her carefree happiness.

Her carefree days had been replaced with meal preparation, cleaning house, and dealing with that big old washing machine. "I'm sure I'll never conquer undoing the tangled mess it makes of father's farm overalls," Aletha said, sitting up on the side of the bed. And that fire-spitting monster she had to use to iron the clothes! How would she ever overcome her fear of it?

The mental picture of her mother's lifeless body intruded into Aletha's thoughts, the rough hands so used to holding a garden hoe now amazingly white and soft.

Was she really dead?

Aletha rose slowly and walked over to the window. Resting her forehead on the cool glass, she stared out at the darkened yard below. She had heard her mother read many verses from her Bible about everlasting life, that those who accepted God's forgiveness lived with him after they died.

Deep down, Aletha believed her mother was in heaven.

At fourteen, Aletha experienced a great sense of aloneness after her Mother's death. Her Granny was not able to take over the housework, so new responsibilities came into young Aletha's life. Aletha describes them in her testimony booklet, *My Confrontation with Death and Life.* "This teen, who had been the 'odd-jobber' around the farm, glad not to know any household skills, now had a rapid course in cooking, cleaning, untangling mangled overalls in the gasoline-powered washing machine, [and] lighting that flame-throwing gasoline iron![i] My

---

[i] See Appendix I: More Information, Just for the Fun of It—"Gasoline Iron."

two brothers and sister were not at home, so I was doing everything from housework to trying to learn to cook, to farm chores, to taking eleventh grade."

But there were times of encouragement as well. Aletha continues, "I remember the day of the funeral, as we came out of the church... a lady stepped from among the people lining the walk and stopped me, the bewildered fourteen-year-old, giving me words of sympathy and love. What did those words say to me? That I was worthy of her notice, that she recognized that I had needs, too, that I was of value! I don't know if I ever remembered her actual words, but I've never forgotten her loving touch and how it boosted my spirits and morale that day." –ALETHA JOICE

"For followers of Jesus, death does not take us away from home. It brings us home." –PHILIP GUNTHER

Again Some Day

The hot afternoon sun felt like it would melt the skin right off her body. Aletha paused from pulling weeds in the flower bed and straightened up. She reflected again about the verses and stories her mother had taught her, the verses that said if she believed in Jesus she would have everlasting life.[i]

"Mother believed in Jesus, so that means she's in heaven. I want to see her again someday, so I need to get to know God and believe like she did." Aletha realized she had spoken aloud.

She turned back to the weeds and as she worked began to sort through how to go about getting to know God the way her mother did. Or the way Granny did; Granny was a picture of God's love.

Granny had told her about the verse that told how Jesus came to earth "to be pierced for her transgressions, to be crushed for her iniquities,"[ii] so that she could know the hope of eternal life when she believed in and accepted Jesus, the Son of God, into her life.

Later that week, having concluded that one should be able to find God in church, Aletha went to a small midweek meeting where she knelt and talked to Jesus, God's Son, who was sent to die for her sins.

"Dear Jesus," she confessed, "I'm scared, scared to die or to live. I've been afraid you would take all the fun out of living. I know my mom is with you forever and I'd like to see my mom again. Forgive me for shutting you out of my life."

As Aletha finished her prayer, she sensed unbelievable peace bathe her wounded spirit. She knew she had been forgiven. God had accepted her as His child!

"At the time of my mother's death" Aletha wrote, "I'd been forced to think of God and the hereafter. She had taught me very carefully about heaven and how to get there. I knew that God had sent Jesus to live and die for my sin. That because He rose from the dead, I through Jesus could go to heaven one day... I knew my mom had gone there.

---

[i] In reference to John 3:16 (KJV).
[ii] In reference to Isaiah 53:5 (NIV).

"So at fourteen, I confessed my sin and accepted Jesus into my life. I remember being surprised and grateful for the peace that flooded my mind and spirit. Jesus says in the Bible, 'Here I am, I stand at the door and knock, if anyone hears my voice and opens the door, I will come in.'[iii] You'll agree that my mother's death had... forced me to consider my mother's teachings.

"The big challenge I faced could have defeated me had it not been for that heaven-sent peace." –ALETHA JOICE

"Granny's lasting... joy... became mine when I too accepted Jesus Christ... when I took that leap into God's all-enveloping, eternal feather tick! And I didn't have to quickly crawl out, but could remain in His love." –ALETHA JOICE

[iii] Revelation 3:20 (NIV).

True Love Forever

The minister opened his book and looked up at Aletha's father standing beside the woman he was marrying. "Walter, do you take this woman to be your lawfully wedded wife?"[i]

Aletha's tears were near the surface again, but she couldn't give in to them.

"To have and to hold from this day forward, for better or for worse, for richer, for poorer, in sickness and in health, to love and to cherish, and to be faithful to her alone, till death do you part?"

"I do."

"Marian, do you..."

Fifteen-year-old Aletha knew her father's reasons, but she still felt like he had already forgotten her mother. It wasn't even a year since she had died. How could he be thinking of marrying another woman so soon?

She glanced over at the boy sitting in the pew across the aisle. He was going to be her brother. Weird. He grinned at her and she quickly ducked her head. Truth be told, he seemed like he might be okay.

"I now pronounce you husband and wife. What God has..."

The questions in Aletha's head began again: What if this new mother doesn't like me? What is going to happen to our family? Dad, wasn't Mother your true love? It's supposed to be forever!

As they were completing the evening chores a few days later, Aletha set her bucket in the aisle behind the cow her father was milking and sat down on a stool. He looked up at her briefly and then put his forehead back against the side of the cow and continued milking. Aletha watched quietly, then taking a deep breath asked her father her burning question.

"Dad, didn't you love mother?"

Her father's hands stopped and he turned to her.

"Aletha, no one can ever take your mother's place in my heart."

Aletha stood up and picked up her bucket and stool. She could dream again. Romantic love was still alive.

---

[i] Wording of wedding vows taken from *The Minister's Manual*, 1983, Faith & Life Press. Used by permission.

"Milking cows together is a wonderfully cozy place for conversation. Dad started reminiscing about my mother... what she was like when they met, etc. One time, he gave me his words, 'Aletha, no one else will ever take your mother's place in my heart.' I got the picture completely. I was fully satisfied and seemed to understand his need to fill the lonely void. And you know, I still believe true love's forever!" –ALETHA JOICE

When Aletha's father remarried, the joining of the two families brought three brothers into the family. "How do two babies of families cope in one family?" she wrote. "Actually Jim and I became good close friends. What one couldn't get as 'the baby,' the other could!" –ALETHA JOICE

What was in Aletha's hand at this point was the decision that she had made to follow Jesus Christ, to trust her eternal life to Him. She did not yet know what the rest of her life would hold, or how much more she would need to yield to Him.

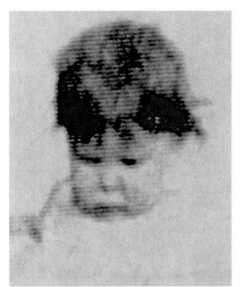

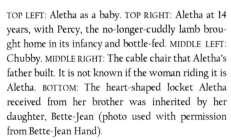

TOP LEFT: Aletha as a baby. TOP RIGHT: Aletha at 14 years, with Percy, the no-longer-cuddly lamb brought home in its infancy and bottle-fed. MIDDLE LEFT: Chubby. MIDDLE RIGHT: The cable chair that Aletha's father built. It is not known if the woman riding it is Aletha. BOTTOM: The heart-shaped locket Aletha received from her brother was inherited by her daughter, Bette-Jean (photo used with permission from Bette-Jean Hand).

"I commit to You..."

Too Much Freedom

"Aletha." Father's unusually quiet voice spoke her name as she sat reading in the living room one evening. She looked up, wondering at the sober look in his eyes. "Aletha, I've noticed how hard it is for you to be at home here."

"I miss Mom so much," Aletha responded, looking down at her book, willing the tears not to come.

Her father reached over and squeezed her arm. "I want you to be happy."

"Everything is so different, Dad."

"I know, but sometimes life changes." He paused and looked out of the window. The summer rain was spatting against the pane. The overcast sky seemed to add effect to the somber mood inside. "I've been considering something, Aletha," her father continued. "I think you should go to Moose Jaw to finish high school." There was another pause as if he was considering whether he would say more. "You would be okay on your own."

"But..." Aletha stopped and looked at her father. She would miss home, but maybe it would be less unhappy.

"I know it's a long way from home, but you could board at the Bible college dorm."

Suddenly the dream of freedom from the struggles with her stepmother presented itself to Aletha. She knew she wanted to go.

Aletha struggled with the way things turned out when her father remarried. She said, "Home was never home again." Thus she was launched on her own at a young age.

Boarding at Aldersgate College, Aletha attended Central Collegiate in Moose Jaw for her senior year. After high school, she attended Tuxedo Teacher's College in Winnipeg, Manitoba and graduated with a Teacher's Certificate at the age of seventeen.

"Living the Christian life is not hard—it's *impossible* without Christ in me."
–Aletha Joice

Peace and Purpose

"Hand me that knife, Aletha. Blade first, if you please."

Bill's sarcasm made Aletha smile. It was really quite enjoyable making supper together when his mother was busy with other things.

"A good thing happened when your mother died," Bill said, slicing into the pan the potato he had peeled. Aletha looked up from opening a jar of fruit preserves for dessert. Having thought he would expand on his comment, when he said nothing else, the hurt of his statement brought unexpected tears to her eyes. Noticing her tears, Bill hastened to amend his statement. "Oh, man, that didn't come out right. I didn't mean it was good that she died. What I meant by 'good' was you had to learn to cook. Now we can make some half-decent meals when my mom isn't here doing it."

Understanding that he was making amends for his earlier comment, Aletha smiled through her tears. She knew Bill was just as good a cook as she was, but it made her feel good to have him compliment her.

Supper over, Aletha went to her room and reached for the college catalogue on her desk. The college in Seattle, Seattle Pacific College, offered degrees in education. Her love of teaching brought the desire to get more training and Seattle College had some good programs. The correspondence course via closed circuit TV appealed to her, too. It would be as if she was right there hearing the professors lecture.

Aletha began recollecting her time at Teacher's College, remembering being ready for the adventure and fun of being away from home. It had turned out to be more freedom than she could handle. She still regretted those poor grades while dating took the upper hand in her life.

"Those blind dates," Aletha muttered to herself, laying the catalogue down. The feeling of disgust she had felt over things some students did at parties rose to the surface of her deliberations. She got up from her desk and went for her Bible.

The routine of daily Bible reading and prayer had become a habit. She again found the peace and purpose for living she had first discovered as a young teen when her mother died.

"I often thought the adventures called for my ways rather than God's ways. So time after time, I tried to live in the fast lane, where my associates were people who sought pleasure at any cost, submerging any thought of the shortness of life and the 'what comes after life' question.

"I was always pulled back by my confrontation with death... and how God had taken me into His family. I remembered my mother's daily ways of Bible reading and prayer and knew that was the only pattern that could keep leading me to heaven and a meaningful life here." –ALETHA JOICE (from *My Confrontation with Life and Death*)

"At that time and many others, my guardian angel, called on by my mother's prayers before she died, I'm sure, was very busy." –ALETHA JOICE

Evaluation

Aletha lifted the felt brush and began erasing the math questions on the blackboard behind her desk. As she went to clean off the blackboard at the side of the room, she glanced over at the superintendent of schools.[i] He unfolded himself from the student's desk he had seated himself in earlier and reached for his coat. Aletha felt glad he needed to be in other classes for part of the day. It was difficult to concentrate on teaching when he was in the class evaluating everything she did.

Aletha finished and went back to her desk. She closed the books she had been using for the last lesson and stacked them on the corner.

What an enjoyable year she was having at this little country school. It was like a big, happy family. The children loved rushing into their ski pants and playing wild games of soccer or anti-anti-over[ii] at recess! It was good exercise for her, too.

What a relief it was to know the superintendent wasn't going to give her a bad time about the window that had broken just before he arrived.

"I will bid you farewell," the superintendent said, coming to the front of the room.

Aletha smiled in response, reaching for his extended hand. "I trust you had a pleasant day."

"I did, thank you." A smile came briefly to his face as he said the words. Placing his hat on his head, he went out the door.

Aletha heard him begin whistling as he disappeared down the hall.

Reaching for her own coat, Aletha contemplated her day. She was sure she had done well, but it was always a relief when the superintendent's visit and evaluation was completed.

"I learned I had inherited organizational and leadership skills as I faced the challenge of teaching seven grades!" Aletha stated in a presentation she made.

In her first teaching position at Garthmore, Manitoba, Aletha had one student in each grade. She spoke of it as being like one, happy family, a starting block for what lay ahead.

---

[i] See Appendix 1: More Information, Just for the Fun of It—"Superintendent of Schools," for more on this type of teacher evaluation.

[ii] See Glossary for explanation of the game anti-anti-over.

"My love of the outdoors and nature, reading, music, and laughter came in very handy. I faced future classes with great optimism and confidence."
–ALETHA JOICE

The next year, Aletha had a Grade 3-4 class at Ochre River, Manitoba. This was a tough class to... manage, including uncontrollable bladders and lice. She wasn't sure how she was going to do it any better than the teachers who'd had the group before. However, with the help of the more experienced teachers on staff, and by becoming a strict disciplinarian, within a few months they were enjoying projects she wouldn't have dared earlier in the year.

"You cannot clean your own field while at the same time counting the rocks on your neighbors." –ALETHA JOICE

"Ten Desk" Sneeze

The snarls and sharp barking of several dogs came through the open window. Aletha rubbed her forehead and tried to bring her mind back to her lesson preparation for the next day. She wanted to make this new section of the Social Studies course as appealing as possible for her Grade 4 class.

"Speaking of appeal," Aletha said under her breath, "I hope I get set up to show that film without a problem tomorrow."[i]

Aletha laid down her pen and stretched her fingers, momentarily drawn back into her memories.

The children in her class this year were not as easily distracted from their work as the Grade 3-5 class the previous year. Dealing with distractions had not been easy, especially when she'd been trying to concentrate on which roller the film went around next when she was threading it through the projector.

She still didn't understand the kicking sprees one of last year's students got into every few days, but there had been some lighter moments last year, too. She smiled at the recollection of twenty-year-old Ben's explosive sneeze. It must have sent papers flying in a ten desk radius. "Well, maybe not ten," she amended to herself, "but I sure had to get out of the classroom with my fit of giggles."

Picking up a little box from the corner of her desk, Aletha raised the lid and lifted a little tie clip off its cotton cushion. The Scotty dog on it was so cute. The clip was a gift for one of her fourth graders—a prize for perfect attendance. What a trooper!

Although he would not have recognized it as a fourth grade student, Dr. Wayne Hindmarsh[5] remembers Aletha's "excellent teaching skills and patience with all of us." He was in her class in Grandview, Manitoba during her third year of teaching.

Dr. Hindmarsh, who at the time of this writing is with the faculty at the University of Toronto, said in a letter, "I liked school so much that year that I

---

[i] See Appendix 1: More Information, Just for the Fun of It—"Film Projection."

had perfect attendance." In fact, he added, "she gave me a tie clip... in recognition of not missing a day of school." The little Scotty dog is still in his possession.

Aletha and Wayne were in touch over the years. She would encourage him and take pride in his accomplishments. "She felt she had a part in my successes," he said. "And she did!"

When Wayne and his wife moved to Regina as a young couple expecting their first child, they became good friends with Glenn and Aletha, a friendship that was to span fifty years. Lois, Wayne's wife, still talks about "her kind, patient, thoughtful behavior" and they remain thankful she was there for them.[ii]

The Scotty dog on the tie clip Aletha gave her student. Photo courtesy of Dr. Wayne Hindmarsh.

[ii]Quoted excerpts are taken from a letter Wayne Hindmarsh wrote about his memories of Aletha.

Changes and God's Leading

"It was a 'tough-living' little village. To have any social life, I had begun to bend my lifestyle," Aletha said to the young man walking beside her. Although Glenn was almost four years younger than she was, she was definitely attracted to this cute fellow.

"It was pretty rough having to leave your job there."

Aletha nodded.

They walked on in silence, each absorbed in their own introspections. Aletha reviewed again, how in the move that year she had begun to spend more time with Glenn. She chuckled to herself as she thought about the first time she had seen one of her students looking up at them standing on the landing, talking. She would have liked to know what was going through the little boy's mind.

Bringing her thoughts back to their conversation, she said, *"I believe God was working things out for me, though. I don't think it was a coincidence that you were attending high school in the same building as I was teaching."*

"I was finding the fast life appealing then, too," Glenn confessed. He smiled. *"My father, a pastor, would remind me occasionally about how I was raised, and ask whether I felt my lifestyle reflected that upbringing."*

"I can't explain why..." Aletha began. *"Well, yes, I can. I think it was still plain selfishness, still wanting to go my own way that kept me from getting back to my mother's values at first. The heady successes of teaching and social life with fellow teachers in the community centered on me, not God."*

Glenn reached for Aletha's hand. *"Looking back on the teaching about God we've had, I feel I would like to have our home based on Christian values. Would you like that, too?"*

Aletha lifted her other hand and tilted it a bit so her ring caught the sunshine. She loved to see the colors changing in the diamond. It was a little like life—things changed, and you never knew what the changes would bring, how God would work things out. But one thing she did know: she loved Glenn and wanted to spend the rest of her life with him.

"Yes, I would. I want to keep the peace and joy, no matter where life leads us."

●●◆●●

Aletha and Glenn's mothers were friends before Aletha's family moved to Manitoba, so their families got together when Glenn and Aletha were still small children. They met again when Aletha was teaching in Grandview, Manitoba. The primary grades were on the main floor of the school, and high school on the upper floor, so they sometimes stood on the landing and talked. It was this young love that Wayne Hindmarsh remembers observing when he was a student in Aletha's fourth grade class. "I watched with interest as a nine-year-old, not understanding love, as she kept talking to the high school boy." It intrigued him that she was "being very friendly" with their pastor's son.

"Anyone who will take time to enter into an intimate relationship with God can see God do extraordinary things through his or her life." –ALETHA JOICE (in reference to John 4:11)

Aletha had faced new fears and changes in her life. She was learning about committing things to the Lord. Although she did not know what lay ahead, she was willing to trust her Heavenly Father with her future.

"May it become your power..."

Wed Mid-Year

The bare evergreen stood in the corner of the living room. Aletha felt like taking the decorations out of the box she had just so carefully packed them into and putting them back onto the tree. The Christmas season had whizzed by on angelic wings. Life was taking on a very different routine.

"Well, why wouldn't it?" she asked herself aloud, going to the kitchen to finish supper preparations.

As she stirred the meat sauce, she considered her newlywed status, continuing her audible conversation with herself. "When you get married in the middle of the school year, things are bound to be different afterwards."

"What's different afterwards?" Glenn came up behind Aletha and put his arms around her waist. Resting his chin on her shoulder, he watched the moving spoon.

"Life," Aletha answered, pausing her stirring and pressing her cheek against his.

"But it's a nice different isn't it, my lovely bride of—let me see..." Glenn stepped back to look up at the wall calendar. "Two weeks," he finished.

"It's a wonderful difference, my groom of two weeks," Aletha affirmed. She lifted a cookie sheet off the counter and transferred the cooled cookies onto a plate.

"Wasn't our wedding day wonderful?" Glenn asked.

"Oh, yes! The sparkle of the trees all covered with hoar frost was so beautiful." Aletha returned to the stove and began stirring the meat sauce again.

"I'm just sorry I didn't have more time off. I would have loved to take you on a honeymoon trip."

"We're honeymooning right here," Aletha assured her young husband. "You don't have to take a trip to do that."

Glenn reached over and took the spoon Aletha was using. Resting it against the side of the pot, he turned her to face him and, wrapping his arms around her, held her close.

Glenn and Aletha were married December 24, 1952 in the same church in Rapid City which Aletha's mother had helped to establish many years before. During the first three years of their marriage, Glenn and Aletha lived in an upstairs suite in Moose Jaw, Saskatchewan.

Aletha finished the year teaching at Caron, Saskatchewan, near Moose Jaw, then taught in Moose Jaw at King Edward School. As part of an experiment King Edward School had initiated during this time, Aletha taught the same group of children each of those three years, progressing to the next grade with them each year. She really enjoyed it, because she got to know the students very well and they got to know her.

Glenn was working at Robin Hood Mills in Moose Jaw, in apprenticeship to be a miller. After beginning as a sweeper, he moved to being a roll oiler. This job meant checking the bearings on the fifty to sixty grain-rolling machines on the roll floor. "Every machine had four rollers," Glenn[6] explained, "each weighing five hundred to eight hundred pounds. The bearings would run hot unless each end of the roll was oiled constantly."

Brush Set for a Bald Head?

Perfect, *Glenn thought, picking up the leather-handled hairbrush. Replacing it in the box, he picked up the hair care set and walked over to Aletha. She looked up from the magazine she was paging through.*

"Look at this," *Glenn said, showing her the set he had brought over.* "This would be a perfect gift for dad for Christmas."

The hair brushes and other things all had soft leather handles. Aletha picked one up and felt the bristles. They were quite soft and pliable.

"I think he'd like this," *she said, replacing the brush.* "It suits his personality somehow."

Bright candle flames leaned and flickered each time someone came through the door. The organist was playing a soft prelude. Only a week had passed since Christmas. A tall, tinsel-clad evergreen still stood off to one side at the front of the sanctuary.

Aletha sighed. Thankfulness for the beauty of the season, the goodness of God in sending his Son to earth, and the joy she had experienced in this first year of her marriage was almost more than she could bear.

Aletha persuaded her mind to come back to the worship service and not let her attention wander. But Christmas, and the memories of all the festivities, kept bounding unbidden back into her thoughts. Her wonderful gift from Glenn... his pleasure with the gift she had given him... the leather brush set they had picked out for Glenn's father. She could still see Glenn's dad's slow smile as he raised his bald head and looked across at them after opening their gift.

Suddenly Aletha had a tremendous urge to giggle. She put her hand up to her mouth to stifle one that nearly escaped. Glenn looked at her with a questioning look in his eyes and raised his eyebrows in a silent question.

Aletha returned his glance, trying hard not to laugh. "Sorry," *she mouthed. Her eyes twinkled as she leaned closer to whisper an explanation.* "I was just remembering your dad opening his brush set."

Glenn looked at her for a moment, unexplainably knowing that if he so much as smiled at her, her contagious silent giggles would cause him to laugh out loud. They both sat up straighter and tried their best not to give in to the laughter threatening to bubble up as the pastor announced the first hymn.

Glenn and Aletha had been so delighted with how nice the leather looked on the gift they bought that they didn't stop to think of the fact that Glenn's dad didn't need a hair brush. He hadn't said much, but just smiled when he opened it. Maybe he appreciated the eye appeal of the gift.

"Oh God, that I would dispense grace this year." –ALETHA JOICE (in reference to Ephesians 3)

Empty Arms

The sun was painting pink lace edges along the clouds as it descended to rest for another day. Glenn and Aletha walked hand in hand without saying anything. The beauty of the winter evening surrounded them, but they could find little of their usual joy in it.

"Homemaking wasn't too big a challenge to me while I was teaching. I didn't do too much of it," Aletha said softly. "I'm sure I could have looked after it, even with a baby. Why did the Lord decide to give us a child and then take it away before we even got to know it?"

"I wish I knew the answer," Glenn responded, squeezing her hand a little tighter. He moved toward the bench in the park and brushed the light snow off with a mitten-clad hand. They sat down on the cold surface.

"I know it would have been hard to fit children in when my priority was teaching, with a list of planning, organizing, collecting, making, planning, organizing..." Aletha paused. "But now I'm not teaching anymore and I know I could have done a good job of looking after our home and a baby."

Glenn could hear the tears in Aletha's voice. He put his arm around her shoulders and pulled her close. "Aletha, I don't understand why either, but you cannot go on blaming yourself. You heard what the doctor said. It is not your fault."

"I won't be holding a living baby tomorrow after it's born..." Aletha began to sob as she spoke. "Knowing should help with facing it today, but... I just... Oh, how will I be able to go home... without our... little one in my arms?"

Glenn felt helpless as Aletha's sobs increased. He wrapped his arms around her as she wept. His own tears wet his cheeks as the deep sorrow of what they faced the next day stabbed at his heart.

Glenn and Aletha's first child was delivered stillborn, January 2, 1957, 6:30 a.m. In one of her Bibles, Aletha records the event: Born to Aletha and Glenn Joice, a daughter, Baby Joice. Burial Friday, January 4.

The doctor had told Glenn and Aletha just after the eighth month of pregnancy that he felt there was a problem. When he induced the birth around the ninth month, he told them their baby would be a stillbirth.

"I will ask you only to do those things for which you have ability and strength... and I, God, am the One who gives ability and strength!" –ALETHA JOICE

Close to My Heart

Aletha got up from the armchair where she was reading her Bible and went to answer the door.

"Hello, Pastor. Come in. Can I take your coat?"

"Thank you." The pastor brushed the snow off his sleeves and handed his coat to Aletha. As she hung it in the front hall closet, he reached down and removed his boots.

"Would you like some tea? I was just going to pour myself a cup."

"That would be super," the pastor said, following her into the kitchen. "Snow's coming down fairly heavy out there this afternoon. I'm wondering if we're going to find ourselves in a great deal of 'whipped cream' by tonight."

I love the way he can illustrate everyday happenings with unusual words, *Aletha thought. She chuckled to herself as she poured a cup of tea for the pastor. She invited him to sit at the table and handed him the sugar bowl. Imagine calling snowdrifts whipped cream.*

"How are you and Glenn doing?" the pastor asked after he had taken a sip from his cup.

Aletha tried to respond before the tears came again, but it didn't work. Her eyes overflowed before her mouth could open.

"I'm sorry. I didn't mean to cause pain."

Aletha reached for the soggy tissue she had laid on the table earlier. Then, realizing it wouldn't help much, she got up to get a fresh one, giving herself time to compose herself.

"Thank you for your concern," Aletha said, returning to her chair. "It has been quite hard, but we're doing okay."

"I'm glad. Perhaps the Lord will grant you other children someday."

Aletha looked at the pastor, but didn't respond. But I wanted this one, her heart cried. She swallowed and willed herself not to let anymore tears escape.

The pastor chatted with her about other things for a few more minutes, then said he would need to stop in to visit a few other people. He had to get going.

Why does my heart ache so? *Aletha asked herself after the door closed behind the pastor. Everyone said she shouldn't have so much sadness, telling her and Glenn that since the child was not home with them before it died, they hadn't had time to get attached.*

"Oh, but I did have my baby with me. I carried her close to my heart for months," she whispered to herself. Why couldn't they understand how much it hurt?

●●◆●●

Because Aletha believed in eternal life, she has been reunited with that first little daughter. In an imaginary scene, one could think of them walking in heaven's beauty, Aletha looking down at the little face and savoring the smiles she was not able to see here on earth.

"Joy comes as a byproduct of confidence in God, not certainty in one's circumstances." –ALETHA JOICE

U.S.A., Here We Come!

Aletha stood looking through their kitchen window in Illinois, her mind replaying the day she'd heard the back door squeak and, unsuspecting, turned to greet a tired, dusty Glenn.

"Hi, my sweet, um... white knight," Aletha had said, smiling.

Glenn had bent to give Aletha a kiss, then straightened up again without doing it. "Let me clean off some of this dust first," he'd said. "I would rather just be a sweet knight when I kiss my beautiful bride. A large quantity of boxes came in today. By the end of the day they were—"

"—all heavier than at the beginning, too." Glenn smiled as Aletha finished his line for him.

"How would you feel about going to the United States?" Glenn had asked, coming back into the kitchen, rubbing his face with a towel.

"You mean to visit?" Aletha had been surprised at the unusual question.

"No, to live. I would like to go to college there in the fall."

"That's a long way from home."

Glenn had nodded. "I know. That's why I want you to think about it."

The days after Glenn first asked her about going to college had moved like quicksilver. There had been so many details to look after to prepare for their move.

Now the days were passing more slowly, and in the quiet of the afternoons, while Glenn was studying, Aletha had to curb her impatience to hold the coming little one in her arms. Maybe it was because she was believing that this baby would arrive safely. The doctor had assured her at her visit last week that things were going well.

Aletha thought back to the day it had been confirmed that she was pregnant again. The doctor had come into the little examining room and closed the door behind him. Seating himself at his desk, he told her the results of the test.

"Mrs. Joice, I would say you are about six to eight weeks along in your pregnancy, and as far as I can tell, everything seems fine." He'd looked up from his file and smiled.

Aletha thanked him, willing her excitement not to spill over.

"Come back and see me again next month," the doctor had said, rising from his chair. "If something seems amiss, come sooner."

Except for the fact that Aletha had wanted to maintain the impression that she was old enough to have a child, she would have skipped when she left the doctor's examining room.

••◆••

When they moved to Greenville, Illinois in September of 1957, Glenn and Aletha had lived in Regina for one year, where Glenn worked at Western Dry Goods Wholesale.

Glenn had two years of credits from Aldersgate College, and at Greenville College was enrolled in Fine Arts, working toward his sociology degree. Aletha was not teaching during this time because of her pregnancy.

"The servant does not tell the Master what kind of assignments he needs. The servant waits on His Master for the assignment." –ALETHA JOICE (in reference to John 21:21-22)

Shorter Than Short

Aletha shook out the haircloth and spread it around Glenn's shoulders. Then picking up the hair clipper, she plugged it in and switched it on. The vibration in her hand made her want to giggle.

"This shouldn't be hard," Aletha decided, putting the electric clipper flat against the back of Glenn's neck and moving it up into his hair just above the cloth. Before she knew it, the clipper had left a clean path in his hair!

"Uh oh," Aletha whispered, dismayed that so much hair had gone so fast.

"What's wrong?" Glenn asked, concerned she had hurt herself with the clipper.

"I—I think I took too much off." Aletha could feel a giggle building inside.

"I do have a brush cut, Aletha. The hair will be short when you're finished."

"I know, but this is really, really short." Aletha held her hand over her mouth, trying to keep the giggle from bursting out. "And I went halfway up your head."

"Let's have a look."

Glenn went to the dresser in their bedroom and picked up the hand mirror. Turning his back to the larger mirror, he looked at the back of his head.

Oh boy, *he thought.* She wasn't kidding when she said she'd made it short. I assumed she knew what she was doing, but I guess I should have asked first.

"Well, it's definitely short," Glenn said to Aletha, coming back to the chair and sitting down.

Aletha looked at the long strip of nearly empty skin on Glenn's head and the giggles finally escaped. "Are you sure you... want me to finish it?" she asked, trying in vain to stop laughing.

Glenn wasn't sure, but nodded. "What's cut is gone. I'll try to explain how to fix it as you go along. My hair line will just have to be higher this time. Start by using the plastic piece with the larger teeth on it so the clipper doesn't go quite so close to my scalp."

"Okay." Aletha sounded a bit doubtful.

"It will grow back," Glenn said, trying to put encouragement into his voice. "Go ahead and finish. It will be fine."

Aletha snapped an attachment onto the clipper. In half a second, she was giggling so hard, she couldn't hold it steady. Putting it down, she walked out of the room, the giggle-induced tears starting to run down her face.

Aletha's short barbering career began and ended in a single day. With constantly giggling and leaving the room because of it, it took more than two hours to finish her first attempt at cutting Glenn's hair. She didn't cut Glenn's hair again after that and, except for a trim on a few occasions while her son Bob was in a band, she didn't cut the children's hair either.

"There are no shortcuts to spiritual maturity. It comes only through hard work and obedience to what God says." –ALETHA JOICE

Miniature Beauty

"She looks like her beautiful mother," Glenn said. He put his arm around Aletha's shoulders against the hospital bed pillow and touched the miniature face of their new baby.

"She is so precious." Aletha adjusted the blanket and tucked the little feet back inside.

"I would venture to say she even looks a bit like an Elizabeth," Glenn said, turning to face Aletha.

"Well, it's a good bit of foresight we had that name picked out then, isn't it?" Aletha teased, smiling up at him.

The infant in her arms stretched and her eyes popped open for a second.

"Oh, look. She hears you talking and wants to see you," Aletha exclaimed.

"But not for long," laughed Glenn as the little eyes closed again.

They observed the sleeping infant silently, taking turns touching her tiny fingers.

"I need to get back to class," Glenn said with a sigh. "I'd so much rather be here with you today, but I have a paper I have to hand in this afternoon."

"I'm so glad you could come even for this little while," Aletha said, handing Glenn their daughter and moving the covers aside so she could get out of the bed. "Let me bring this bundle back to the nursery. I'll walk with you to the entrance."

"I would be most delighted to have you accompany me," Glenn said in a dignified, formal-sounding voice.

Aletha giggled at him as she went through the door of her hospital room and down the hall to the nursery.

Elizabeth Jean Joice (Bette-Jean) was born in a small hospital in Highland, Illinois near Greenville, January 23, 1958.

"College wives were pretty sophisticated," Aletha wrote in some study preparation notes. "Those babies were scheduled by the book. If your child didn't get her first tooth, or sleep through the night, or wasn't potty trained or whatever on the exact right hour of the right day of the right month, you weren't in! That was too extreme for me. I thought that if I was an individual, so was Bette-Jean. She slept so little, day or night, that I had to fall in with her individual tastes, and somehow she seemed to hit or miss as many 'norms' as did any of the college babies.

"What I'm trying to say is that you'll have enough frustrations and things to learn without getting ulcers over what others are telling you to do or say. Hear God's Word from the Psalms: 'I will instruct you in the way you should go; I will counsel you and watch over you.'"[i] –ALETHA JOICE

Bette-Jean was given her name after her grandmother, Elizabeth Rogers, a name that means "consecrated to God."

---

[i] Psalm 32:8 (NIV).

Use the Time Wisely

"Bette-Jean, stop that." Aletha's voice rose as Bette-Jean's dirty fingers reached into the planter again and lifted a little more dirt to put into her toy cup. "Bette-Jean! I said stop it." Aletha grabbed her daughter's arm, stopping her in mid-motion, scattering the dirt on the floor. Bette-Jean began to howl. Exasperated, Aletha picked her up and headed for the bathroom.

Glenn had been out of town for most of the week. Aletha was feeling too rotten to leave the house or to have someone in! And this child took nearly every ounce of strength and almost all of her time. Some mornings she didn't even want to get out of bed.

When she had finished washing the little hands, Aletha put Bette-Jean into her crib and shut the door on her wails. Going back into the living room, she sank into the armchair and wept.

"What am I going to do, God?" she cried. "It is so lonely and hard without Glenn here. It isn't Bette-Jean's fault that I'm sick. I want this new child you are going to give us. I didn't mean to be so rough on my little girl. Forgive me."

"Use the time wisely." The words she must have read somewhere went through Aletha's mind. What did it mean?

"Are you telling me something God?" she asked aloud. "I do need to use this as a special time for Bette-Jean, don't I, Lord? It won't be long before a little brother or sister will take some of my attention away from her."

The sobs from the other room and the ones in the armchair quieted. Quietness began to settle over Aletha's spirit, too.

"Use the time wisely." The words came again. Suddenly, Aletha realized that she not only needed to spend special time with her daughter, but also with her heavenly Father. And what better time than when Bette-Jean napped?

"One of my loneliest times was when our daughter was two and a half... and I was expecting our second child. When Bette-Jean napped, I took my Bible and my notebook and I did character studies, topical studies, read a Psalm or a chapter of Proverbs a day, and so on. I was able to give Bette-Jean good care and even some fun days and not be a basketcase when Glenn got home.

"Since then, have I not had lonely times? Yes. And have I always encouraged my family? No. But I found that complete abandonment to God through His Word brought no disappointment. It brought tough lessons, often still does, accurate pictures of myself that were painful, but always words that build up! He is the Master Encourager." –ALETHA JOICE

"Lord, help me to obey what I learn from Your Word... to expect some mountaintops this year, even though I know there will be valleys." –ALETHA JOICE

When Does My Hair Turn Black?

Glenn and Aletha sat watching three-year-old Bette-Jean trying to do somersaults on the lawn, her red blonde hair catching more blades of grass each time she tumbled off to the side.

"She certainly doesn't give up, does she?" Glenn chuckled as Bette-Jean righted herself for the umpteenth time.

"My goodness, you will soon look like the straw man," Aletha said as Bette-Jean came running over to them. She began to pick at the blades of grass in Bette-Jean's hair as she spoke.

"Mom, when does my hair turn black?" Bette-Jean asked, leaning against Aletha's knees.

"Why, it won't ever get black," Aletha answered, wondering at the reason for the question. She didn't have long to wait.

"Awww. I want black hair like yours. I want mine to be black and shiny, too."

"Well, sweetheart," Aletha began, turning Bette-Jean to face her, "God designed it so children are born with a certain color of hair—dark hair or light hair. Some children have the same color of hair as their parents."

"Like Todd?" Bette-Jean asked. "His is black and his Mom and Dad have black hair." Aletha nodded. Bette-Jean reached up and touched Aletha's hair, still looking puzzled. "But your hair is black, Mom. Why isn't mine black?"

"God gave me my dark hair before I was born and He gave you your beautiful red-blonde hair before you were born."

"But, Mom," Bette-Jean protested, straightening and putting her hands on her hips. "Todd has black, shiny hair just like his Mom. Why isn't mine the same as yours?"

Aletha sighed. How do you explain the x's and y's of hair color to a three-year-old?

"Well, honey, sometimes the color of a person's hair is like the kind of hair their grandparents had, or even their great-grandparents."

Bette-Jean screwed up her forehead and pursed her lips. Aletha knew most of what she had just said was causing more questions than answers, but her little girl would persevere in trying to understand, just as she tried to do many other things.

After moving back to Canada from Greenville, Glenn and Aletha lived in a number of Canadian cities. The first was Prince Albert, a city in northern Saskatchewan, where Glenn 'supplied' (pastored) a church for a year and Aletha was a substitute teacher in the primary grades about two afternoons a week.

Then, it would be on to Moose Jaw.

"Thank you God that you are still creating—renewing the earth, creating new people in Christ Jesus, renewing our minds!" –ALETHA JOICE

Toothless Smile

Bette-Jean stood with her face pressed against the bars of the crib, watching Aletha. "Mom, can he come out and play?"

"Oh, no, Bette-Jean. He can't walk yet!"

"He's got legs, same as I do. How come?"

Closing the sleeper on her infant son, Aletha stooped down and put her arm around her inquisitive little daughter.

"Bob was just born three months ago. He has to grow a lot before he is strong enough to walk. There will be other things he'll do first, like wave his arms when you talk to him, or smile at you."

Aletha lifted Bette-Jean so she could look over the edge of the crib. Bob looked up at them, kicking his little legs.

"Look at you," Aletha said to him. Bob responded with a big toothless smile.

"Mom, he smiled at me!"

Aletha decided exactly who the baby had smiled at wasn't important.

"He sure did," she answered. "Know what? Soon he'll laugh for you, too."

Glenn and Aletha had lived in Moose Jaw earlier in their marriage, but this time Glenn began using his training in sociology. Aletha was not teaching, because it was here their son was born.

On March 8, 1961, infant Robert John made his presence known to the world. Dark haired Bob was three years younger than his sister Bette-Jean, and as would be revealed in the years to come, had a much different personality.

A year later, the family was off to Winnipeg for two years, where Glenn worked on his Masters at the University of Manitoba, majoring in social work. Graduation was followed by a move to Weyburn, a small city in southern Saskatchewan.

Although they lived in Weyburn, Glenn was responsible for a generic childcare caseload in the city of Estevan. This included protection, foster care, juvenile probation, and adoptions.

●●◆●●

The meaning of Robert, "of bright shining fame," and John, "God's gracious gift," seems to give a feeling that Glenn and Aletha felt confident of the future and blessed by the arrival of their new son.

Skates and Books

"Almost time for bed, Bette-Jean." Aletha sat down on the couch beside her daughter. There was no indication she had heard until Aletha pulled her book down.

"I know, Mom. I just want to finish this chapter."

"Okay, but before you do that I want to talk to you about something. Your teacher called today. She told me she suspected you have not been paying attention in school because you are hiding a storybook inside the textbook you are supposed to be reading." Bette-Jean looked up at Aletha without saying anything. "You are pretending to be doing something you aren't. That isn't truthful."

"I'm sorry, Mom."

"I'm glad you are repentant, but you need to tell Jesus you are sorry, too." Bette-Jean nodded. "Now finish that chapter and get into your pajamas."

"Mom, remember those strap-on rollerskates[i] I bought with my own allowance when I was five?" Bette-Jean asked as Aletha was tucking her in later. "They helped me learn to ice skate, right?" Aletha nodded, remembering how insistent her five-year-old had been that she didn't want figure skating lessons, but wanted to play hockey. "Well, how come I could learn to ice skate better because I had rollerskates, but I can't learn school stuff if I'm reading a storybook instead of my Social Studies book? Those are both reading, the same as roller and ice ones are both skates."

Aletha laughed, and tickled Bette-Jean. "Time to go to sleep." How could you even try to answer logic like that? "No school tomorrow, but it's a big day. We have to start packing."

"Mom, how are we going to take Frisky along?" a worried voice asked as Aletha pulled the blanket up.

"We'll find a good box with lots of peep holes so she can breathe. She'll be fine."

"What if she runs away on us and gets lost?"

"You've been reading too many animal adventures," Aletha laughed, tucking the blanket around her daughter and giving her a kiss. "I know you'll take care of her. She'll be fine. Now, close those big eyes."

---

[i] See the end of this section for a photograph of this kind of roller skates.

Frisky the cat would go along from Weyburn to Swift Current without mishap, and for a few years produced a single offspring per year. But after the move to Regina, it seemed she knew she could settle in for a while, and that year she had five. Glenn and Aletha decided if she had more than one kitten annually in the years to come, there would be too many to find homes for, so they gave her away, along with her kittens. Some years later, when Bette-Jean came home from college, a kitten named Woody[ii] came with her. Woody was with the family for eighteen years.

"God will not send us where He will not sustain us." –ALETHA JOICE (from the margin of her Bible, referring to Genesis 6)

[ii] See Wall of Memories for photograph of Woody.

'Heavy' Boxes

"Bring that little box," Glenn told his young son, picking up a larger box himself. "Let's go put these into the truck."

"It's heavy, Dad," Bob said, picking up the box Glenn had told him to bring.

"But you are a strong boy," Glenn said, smiling at Bob over his shoulder. "I know you can carry a puny little box like that."

Bob smiled up at his dad and trotted along behind him to the moving truck.

Later that afternoon, as Glenn closed the big doors on the truck, he looked up at the sky. It looked a bit like rain. Hopefully, it would be over by morning and traveling weather would be good. He slapped the truck lightly and went back into the house.

"Dad, can you read me this story?" Bob asked, climbing into Glenn's lap when he had seated himself on the bare living room floor.

Glenn took the book and opened it to the first page of the story. Holding the book with one hand, he held Bob with the other and scooted back a bit so he could lean against the wall. The house was so empty. Everything they were able to load tonight was in the truck. They wanted to get an early start in the morning. Lord, could you settle us down this time? Glenn prayed silently. I'm getting so tired of moving.

"Read, Dad." Bob's voice brought Glenn's attention back to the book in his hand.

In the early years of their marriage, the Joice family moved a lot.

Bob has few recollections of their moves, as he was quite young. By the time he began kindergarten in Swift Current, his family had already lived in many places and moved a number of times. His six-year career in moving ended in Regina in July of 1967. Bette-Jean and Bob would both call Regina their home until adulthood.

At the time of this book's writing, Glenn still lives in the house they purchased at that time.

"God cares enough for me to do what's best for me." –ALETHA JOICE

Can You Hear Him Talk?

Aletha looked up from reading her Bible to see Bette-Jean standing in the doorway. Aletha smiled and beckoned to her.

"Do you talk to Jesus in your mind when you pray, Mom?" she asked, coming into the room.

"Yes. Sometimes I pray out loud, too."

"He's a real person, huh?"

"Sure."

"Can you hear him talk to you?"

"Not the same way you and I are talking to each other, but I hear him because I read His words in the Bible."

"Does He tell you things?"

"Yes. Like the part I was reading just now. He told me He was 'the Way, the Truth and the Life'.[i] Yesterday I read a part that told me when His Spirit came to live in us we would be able to be loving, patient, kind, good, faithful, and have self-control."[ii]

"Those are all really good things, right?" Bette-Jean asked very seriously.

"Yes, they are."

"Is that why I was very happy when I asked Jesus to come into my heart at the crusade?"

Aletha nodded, remembering the determined little person finding her way down out of the bleachers, disappearing out of sight, then reappearing again, walking up the long aisle to the front of the big auditorium.

Aletha's response to Bette-Jean's conversion? "She was thrilled. I knew that my parents believed Jesus was someone you could talk to like a real person and I talked to Him at meal times and at bedtime.

"When I was nine, Layton Ford had a crusade in Swift Current. He told about Jesus forgiving my sin and me being able to have a relationship with Him. I had heard this message before, but had not done anything about it. When we

---

[i] Scripture phrases from John 14:6 (NIV).

[ii] Scripture phrases referring to Galatians 5:22-23.

lived in Weyburn, an evangelist had come to our church. He had explained the way of salvation and asked people to come forward. I knew I should, but didn't want to. Mom was exasperated with me at the time, because I was a six-year-old in tears, but wouldn't go. Now, three years later, I went forward to pray that Jesus would forgive me. I was independent in a lot of things, so didn't mind going forward, at the crusade, on my own—I came to the beginning of faith. I remember being very happy and realizing that the joy came from having Jesus in my life." –BETTE-JEAN HAND

When the angel of death saw the blood on the doorposts of the Israelites' homes,[iii] they were redeemed, or saved by it. A lamb shed its blood for the people. "When God sees Christ in us—the blood on the door post of our hearts—we are redeemed, consecrated to Him." –ALETHA JOICE

[iii] In reference to story in Exodus 12.

Solo Fear

Aletha stood at her classroom window, watching her daughter's slow steps. Bette-Jean had been unusually quiet this morning, and now as she watched her trudge along the sidewalk to her own school, her head down, Aletha was a little concerned.

I hope she isn't coming down with something, *she thought.*

The morning was long and tiring, and Aletha was glad to see the last of her class go out the door. She laid out what she wanted to use for the afternoon's lessons, then reached for her sweater and headed home for lunch.

"I hope this afternoon goes well," Aletha said as she and Glenn finished their coffee. "It's been a long week. Sometimes these longer substitutions are harder than teaching full time."

"Did Bette-Jean say anything to you about a solo?" Glenn asked, setting his mug onto the counter.

"No, why?"

"Today when I came home at lunch she had the table set and lunch ready. When I asked her what was going on, she just said, 'Well, there's a first time for everything Dad.'"

"So did you find out what it was about?" Aletha asked, setting her own mug into the sink and reaching for the dishcloth to wipe the table.

"It took a bit of gentle prodding, but I finally got a tearful explanation. Instead of walking to her school this morning, she walked home."

"I wondered about her when she left my classroom. It seemed as if she wasn't feeling very well."

"She probably wasn't, although she wasn't physically sick. You know that music teacher she is so afraid of...?" Aletha nodded. "Well, just before class was over last week, the teacher told the class she wanted them to sing to her individually, and if they didn't sing well, she would punish them. Bette-Jean immediately decided she was not going to go to school that morning!"

Aletha shook her head.

"What a way for a teacher to talk to her class," she said. "I certainly hope she wasn't serious about punishing them for not singing well. No wonder Bette-Jean was terrified. I'll go along with her on my way back to school and talk to her teacher."

"Even as a child, I had, and it has been my experience that all children have, a great sense of fair play and of justice—of right and wrong. Kids see truth readily and tell the truth readily and can lie just as easily to suit their own means.

"Although I had been ready to handle this problem on my own, it was a relief to know that my dad knew the truth and that I was forgiven for skipping school and for lying." –BETTE-JEAN HAND

"But when we're looking for ways to give verbal encouragement, it occurs most effectively when opportunities are seized, rather than created." –ALETHA JOICE

Any Ice Left?

"I say we head out this evening and work on the cabin this weekend. Anybody want to go along?"

"Can I see if Heather can come?" Bette-Jean asked, jumping up from the table and going to the phone before Glenn had a chance to answer.

Aletha smiled. It was not difficult getting enthusiasm up with Bette-Jean. Channeling it was more of a challenge.

"I'm coming too, right, Dad?" Bob asked while Bette-Jean was on the phone. "I help well. Remember how I took nails out of the boards for you?"

"That was a great help," Glenn replied, smiling at his young son. "I'd love to have you come along and help us build on the cabin."

"He is? Oh, great." Bette-Jean covered the mouth piece of the phone receiver. She turned to Glenn and reported. "Mr. Campbell was thinking of going out to work on theirs this weekend, too. He was going to ask you if he could get your help on something, Dad."

"Fine, let's do it then. Let me talk to him when you are finished with Heather."

Bette-Jean nodded and turned back to her telephone conversation.

"They nearly played those kittens to a frazzle," Glenn told Aletha Saturday evening when they returned. "I'm not sure how the mother cat felt about it—she sat calmly on the straw in the ice house and watched them—but the girls sure enjoyed it."

"I'm glad they had a good time. How did the work go?"

"We made good progress. We should be able to use it this summer."

"Is there still lots of ice left in the ice house?" Aletha asked, her question appearing unrelated to the conversation.

Catching on quickly, Glenn replied, "The cabin isn't quite ready for company. You won't have to be concerned about that yet."

"Oh, but Glenn, the main purpose for the cabin is to have people over. I'd want to be sure the food stayed cool in the icebox."

Glenn smiled and put his arm around Aletha. "My wife, the servant," he said, smiling down into her face.

Glenn and Aletha built a cabin[i] at Arlington Beach when Bette-Jean and Bob were young. Glenn and the pastor of the church at the time collected materials for the cabin from the wood of an old barn they tore down. This was a case of finding new uses for old materials to cut costs, before the term recycling was well-known.

Glenn, Aletha, and the family went out there a lot in the summertime. When the cabin was just a shell—four walls with blankets dividing the area into 'rooms' and no indoor bathroom—they had their first guests, the Neufeld family, over for a weekend.

Other family friends recall one Saturday evening when the Joice family drove onto their yard on the way back from the lake. In a hurry to get home to prepare for Sunday, they just made a circle around the Reimche's yard, all yelling hello from the car before driving off again.

---

[i] See the end of this section for a photograph of the cabin.

I Want to Finish My Airplane

Eight-year-old Bob bounced out of the car at a run, on his way toward a crowd of children watching something going on at the lake's edge.

"Hold up, son!" Glenn called. "Registration first."

"Aww!" moaned Bob, coming back to the car.

Aletha handed Bob his duffle bag and picked up the bag with his baseball glove. She closed the car door and walked toward the front of the main camp building.

"This sure is a beautiful spot," Glenn said, coming along beside her with Bob's bigger suitcase from the trunk.

Aletha nodded, looking around. "It's no wonder the hotel was built at this spot. I would have liked to have been here in its glory days."

The week went zipping past, and before she knew it Aletha was putting the duffle bag back into the car.

"Did you have a good time?" she asked

"Yes!" was Bob's quick answer. He danced a little jig around to the other side of the car. He got in and then waved and shouted his goodbyes to some friends nearby. "Dad, did you know there used to be a paddle wheeler running on the lake?" Bob asked as Glenn turned the car out onto the highway. "It stopped in front of the hotel."

"I believe I did," Glenn responded.

Bob was quiet for a time, looking out of the window as they drove.

"Missing it already?" asked Aletha.

Bob shook his head. Puzzled at his unusual quietness, Aletha couldn't resist asking if he felt okay.

"Yeah, I feel fine," he answered, without turning from the window.

After a few more miles of silence, Bob spoke softly. "I became a Christian," he said, "I'm going to meet Grandma in heaven when I die now."

"That's wonderful son," Aletha said, turning to look at him. "That's really wonderful."

"My counselor told me all about Jesus wanting me to come and live in heaven with Him— so much that He died for my sins. All I had to do was ask Him, and He would forgive me."

"So did He?" Aletha asked, wondering whether Bob's sense of assurance had accompanied his newly attained knowledge of how to become a Christian.

"Oh, yes, I asked Him to this morning," Bob answered. "But I hope I won't die today. I want to finish the model airplane I started before I went to camp."

Aletha smiled. More teaching needed, *she thought.*

Bob remembers becoming a Christian at children's camp at Arlington Beach, a Bible camp run by the Free Methodist church. The facility the church purchased was an old lakefront hotel on Last Mountain Lake, north of Regina.

"As growth is natural to the physical, may I keep growing spiritually." –ALETHA JOICE

"Oh, Glenn."

"Come on in, folks." Aletha moved aside as their company came into the front entrance. "Go on up," she added, closing the door. Anne set the Chinese checkers game on the coffee table, then joined Vern, who had gone straight into the kitchen where Glenn was carving a roast.

"Say, that smells intensely good," Vern said, taking a deep breath. He stepped aside as Aletha reached past him to open the cutlery drawer.

"We're almost ready," Aletha said with a smile as she began dipping the mashed potatoes into the serving bowl.

"That was a lovely meal as usual, Aletha," Glenn complimented, patting his chest after a faux burp.

Aletha couldn't keep from grinning. "Sometimes you are so silly." Pretending to be cross-eyed, Glenn feigned fumbling attempts to find her hand. "Oh, Glenn," she admonished playfully. Raising both hands and making a shooing motion at Glenn, Aletha shook her head and laughed.

In the kitchen a little later getting the dessert, Aletha could hear Glenn begin telling a joke. He was such a character. I wonder if he'll get the punch line right? *she thought, placing a piece of cake on a plate.*

When everyone had finished licking their lips, to get the most out of the delicious dessert, the women began clearing the table.

As the two men sat down in the living room, Vern reached for the Chinese checkers game. "So are you up to the challenge?" he asked, opening the box.

"Most certainly," Glenn said, rubbing his hands together in anticipation. "Hand me those marbles and let's get this set up."

Aletha enjoyed laughter. She laughed at Glenn's jokes, and on occasion corrected him. One day he was telling a joke about two fellows seeing parts of a body as they walked along. As they passed each one, they commented about the parts being Joe's arms, legs, torso, etc., and finally the head. At that point, Glenn bent down, pretending to be the person seeing the body parts, and delivered the punchline: "Joe! Joe, are you hurt?" In her involvement in the joke, Aletha corrected him, saying, "No, that's not the way it's supposed to end. He says, 'Joe, Joe. Pull yourself together, man! You are all in pieces.'"

Glenn and Aletha met Anne and Vernon Neufeld when they lived in Swift Current in 1965. When they moved there, housing was hard to find, so they spent the first few months living in the Swift Current Bible Institute's dorm/motel, sharing the use of the Bible school's kitchen with the Neufelds. The children enjoyed riding their tricycles around in the big dining hall where they ate their meals.

Call to Subtitute

"I will be your teacher today, Bob," Aletha said, hanging up the phone. *"I just got a call to sub for your class."*

"Hey, cool!" Bob said, reaching for another piece of toast. *"Can I get a ride?"*

Aletha reached over and tousled his hair. *"You silly... of course not. You can walk ahead and show me the way."*

Aletha glanced out of the window. It would be a beautiful day to walk. She enjoyed walking when she taught at the nearby school Bob attended. For some calls, she had to go farther.

"Come on, Mom. Stop your wool gathering. You're going to be late."

Aletha turned to look at Bob standing in the kitchen doorway, grinning.

"Using my own lines against me, are you?" she asked, walking over to him and squeezing his chin in her hand. Bob laughed at his mother's teasing.

Aletha watched as he bent down to tie his runners. He seemed happier now that she had told him about her decision not to teach next year. How she had loved teaching over the years! The decision to be a substitute had been a hard one, and no longer teaching at all would be even harder.

The doorbell rang as Bob finished tying his second runner. *"See you after school, Mom,"* he called as he dashed down the steps and out the door.

Aletha picked up her Bible and put it on top of the fridge. There was so much she was learning from God's Word in her daily Bible reading and prayer, especially when she confronted difficulties. And facing full-time homemaking would certainly be a difficulty..

"Lord," she prayed, as she prepared to leave for school, *"show me how to find fulfillment. I loved teaching in the classroom, but I want to teach my children about love, too, so I know right now this is what you want me to do. Give me peace and joy."*

Aletha was still teaching full-time in Swift Current when Bob started Kindergarten, but discovered how hard it was for him. She began teaching part-time when they moved to Regina and he was in first grade. She loved teaching and becoming a full-time homemaker was a tough decision for her. She wrote in her journal, "Bette-Jean's independent spirit could handle it (teaching full-time), but not so our son... the adjustment has been a big challenge."

There were a few occasions on which she was called to substitute for Bob's teacher. Bob said he had not had a problem with his mom being his teacher.

"Oh God, fill me with Your love that I may be able to serve someone who needs Your help." –ALETHA JOICE

Tears of Longing

"I can't believe my little girl is in junior high already," Aletha said to herself as she watched Bette-Jean come up the sidewalk with a couple of friends. She could hear their laughter before they opened the door.

"Hi, Mom! Is it okay if we have—"

"—some milk and cookies," Aletha said, putting a pitcher of milk and plate of warm cookies on the table before Bette-Jean could finish her request.

"Mom, I signed up for Phys. Ed. instead of Home Ec. We get two afternoons off a week to bowl, play tennis, golf, snowshoe, cross country ski, downhill ski, and play hockey. It's going to be great!"

Aletha smiled at her excitement. She had a great exuberance for life, but also a gentle caring spirit. As the girls chattered, Aletha went back to the stove to take the last pan of cookies out of the oven.

Bette-Jean was getting so grown up, too. Aletha's thoughts went back to the day Bette-Jean had come home and seen her in tears. Now that she wasn't teaching full-time, she had been feeling such an overpowering need to minister to someone, to do something that would help someone to come to the Lord, that she had been weeping about it. Bette-Jean's concern had been so mature.

It was that day that she decided to find some way to teach God's Word.

Aletha first found a way to teach God's Word through her discovery of Friendship Bible Coffee. She was filled with a longing to reach out to those who did not know the Lord.

Bible Study was important to her, and in this way she found she could not only study and teach God's Word, but also minister to non-church people. "She would be disappointed if people who hosted Friendship Bible Coffee only invited Christian friends," her daughter Bette-Jean said.

"Remembering my mother's practice of daily Bible reading and prayer set me on a course of learning and enabling through the years. Friendship Bible Coffee was a 'lifeline' to me as a young mother at home and no longer teaching school. It impacted my life as no other."—Aletha Joice

Jewels Within the Lines

Glenn grunted as he lifted the box of books into the trunk. "I wonder if the library has any books left on their shelves," he teased. "Seems we may be taking them all to the lake."

"Jewels are found within each line, written words..."

"...are joy sublime," Glenn finished as he turned to Aletha.

"One of the things I love about you is that insatiable thirst for knowledge. Another thing I know... you'll never be bored."

"We'll need to clear the broken branches off the walkways from the storm last night," Aletha said as she swept the floor after breakfast the next morning.

Silence greeted her statement. She looked around at her family and a smile spread across her face. Everyone had finished their assigned tasks and were sitting in various spots around the room, reading. They all thought they could get away with doing less work if they were reading when something came up. It was true that they could, but she was the winner anyway. It delighted her to see them benefiting from the reading they were doing trying to avoid extra work.

Reaching for her Bible, Aletha went out into the sunshine, and walked toward the beach. "Thank you, Father," she whispered, "for giving me a family that loves to read. Give them a love for reading Your Word as well."

Aletha felt books were important. There were always books out at the lake. She would give books as gifts for birthdays or Christmas. It was just as likely as not that if someone received a book, it had already been read, or someone would say, "When you are done with it, I want it next."

Aletha read to her kids every night—even when they were in high school, when she read Shakespeare to them. "I had been wondering," said Dawna Friesen,[7] friend of Aletha, "how old my kids should be before I stopped reading to them. I realized you don't have to quit reading to your kids if you don't want to."

"I pray for opportunities to share what you give me in my quiet times with you. Oh God, help me to walk in the light of your Word. Make me a faithful reflector of your glory!" –ALETHA JOICE

Snippy and Slam

"You've got good, warm boots," Aletha said as Bette-Jean zipped up her jacket. "Why are you going to school in runners?"

"Mom, it's not a big deal! There's not much snow."

"Your feet will get just as cold as if there was a lot."

Bette-Jean picked up her books and turned toward the door. "It's easier to wear my shoes than carry them."

"That doesn't keep your feet warm," Aletha continued, standing at the top of the steps to the back entry.

"When I wear my runners, I don't have the hassle of changing at school," Bette-Jean shot back, irritated.

"And look at those jeans. They cost good money. Why do you let them drag on the ground?"

Bette-Jean looked down at the frayed hems of her jeans. Why was she getting this interrogation this morning? "I like them that way."

"Don't get snippy with me, young lady."

"I'm not, Mom. I just don't see that it's a big deal," Bette-Jean said, opening the door. "I have to get going."

Aletha jumped as the door slammed behind Bette-Jean. Going back into the kitchen, she began clearing the breakfast table.

Why couldn't Bette-Jean understand the importance of dressing properly? Yesterday they had argued over the shirt she was wearing. Aletha sighed. Last week, they fought over how long Bette-Jean soaked in the tub. She winced as she thought about her comment that Bette-Jean's room looked like a pig pen.

Why was she fighting with her daughter? She was determined to be a good mother, to show her children she loved them. She wanted them to remember hugs and kisses and the words "I love you"—words she hadn't heard from her own mother. Yet here she was trying to win a battle with her tongue again.

"Lord," she whispered, pulling a chair out and sitting down, "I've gone and blown it again. How can I show Bette-Jean I love her when we have these royal verbal battles over the most unimportant issues?"

"I learned through God's Word and prayer that God loved my kids more than I loved them; that if I'd just shut my mouth and let Him (God) love them through me, God would get a chance to change me. I'd find that these kids weren't so bad after all." –ALETHA JOICE

"We know we are not perfect. Our children know we're not perfect. 'I'm sorry' not only helps mend broken relationships, but it frees our children to fail, without fear of rejection." –ALETHA JOICE

Sitting to Learn

"Mom, is supper almost ready?" Bob asked, coming into the kitchen where Aletha was setting the table. "I'm so hungry I could eat spinach."

"Really? Well, supper is nearly ready. Once the table is set, all I have to do is get the food out of the pots and onto the table. With you helping, supper would be on in half a nick of time."

Bob knew a hint when he heard one. He went over to the cupboard and reached for the dinner plates. "We have an old guy coming to youth tonight. I wonder what he's going to talk about that will be of any interest to us young kids."

"Now, son. Give him an open mind and a listening ear before you pass judgement on what he says."

"Oh, all right."

"Someday you will have old guys for parents you know, and we'd still like you to listen to us once in a while then, too," she said. Bob grinned. "By the way, how about we have a gander at that report card you got yesterday."

"Man!" Bob put down the last plate. "Sometimes I wish my mother hadn't been a teacher. Report cards can never go unnoticed. They always need to be reviewed—even at the end of the year."

"Robert!" Aletha's tone told Bob he had said enough. He went to get his report card and laid it on the counter beside Aletha, just as Glenn walked in from the back entry. His father came and looked over Aletha's shoulder as she picked up the report card and opened it.

"You need some work on these grades, son," Glenn said, turning to Bob.

"Yeah, Dad, I know. But being in school is such a drag. I wish I could learn the stuff without having to sit in a desk."

"Sorry, not possible," Glenn said as Aletha handed him the report card. "We'll have to take a serious look at your study habits."

"Okay, Dad. In the fall." Bob lifted the lid of the pot on the stove. "When can you take me out to Arlington?" he asked, turning to face Glenn. "I need to be there for counselor training at the beginning of the week."

●●◆●●

In one of her journals, Aletha made an entry regarding praying about Bob's marks. Asked if he knew she prayed about this, he responded that it was because he started working when he was in tenth grade and his parents were concerned about him finishing high school. Aletha hadn't nagged him about his marks, but his dad, Bob said, "would push more and express concern."

Aletha would be proud of Bob now. He has recently completed further education and obtained his Certificate in Purchasing with PMAC.[i]

"The Queen of Sheba made a difficult journey to know the truth. How much do I inconvenience myself to learn about God and His will for me?" –ALETHA JOICE

---

[i] PMAC stands for Purchasing Management Association of Canada.

Doors and Good Things

"What was it Bob was saying as he left earlier?" Glenn asked. "Something about they were finished fixing the door? What door?"

"The big folding door," Aletha answered from the kitchen, where she was getting some batter ready for some of Glenn's favorite apple muffins.

"I didn't realize it was broken. Why were they fixing it?"

"They fell through it this afternoon."

"How in the world did they do that?" Glenn asked, coming into the kitchen.

"They both jumped on an armchair at the same time and it tipped over, sending them through the door. The door came off the hinges, so they were putting things back together."

"Those two get into more trouble..." Glenn said, shaking his head. "Did they damage anything in the puppet area?"

"No, it's fine," Aletha answered.

"That young friend of his has too much time alone in the house with his mother working outside the home and his older brothers already moved out. When the two of them hang out together, mischief seems to be a second name for both of them."

Aletha smiled. "They'll grow up soon enough and be gone from home," she said. "They don't mean any harm. Besides, think of all the fun they have doing good things. It amazes me when I think of how far Bob bikes to get to Dave's house. It's nearly all the way across the city."

"And when he gets a ride out to the farm so he can ride horses," added Glenn. "That's good fun, too."

"Bob was a challenge," Audrey Wood[8] stated. "Full of energy. When he and his friend... would get into trouble, Aletha would get upset, but then laugh. She wanted the best for her children. Sometimes she would cover her eyes with her hands and say, 'Oh my goodness!'" –FROM AN INTERVIEW WITH GAVIN AND AUDREY WOOD

"The riches of His goodness never fail." –ALETHA JOICE (in reference to Romans 2:4)

Past Cute and Cuddly

I just want to run away, *Aletha said to herself, fresh tears running down her cheeks.* I don't want to be here to see Bette-Jean's heartache if she keeps getting more serious about the boyfriend she has now. Just last week, she told me again about her commitment to God being important to her. How can she say that and be dating a non-Christian fellow? I wish I could find the happy medium between good advice and interference. I'm such a failure.

Just as clearly as if they'd been said aloud, words came to Aletha. "But you serve a God who is not a failure."

She reached for a tissue and wiped at the tears. But Lord, she is going to mess up if she keeps going this way.

"Do you trust me?"

But Lord, I want so much to help her see where she's headed.

"Do you trust me to know what is best for your daughter, that the lessons I prepare for her are designed for the things she needs to learn?"

Slowly the questions began to sink in and Aletha decided she didn't need to run anywhere... except to God in prayer. How many times had she gone to garner strength from the Lord in the last while? Her children weren't always lovable, that was true. But her goal of loving them was not dependent on them; it was an achievable goal if she allowed the Lord to help her and teach her.

Someday her children would be adults and on their own in the world. If she didn't trust her heavenly Father to look after them, how would they see that He was a heavenly Father they could trust?

"It was easy to show love to the children when they were little, cute and cuddly. It was another thing to persevere when they hit their teens.

"...We should persevere, but with love and with 'wisdom from above.'

"...Here she (Bette-Jean) is today—capable, a well-loved teacher, still ready to take on the world—a best friend whom I love dearly." –ALETHA JOICE

Eyes!

Dave nudged Bob in the side. "That's a cute chick over there," he said. "I'd try and get her eye if I were you."

Bob looked over to where the girl Dave was talking about was standing with a few of the other youth.

"So she's cute. Why tell me? I've got a girlfriend. You try and get her attention yourself." He turned back to finish fastening the spotlight onto the pole.

"Is everything set up and ready to go?" Aletha asked, coming onto the stage from a side door, and looking around.

"Pretty much shipshape," Glenn answered. "The tape is ready to roll."

The performance went well, and after the audience had left the sanctuary, the dark-haired youth leader came back to the front platform where the puppeteers were packing up their equipment.

"Could I get everyone's attention?" he asked.

Aletha and the puppeteers stopped what they were doing and looked up. The youth pastor continued, "Our youth group would like to invite the God Squad puppeteers out for pizza."

"Man, now that's what I call a good sound." Everyone laughed at Bob's comment.

"Hollow leg?" the youth leader asked, turning to Aletha and the others and grinning. They all knew about Bob's appetite. She nodded and smiled at Bob.

Glancing back at the youth leader she asked, "Could you give us another ten minutes to finish here?"

"Certainly," he said. "I'll gather up our crowd, and we'll meet you at the front doors in ten."

Dave nudged Bob again when they were getting seated in the restaurant.

"Here's your big chance, guy," he said. Bob looked at his friend without saying anything. "Don't you want to meet her?" he asked, ignoring Bob's silent affirmation of his nonexistent interest.

Bob's forehead puckered with obvious annoyance.

Dave shrugged. "Well, my friend, it's your loss. She was eyeing someone up there on the puppet stage during the introductions, and it wasn't me. She followed you with her eyes every time you moved afterwards, too."

Bob did meet the 'cute' gal, Shelley Bowman, after all. After God Squad finished their performance at the church Shelley attended in Saskatoon, Saskatchewan, the youth invited the troupe out for pizza, where Shelley sat across from Bob.

That summer, Shelley worked at Arlington camp, the same camp where Bob was on weekends and holidays. The relationship grew, and after high school Bob and Shelley attended Aldersgate College in Moose Jaw, where they dated.

Blinking Lights

Aletha switched off the light and went down the hall to their bedroom.

"I hope Bette-Jean arrives safely," she said to Glenn as she pulled back the covers on the bed. "I get so worried about her traveling back and forth from college."

"She'll be fine, I'm sure," Glenn responded.

"Sometimes I wish she wouldn't have decided to attend a college so far away."

"But letting her go out on her own is part of growing up, Aletha."

"It's hard to have her so far away."

"Sure it's hard to do, but she's learning more than just academics. Last time she was home, she talked about realizing that just because it was a Christian College not everyone would see eye to eye. She said her faith was constantly challenged by kids who came from all sorts of backgrounds."

Aletha stopped brushing her hair and looked at Glenn. "I guess being challenged is a good thing."

"Yep."

They continued talking about other things as they finished preparing for bed.

"I wonder if I'll sleep tonight," Aletha said as she pulled the covers around her neck.

The quiet of the night settled around them, but Aletha found she wasn't getting to sleep. At last, she got up and went to the front door. Looking out, she saw the blinking lights of an airplane rising in the night sky. A mental picture of the plane in the palm of God's hand came to her mind. That's how it will be with Bette-Jean's flight! *she thought.*

Aletha recalled a phrase she had read that morning in her personal devotion time—"Our times are in His hands...!" She knew she could trust her heavenly Father.

With a prayer for Bette-Jean's safe arrival, Aletha went back to bed, a sense of peace filling her mind.

After one year at the local university, Bette-Jean went to Greenville College to finish her postsecondary education. She was a long way from home, but it helped her to know that, at about nine o'clock each morning, Aletha would be having her quiet time, praying for her.

"I can see you sitting in your bedroom, in your rocker, with your Bible on your knee, reading and praying," Bette-Jean wrote in a letter home.

"She never told me specific incidents that she prayed about," said Bette-Jean, "[but] I knew she prayed for me. It meant the most when I was in college. I felt very much cared for through that."

"If you pray regularly, your child will know and find security in that knowledge," Aletha recorded in one journal.

Well Done!

"Mom?"

Aletha looked up from the songbooks she was going through at the dining room table. Bob leaned around the doorway to the back door, a grin spread across his face. It was good to have him home for a while before he went back to school at the technical institute in Moose Jaw.

"Dad wants you to come and look at what he did to get the bird to flap its wings."

Aletha laid her pencil onto her page of notes and got up. "He's finished already?" she asked.

"Yep." Bob went back out the door and let it slam behind him.

Aletha reached for her sweater on her way out to the garage. The late summer evening was quite cool, and the garage wasn't heated.

Aletha smiled as she came back to her preparations after viewing the prop Glenn had prepared for the puppet skit God Squad had coming up. What a help he was with her puppet ministry. Such a mechanically inclined mind. She was very glad she could rely on Glenn to take the ideas of what she wanted to do for God Squad and make them into a working, moveable reality for her.

Taking the white-tipped pointer,[i] she tapped out the syllables as she hummed the songs to herself.

What fun to lead the singing in Sunday School, Aletha thought, putting her books and notes away a bit later. Soon she would be getting ready for a Christmas program again. Children got so excited about Christmas. This had been a challenging year working in Christian Education at church, the library, Christian Women's Club, and coordinating Friendship Bible Coffees. But she wanted to serve wherever she could. What if she shirked what the Lord was asking her to do, and when she got to heaven He would not be able to say "Well done" to her?

---

[i] See Glossary for explanation of pointer.

Aletha served in many positions in the churches she attended, often several at the same time. When first coming to Regina, the family attended the Sherwood Free Methodist, then later Parliament Community Mennonite Brethren.

Entries in her journal describe concerns and hurts occurring when working with other people, but Aletha also recorded prayers for those same people. Her one desire was to bring glory to God.

A Fine Young Man

"He's from Georgia, is that what Bette-Jean said?" Glenn asked, turning into the gas station.

"Savannah, I think," Aletha replied.

"Isn't it funny," Glenn said as he stopped the car, "how Don came to the audition to do puppets and met Bette-Jean? It's like the Lord had that in mind when Bette-Jean first got interested in doing puppet performances."

"It is interesting how the Lord introduces people to each other," Aletha asserted.

They were on the way to attend Bette-Jean's graduation from college.

"I hope we meet his approval as future parents-in-law," Glenn said, switching off the motor.

"He could have no better father-in-law," Aletha said, squeezing Glenn's arm.

"Thank you, my de-ah," Glenn quipped, rolling down the window as the attendant came up to the car. His attempt at using a southern accent produced a chuckle in Aletha.

Glenn turned to the gas station attendant. "Fill 'er up." After the attendant had started filling the tank, Glenn went on, "He seems comfortable with us. I think she's picked a fine young man to marry."

Aletha smiled and nodded. "I think I'll get out and stretch," she said, squeezing her feet into her shoes.

After they had been on the highway for a while, Glenn spoke again. "Bette-Jean sure loves working with puppets."

"She does," Aletha responded. "I asked her once why she didn't do something else at college, and she said, 'But, Mom, I love it!'"

"Dad, how about we stop and get something to eat?" Bob asked from the back seat.

"Not for a while, son," Glenn replied. "We'll stop when we get to Fairbolt. That gets us about halfway there." Glenn understood. He was beginning to feel the length of the two-day trip, too.

God certainly answered our prayers about a spouse for Bette-Jean, Aletha thought as she took a final sip of her drink and began cleaning up the papers and cartons from their lunch. I wonder who He has in store for Bob. Maybe the gal he met in Saskatoon.

She watched as Glenn and Bob tossed the frisbee back and forth. Bob was becoming such a handsome young man.

Bette-Jean and Don were married on a rainy day, August 16, 1980, at Sherwood Free Methodist Church in Regina. After a honeymoon at the cabin at Arlington Beach, they made their home in Greenville, Illinois, where Don completed his education at the college. They have since returned to Canada, and at the time of this writing are living on a farm near Moose Jaw. Don has taken up farming and selling real estate, and Bette-Jean continues to teach.

What Will My Treasure Be Now?

Aletha put her arm around Bette-Jean's shoulders. How could she comfort her? She thought back to the baby they had lost before it was born. Although she knew her daughter's pain was her own, Aletha realized she could feel greater empathy than someone who had never experienced the loss of an unborn child. Aletha had told Bette-Jean and Bob that children were a treasure. But what happens when things turn out differently than you anticipated? *she asked herself.*

"My view of life was, you get a good education, get married, and have a family." *Bette-Jean spoke softly.* "That's what everybody does. It just happens."

Aletha nodded, not sure if Bette-Jean expected a response.

"So now what is supposed to be my treasure?" *Bette-Jean continued, beginning to weep again.*

"What did the doctor say about why it happened? " *Aletha asked, after Bette-Jean had calmed a bit again.*

"He said there was nothing wrong. It just happens sometimes." *Bette-Jean rose and went over to the window.*

A reflection of how she feels, *Aletha thought, watching Bette-Jean standing and looking out where early summer rain was falling from the grey sky.*

"I think I'm finding it so hard to get over this because a miscarriage isn't really treated as a death. People expect you to be pregnant again. They keep asking when we're going to have a baby." *The tears began again.* "I so much wanted to show off our baby to you."

Aletha went over to stand beside Bette-Jean and put her arm around her.

"I know, sweetheart. I so much wanted to see your baby, too."

"You do know, don't you Mom?"

Aletha nodded. Lord, would you grant my daughter the joy of children someday? *she prayed, squeezing Bette-Jean in a mother's hug.*

Because of her experiences with how insensitive some people could be when relating to parents who experienced a miscarriage or stillbirth, Aletha was sensitive to how Mother's Day services were conducted. After one service where the youth pastor, Jason Unruh,[9] [xx] commended not only the mothers, but also the other women of the church, Aletha wrote a short, affirming note to him: "We who are mothers are blessed. Those... women who never have or probably never will conceive, while they do not face the stigma as in years past, still have a deep longing to be a Mom. Mother's Day becomes one of the hardest services to attend. Many single women and childless married women have mothered countless children. It's a good day to pay tribute to all who 'mother' and to include them when you are giving out the flowers."

"Aletha was glad Bette-Jean could teach full-time and not have to juggle that with family, but was still disappointed they were not able to have a child." –GLENN JOICE

Intravenous and Prices to Pay

Aletha shifted in her hospital bed. The pain she was in now after the surgery was as bad as before, when the doctor had told her she needed a hysterectomy. But I guess it was something I needed to insure future good health. Now I need to work at getting better.

"How do you feel about not having any more children?" the doctor had asked. What a silly question, when her youngest was twenty years old!

"I wanted children very much and, after losing our first baby, I consider the two children we have as gifts from God," she answered. "I have taken endless delight in their development. So no, being sorry I won't have any more children isn't a hurdle for me in considering the surgery."

For her, it wasn't, but it might be different for a young woman just starting a family. It would have been quite different if she had been asked the same question before she had any children at all. Then her sorrow would have been a great factor.

A nurse walked into the room, interrupting Aletha's reflections.

"How are you feeling, Aletha?" the nurse asked, checking the tubes from the IV.

"Like I don't want to move, so the pain is less," Aletha said, watching the nurse write something on the chart in her hand.

"That will take a bit of time, though by next week it should be a lot better."

After she left, Aletha's thoughts turned to the new speaker system she was working on finding for God Squad. She had gone from place to place collecting prices so they could make a good decision about what to get. Glenn and Bob—

"Hi, sweetheart."

"Hi, Mom."

Well, if thinking of them didn't bring them in person!

Due to her experience with the stillbirth of their child, and Bette-Jean's loss of her own baby, Aletha had great empathy for other women who lost children. Not only did she express herself regarding attitudes to childless women, she often expressed sympathy to those who had lost a child.

When she was told she would need a hysterectomy and could not have any more children, she also understood that it was less traumatic for her than for young women whose hopes of having children were dashed by the same news. Her expressions of empathy extended to them as well.

"God said, offer me the hard parts of what you do." –ALETHA JOICE

Lesson in Humility

The minister's deep voice spoke the words which would bind Bob and Shelley together for life. As they walked over to the table to sign the register, Aletha let her mind drift. My last child married and away from home. I'm so happy they will be living nearby.

"Shelley looks so beautiful," Aletha whispered to Glenn.

"She's a beautiful young woman inside, too," Glenn whispered back.

Aletha nodded, then watched the young couple again, smiling as she recalled the first time Shelley had been with them for supper. It had showed just how different their two families were. Shelley's mother preferred waiting on everyone, while in the Joice family, if anyone wanted anything else after a meal was prepared, they looked after it. That day, Glenn had wanted coffee, so while he'd gone for the pot, Aletha had gone for the cups. Bob had gone to get himself some juice, leaving Shelley alone at the table.

Shelley rose from signing the register and the bridesmaid reached for the pen. Aletha's thoughts went back to how Bob and Shelley had met. Maybe they wouldn't have met if I hadn't continued working with the puppet group after Bette-Jean went to college, if I hadn't kept Bob involved.

"Still need some lessons in humility?" The question her Heavenly Father put into her mind made Aletha smile.

No, thanks. *He would have arranged the meeting without her help, she was sure.* I wonder what other method the Lord would have used to bring them together, *she mused.*

The minister stepped aside as Bob and Shelley walked to the front of the platform. "Ladies and gentlemen, I would like to introduce to you Mr. and Mrs. Bob Joice."

Aletha wiped at a few tears trying to sneak down her cheek as the smiling couple walked quickly down the aisle. She was so proud of their son. And now she had another daughter to love.

The wedding guests followed the newlyweds out of the church.

"The sun must be out there somewhere," Glenn said as they stepped outside and felt the heat. "You'd never know it though with the haze out here."

"Could be the smoke from the forest fires," Aletha responded, looking up at the sky.

Bob and Shelley were married July 31, 1982 at the Lakeview Free Methodist church in Saskatoon. Glenn and Aletha had given their blessing and the occasion was a joyous one. They had been dating for three years, and engaged for one.

Although they were concerned about their pictures turning out because of the overcast day, they turned out beautifully. It seemed the muted lighting only served to enhance them, making them better.

And the parents-in-law? "When they thought something had been said which was overly critical, they would call and apologize even if it was something which may not have bothered us and we hadn't noticed," said Shelley.[10] "They were sensitive to their children, wanted a good relationship with them, [and] always let us know they loved us, cared for us."

A Trunk and Classes

Bob grunted as he and Shelley lifted the heavy trunk out of the car. If there was no other way to tell if the trunk was an antique, its weight gave it away.

"It's so warmly finished," Shelley said, running her hand along the top of the trunk after they had set it down in the living room. "I'm so glad we stopped at that antique place. That big barn held the mother lode of antiques."

Bob smiled and nodded.

Shelley opened the dome-shaped lid of the large, old trunk. "I can't believe it still has the original print inside it. And the hat box! What a find!"

"If you like it, I'm glad we got it," Bob answered. He was finding out many things about his new bride. He was also discovering that he would be involved in what he found out about her. Her interest in antiques, for instance, meant the need for a strong back.

"What time will you have to leave for classes in the mornings?" Shelley asked a little later as they sat at the kitchen table, finishing their supper. They had been talking about the classes in Purchasing Management Bob was going to be taking at the technical institute.

"Eight should be early enough," Bob answered. "What a rude awakening classes are going to be," he added. "After getting married and spending so much wonderful one on one time with my beautiful, new bride, it's going to be rough."

Shelley smiled. She loved him so much. And what a joy it was to be part of his family.

Following their honeymoon at Kenosee Lake, Bob and Shelley made their home in Regina, Saskatchewan, where at the time of this writing they still live. Shelley's antique trunk stands in a prominent place in their living room.

Shelley spoke well of Aletha as her mother-in-law. She said Aletha and Glenn were careful to give them their space. They never interfered. They gave suggestions, but never told them how they should do things, such as in raising their son.

Jacob John

The little fist curled around her finger as Aletha touched the newborn's hand. "Thank you, Father," she whispered. "He is so precious."

Aletha looked up as Bob and Shelley came into the house from the deck.

"Mom, you are going to give him back before you go, right?" Bob teased as they came over to where she sat cuddling Jake in her arms.

Bob and Shelley had invited them over for the afternoon, and although she was reluctant to have her little grandson leave her arms, she knew Shelley was tired and that she and Glenn should be heading out soon.

Aletha looked up and smiled. "You really want him back that much, huh?" she teased back. She knew Bob was very glad to be a father.

The little boy who lay in her arms was extra special to her because it seemed this would be the only grandchild she would ever have. How she had longed to see her children's children running up to her and reaching out to give them a hug. But if the Lord only gave her this one grandchild, she would praise Him and be the best grandmother she could be.

"Bob and Shelley are so relaxed with J.J.," Glenn said on the way home. "The little fellow seems very content with them, too. I'm sure he's glad to be home after sleeping under those ultraviolet lights."

Aletha nodded. "They will be good parents," she said, after a pause. "They're quite laid back. So many parents feel overwhelmed when those little people arrive and disrupt their homes with their cries for nourishment and attention."

"Well, he'll get lots of our attention," Glenn said, turning to Aletha with a grin.

Aletha smiled back at him. "You'll be a wonderful grandpa," she said lovingly.

Bob and Shelley gave their son the full name Jacob John, but for many years family and friends called him by the nickname J.J. One of his youth group friends, however, later found out J.J.'s full name and began calling him Jake. Rather liking it, J.J. asked that his parents and grandparents start calling him

Jake. J.J., acquired in his babyhood, stuck for many years, but at his request they began using Jake.

What kind of grandmother was Aletha to Jake, who would be her only grandchild? Friends Gavin and Audrey Wood used the phrase, "She adored J.J."

"She showed that what J.J. had to say was important. She really listened to him and spent time with him. She knew him quite well as a person, not just a grandson. She encouraged him to find out what his gifts and abilities were." –BOBBY JO STENZIL[11]

Old Toys and a Special Grandson

"That's cool, huh, Grandma?" J.J. said, pointing to a large blue remote control car.

"Well, I suggest it go on your list then," Aletha responded, tapping the paper J.J. was carrying. They were wandering through the toy store, looking at the heavily laden shelves, primed and ready to spill forth into the hands of all the Christmas shoppers. Aletha and J.J. were on their annual shopping trip, to do a 'look see'. That way Aletha knew she would be getting him something for Christmas that he liked.

"Hey, check this out, J.J." Aletha stopped in front of the games shelf and lifted a box with a picture of a family seated at a table playing the game. "Looks like this family is having a good time. This must be a good game."

"Nah. I've played that with my friends. It's not that much fun. That picture doesn't tell you much about the game."

Aletha smiled and nodded. "It's a good thing we do this every year," she said. "It saves me from getting you a boring toy."

"And it's fun just looking, too," J.J. said, turning the corner at the end of the aisle.

"Not only that, I get to spend time with my most special grandson."

"Grandma, how could I be the most special grandson? I'm your only grandson."

Aletha laughed. "So you are," she said, "but you are still the most special one. No one else's grandchildren are as special to me as you are."

"Oh, I get it now," J.J. said, reaching for a package from the display and examining it more closely.

"Anything special happening at school?" Aletha asked, as they turned down the next row of toys. "How is that project coming?"

Being the only grandson was a very special spot, according to Jake.[12] "The attention was not spread out. It was special because it was 'just me.' Sometimes at gatherings, 'just me' was a bit boring, but mostly I liked it."

Some of his memories include times when Aletha (and sometimes Glenn, when he wasn't working) babysat him. "There was this box of old toys in the basement. She would sit down on the floor and play with me," Jake recalled. As he got older, Jake said more of the time he spent with his grandmother was in conversation—a lot of it while they were eating.

Birthdays and Christmas meant making a big list while window shopping with Aletha. When he got older, they didn't go to the store together anymore, but she would still choose their gift for him from a list he gave her.

What kind of Grandmother was she? "Fun. I'd say loving. It was subtleties really—the way she did things." –JAKE JOICE

Trust in her heavenly Father was increasing in Aletha's life. More and more, she was reaching out to the Lord with what was in her hand, giving it over to Him to be filled with His strength and not her own.

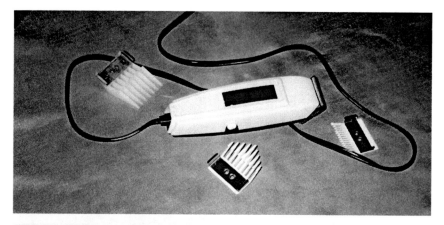

TOP: An electric hair clipper similar to the one Aletha used to cut Glenn's hair. MIDDLE LEFT: Aletha with Bette-Jean at four months, in front of their house in Greenville. MIDDLE RIGHT: Young Glenn, seen here with Bob as an infant of six months, in Moose Jaw. BOTTOM: All dressed up, Bette-Jean at three years old certainly has someplace to go.

TOP LEFT: The kind of roller skates Bette-Jean purchased (photo taken with permission of the Antique Mall of Regina). TOP RIGHT: The wonderful old trunk Shelley and Bob purchased on their honeymoon (photo taken with permission). MIDDLE: The Joice family in 1989. (l-r) Aletha, Glenn (holding Jake), Shelley, Don, BOTTOM: Bette-Jean and Don on their wedding day, August 16, 1980.

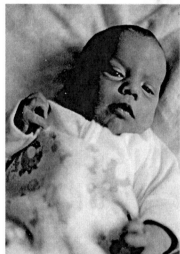

TOP: "The cabin later became a cottage with three bedrooms, spacious living, a dining room, full bath, and modern kitchen." –GLENN JOICE MIDDLE LEFT: Bob and Shelley on their wedding day, July 31, 1982. MIDDLE RIGHT: Contented Jacob John, born on April 9, 1988, seen here at one month. BOTTOM: The Bible was a special book to Aletha. God's Word was her guidebook, became her personal treasure. Aletha underlined countless verses and squeezed out as much space as possible when writing in the margins.

"To your glory..."

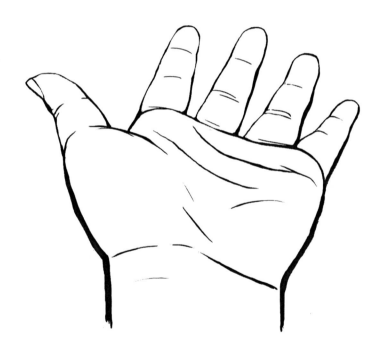

Words Have Power

Aletha quickly flipped the page of her book and continued reading.

> The doctor pulled the curtain closed and sat down on the edge of Connie's bed. "The tests all came back positive. I'm sorry, Connie."
>
> Tears came to her eyes as Connie looked up at the green-clad surgeon.
>
> "Isn't there something else you could try? I don't want to leave my little boy. He needs me."
>
> "There is nothing I can do," the doctor replied. "Someday maybe we'll have more cures. I wish it would happen today. But..." He stood without finishing, the pain of helplessness showing in his eyes.

The big clock chimed the half-hour. Aletha lifted her eyes from the book and looked up at the clock. Five-thirty! Oh, my goodness. Glenn will be here soon and supper isn't started.

Tempted to read to the end of the chapter, Aletha instead put the bookmark between the pages and laid the book on the coffee table.

When supper was finished, Glenn reached for the Bible to read the daily portion. Aletha's mind returned to the book she had been reading. She could hardly wait to get back to it. What a woman the heroine was, *she mused.* I wonder if I would be that brave if I was dying of an incurable disease.

Aletha's childhood love of words continued into adulthood. She loved working in libraries at the church she attended, and read every book she bought for the library—whether for adults or kids. "If it was not suitable, she would return it and ask the bookstore why they sold that kind of book. Sometimes she would put a little review inside the book cover, explaining something. For example, in the medieval times, the word 'bastard' was an acceptable word. So she would indicate which page the word was on and explain its usage." –JANEY GOERT-ZEN[13]

"When the *Reader's Digest* comes, the first thing I do is the word quiz, [called] *It Pays to Enrich Your Word Power*, and I'm greatly encouraged the few times I rate 'Excellent', and quite encouraged when I rate 'Good'." –ALETHA JOICE

Children and Missions

"Come on in." Aletha pulled the door wider so Marilyn could step inside. "Let me take that," she added, reaching for the box Marilyn was carrying and setting it on the steps.

Marilyn stepped out of her shoes and took off her jacket. She handed it to Aletha, then picked up the box and went up the steps.

"Have a seat," Aletha said, going into the kitchen after hanging Marilyn's coat in the hall closet. "I'll get the tea."

Marilyn sat down on the couch and set the box of meeting records down beside her and leaned back. Aletha's home never failed to touch her. The peacefulness wasn't just something caused by the attractive furnishings and draperies. It was the spirit of kindness with which she was greeted at the door.

"How many children do you think we should plan for this year?" Marilyn asked, accepting the mug Aletha offered her. "Mmm, this is good," she added after she had taken a sip of tea.

"It's always so hard to tell how many children will be there, isn't it?" Aletha asked in answer to Marilyn's question. "What number did we have last year?"

Marilyn set her cup down on the end table and, opening the box, took out a binder with last year's minutes.

"By the way, how is your brother doing?" Aletha inquired as she seated herself in the armchair across from Marilyn.

"Wonderful news!" Marilyn exclaimed, laying the binder on her lap.

"Oh, tell me!" Aletha responded, nearly spilling her tea as she moved quickly to set the cup on the table beside her. She leaned forward expectantly.

"Darcy was healed!" Marilyn answered. "The cancer is gone."

"That is wonderful news!" Aletha affirmed, tears pooling in her eyes. "I'm so glad!" Marilyn smiled, the joyful tears coming to her eyes as well. They had prayed so much. "Tell me about it," Aletha said, reaching for a tissue. "And then let's spend time thanking God in our prayer time." Smiling across at Marilyn, she handed her a tissue, too.

Tea and planning were momentarily forgotten. Drawn into the emotional embrace of Aletha's attentiveness, Marilyn shared the details of the answer to their prayers about her brother.

●●◆●●

"Aletha and I were friends related to the missions committee," related Marilyn Dyck.[14] "We got together at her house to plan the children's aspect of the missions conference. We would have conversation and tea before starting the meeting. She would ask specific questions... [and] knew what was on my heart. She shared a bit with me of herself. The meetings sometimes lasted the whole afternoon. She had a deep compassion for spiritual growth, as well as interest in missions information for the children. She wanted children to hear God's Word."

"Aletha was always concerned that the children would have a good program at the fall missions conference. She would have the children's activity planned by June and would write the plans all out in detail... " –HELEN BRAUN[15]

More than Missions

A floral border surrounded the words Aletha was writing. After signing her name to the letter, she looked up at her bulletin board. Hmmm, *she said to herself, removing the card with a record of the letters she had sent.* I must get a few more done today. It's entirely too long since I sent the last letter to the Brauns and Godards.

She folded the letter and, reaching for an envelope, put the pages inside. After she had addressed the envelope, she set it aside and reached for another piece of stationery.

It is so much nicer to send a handwritten letter, *Aletha thought as she began to write again. This note was going to Guatemala. One of the boys from God Squad was there doing a missions project. She had a special place in her heart for him and what was happening in his life.*

A few more letters completed, Aletha stretched and looked at her watch. The letter to the Godards would have to wait until after lunch. She wanted to spend some more time praying for them while she wrote. The sense that they needed prayer was beginning to weigh very heavily on her heart. I wonder if I should talk to Steve Klassen[i] about it, *she mused as she went to prepare a sandwich.* I feel I need more people praying.

"How are you feeling?" Aletha wrote later that afternoon, the hand holding the pen beginning to ache a little. This was the fourth card, yet it only touched the edges of the group of people to whom she wanted to send encouragement today. "I hope the doctors will soon find the answer to your problems. It must be very hard to cope with all that pain every day."

When she finished the last letter, this one to a young teacher friend, Aletha laid the pen down and read through what she had ready to mail. Although they were far apart in age, they had that common bond of a love for teaching. "Always include something positive for every child," she had written. It was report card time, and Aletha still remembered how difficult it could be to find positive things to say to some children in a tough class.

---

[i] Steve Klassen was Director for Constituency Relations with Mennonite Brethren Missions and Services International (MBMSI), the missions organization which a number of missionaries Aletha wrote to were associated with.

"She had a great ability to remember things. After six months of not seeing a person, she would ask about some little detail you had told her. She corresponded with a lot of people and when you think of the number of people she wrote to, it was a lot to remember."—Doreen Butterfield [16]

When Aletha wrote her letters, she would include specific, personal comments to the person to whom she was writing. That thoughtfulness had an effect on teacher Bobby Jo Stenzil. "With some children… it is hard to find something positive I can say in their report cards, so I need to remember things. I keep a file on each child, and now if I see something positive they do during the day, I write it down and put it into the file. If I notice something they are doing that is positive and I can put it into their report card, it may affect them for the rest of their lives."

Aletha found it important to contact anyone who went away, to tell them she was thinking of them and praying for them. "I appreciated that," said Josh Bekker.[17] Aletha corresponded with Josh while he was away at Bible school in Austria, and also later while he was teaching in Guatemala. "She was interested in my stories, what was going on in my life," Josh added. "When I was in Austria and Guatemala… she was one of the few who wrote."

Each time she wrote, Aletha recorded on a file card the name of the missionary, missionary couple, or young person who had gone on short-term missions to whom she had written a letter or sent a card. Satisfying your curiosity about the number of letters she wrote each month or year could be easily assuaged by using a database. You would see each missionary name reappear every few months of the year, and that from three to seven times in a month a letter had been written to someone.

The overseas missionaries who received correspondence from Aletha were impressed with her faithfulness in writing letters, thankful for her encouragement, her prayers, and her faithfulness to the Lord.

"I remember the faithful encouragement Aletha was. You could expect it regularly. Her letters were like an anchor on a rope, keeping the lines of communication from the church connected. It would brighten my day when a card or letter came, because I knew it would uplift me." –Carolyn Gartke[18]

At times, Aletha sent notes and encouraging little cards, but missionaries loved her letters. Not just short little notes, but long, newsy letters. Those handwritten letters, coming on a regular basis, keeping them up to date about church life back home, were a real encouragement to them. For those in the mission field, Aletha's letters communicated the love of the church.

"Aletha's lengthy letters required the pages be numbered," was Carolyn Gartke's observation. She would "fill the front sides of the pages and then go back and fill the back sides. You had to watch that you kept track which page was next."

Although email was quick, her long handwritten letters were special. "We got about six or seven letters a year... always... in longhand," Julie Siemens[19] recalled. "Others would write an email, but Aletha would write in-depth. Her letters were informative... pages about what she was doing, events in her life, and God Squad... what was happening with the membership, the ladies' group, the youth."

Getting letters on the mission field was especially exciting in outlying areas. Garry and Rita Mae Braun[20] "got into Bamako about once a month," so they "always hoped for a nice stack. Getting letters from Aletha was an emotional boost." They knew some kind of encouragement would be in them.

Aletha also wrote specifically to children of missionaries, who were often away from home going to schools for missionary children.

"She would send cards to the kids at school," said Rita Mae Braun. "They loved getting mail anyway. The mail would come in around noon everyday. There was a long table in the dorm where the dorm mother laid out the mail. The kids would go to that table first thing at noon when they got out of class."

Birthday and holiday greeting cards were part of the correspondence Aletha conducted, so the children were recipients of those as well. Julie Siemens remembers one Christmas card their girls received. "It was so cool. It was very Canadian," she said.

Often her letters to the children included a special little gift. Aletha would send little extras, something flat that fit into an envelope. "She would send stickers," said Rita Mae. "At Valentines, she would send a few extra little Valentines that they could give to their friends."

Not limiting herself to sending only things that fit into envelopes, when someone was going to that mission field for a visit, Aletha used the opportunity to send along a small gift for a missionary. "When I was in Honduras, she sent a small gift along with my mother. It was four little travel containers with hairspray, shampoo, conditioner, and gel. I still use the containers when I travel."—NANCY JO (RUSSELL) ZIEGLER[21]

Missionaries referred to in this chapter and in the chapter *Burdens and Intercession*:

- Garry & Rita Mae Braun, who served in Mali under Gospel Missionary Union.

- Carolyn Gartke and her husband Tim, who were missionaries to Lithuania with Mennonite Brethren Missions and Services International.
- Trever and Joan Godard were in Columbia with Mennonite Brethren Missions and Services International.
- Julie Siemens and her husband Scott were in Kentucky under the Mennonite Central Committee.
- Nancy Jo (Russell) Ziegler was in Honduras with Samaritan's Purse.

There are more comments from missionaries in the Appendix 4: Lasting Impressions.

Party Line Ministries

There should be a good number out at the training session this morning, *Aletha said to herself, putting the list of Friendship Bible Coffee guides back into the folder and going to the closet for her jacket. She was looking forward to meeting the women who would be new to guiding, as well as renewing acquaintances from last year.*

"Before we get into the training," *Aletha said after the ladies were seated around the room,* "how about some of you share some experiences of your guiding with the rest."

A number of women told how they had solved some kind of problem, how the Lord had looked after small details of planning and time management.

"One more," *Aletha said, when there was a pause,* "and then we'll get to work."

A softspoken grandmother looked around the room and then spoke. "Never underestimate how the Lord will bring ladies to the study," *she began.* "I live on a farm and we still have a party line. This means that when I pick up the phone to call someone, my conversation can be heard by anyone else on my line who picks up their phone while I am talking."

"Good old 'rubbering'," *one lady interjected. The other women chuckled at the word that described what the grandmother had been talking about.*

The woman who had been sharing smiled and then continued, "One day I had a phone call from a lady who wanted to begin attending Friendship Bible Coffee because she had overheard me talking to someone about a study. Now she is a regular attender."

"Thank you for sharing that," *Aletha said, opening her folder.* "Thanks to all of you for again being willing to teach God's Word. Let's begin by asking God to bless our efforts."

After first discovering it as a young mother, Aletha's involvement in Friendship Bible Coffee lasted for many years. In addition to guiding, or teaching and hosting studies in her home, she also held the position of consulting coordinator, where she was responsible for organizing studies, finding hostesses, providing material to guides, and recruiting and training guides. Those who trained under her said she was very thorough. "She would train for a while in the morning," Sonja Weir,[22] fellow Friendship Bible Coffee Coordinator said, "take a break for lunch, and then have another training time in the afternoon."

The aim of Friendship Bible Coffee, to introduce non-Christians to studying God's Word in the home of a friend, matched Aletha's desire to reach as many women as possible. In her notes for a talk she gave about the history and purpose of Friendship Bible Coffees, she wrote this: "We live in a changing world. More women are working outside the home. More women are going back to school. Should we give up? No, they still need God's Word, the Good News of Jesus Christ. We must adjust the times to fit the schedules of today's women; for example, short lunch hour studies at work."

"If Aletha trained you," stated Irene Sotropa,[23] "you knew everything you were supposed to do. If you did it or not was up to you."

At the Podium

Aletha read the lines printed beneath a picture of herself in the newspaper article:

> *"Aletha Joice, teacher, homemaker and presently Friendship Bible Coffee Consulting Co-ordinator, will be guest speaker at a Deck the Halls dinner... Tuesday at 6:45 in the Elizabethan Ballroom of the Regina Inn."*

Aletha laid the newspaper down on the coffee table.

A ballroom, *she said to herself.* Will what I say be more impressive than my surroundings? Lord, give me the right words, *she pleaded, picking up the notes she had been working on in preparation for speaking at the dinner.*

A few hours later, her hand cramping from holding the pen so long, Aletha got up to prepare supper for her family. There were more words on her page now, but her prayer was still the same: Lord, give me the right words.

Aletha "was a very good speaker. She spoke on something she believed in. She was always well-prepared... being a teacher came out in what she did."—Vivian Norbraten,[24] fellow Christian Women's Club worker.

"I found her to be excellent in any speaking she did. She was always well-prepared and methodical, and I knew these things were backed in prayer preparation as well. I was grateful for her excellence and the knowledge of her deep commitment to the Lord. She had a deep faith which was founded on her knowledge of Scripture and... only the Lord knows the full impact of what she did." –Betty Anderson[25]

Sometimes Aletha would have a full day of speaking. Until recently, coffee times, luncheons, and evening meetings were all held on the same day. The person who was speaking would give their talk at all three meetings.

In addition to speaking at functions, Aletha served in many capacities with Christian Women's Club (CWC) over the years—telephone chair, project coordinator, prayer advisor, district counselor, area representative, and consulting coordinator for Friendship Bible Coffee and CWC executive chair.

"She had some kind of position every year," said Vivian. "She was consistently involved."

Aletha spoke not only at Christian Women's Club, but was asked to speak at ladies' group activities at church.

On occasion, Aletha shared the podium with her daughter Bette-Jean, also a gifted speaker.

Do It Well

"Disciplining myself to pray every day has been hard." The lady speaking dabbed at her eyes, *and paused to collect herself. "But it's become easier now that I have someone specific to pray for, knowing that person is also praying for me." A smile came despite her tears. "The three other people praying for me have a lot more work than I do praying for them."*

The other ladies smiled with her. They knew about the many struggles she'd had in the last year, and how the Lord was working in her life. She is a stronger person, Aletha reflected, *even though she does not realize it herself.* Last year, she would not have had the courage to share her struggle with anyone else.

"Are there any others who want to share a specific thing about being a prayer partner this year?" Aletha asked after a pause. When no one spoke, she continued. "Last week, I asked that each of you prepare a special blessing for your prayer partners using a Scripture passage as the basis for what you wrote. Let's begin reading those now."

One after the other, those who had their blessings ready rose and went to stand beside the person they had written it for and read it aloud.

The tears were flowing freely by the time her prayer partner stood beside Aletha. "I thank God for you," Elaine read. "When I think of you, what comes to mind is your work of faith, your labor of love, and your patience of hope in following our Master, Jesus Christ. It is clear to me, Aletha, that God not only loves you very much, but also has put His hand on you for something special. Although you have experienced trouble in your life, you have been able to take great joy from the Holy Spirit—taking the trouble with the joy, the joy with the trouble. May the amazing grace of Jesus Christ, the extravagant love of God, and the intimate friendship of the Holy Spirit be with you, Aletha."[i]

Aletha led many Bible studies in the women's group at her church. She was very open about what was happening in her own life, and this sharing of herself gave the ladies in her class the freedom to share concerns they had. Very conscientious about good preparation, her notes from the various studies she led filled

---

[i] In reference to I Thessalonians 1:2-6 and 2 Corinthians 13:14, quoted from a note written by Elaine Wiens.

several binders. Her policy was that if you were going to do something, you might as well do it well.

Always eager to enable others to teach well, Aletha took on researching the type and availability of Bible study materials for small groups one year. She prepared an extensive reference binder, with information about what kind of studies were available, and placed it in the church library.

"Am I clean as I approach God's house and as I serve? The blood of Jesus cleanses me!"[ii] –ALETHA JOICE

[ii] In reference to Psalm 15.

Little Things

"They can't be lost, they just can't be," Aletha said to Glenn at supper. She had looked for the pictures they had taken at the lake every place she could think of to look.

"They'll likely show up in some unusual spot," Glenn said, setting his coffee cup down and reaching for Aletha's hand.

"Some of them are so special, I really would hate to have lost them," Aletha responded, blinking back a few tears.

When the breakfast dishes were all put away, Aletha pulled the vacuum into the living room. As she vacuumed, her thoughts repeatedly went back to sorting out where she could have put the pictures. Knowing her heavenly Father cared about the little things in her life, she spoke to Him in a short prayer. "Dear God, I can't find those pictures we brought from the lake. I don't know where else to look. Do you mind helping me? Thanks, Amen."

Early the next morning, as Aletha was brushing her hair, some words came to her mind: "Go look in the suitcase again. Check under that flap in the part that you don't often use."

"Aletha," Glenn called interrupting her contemplation, "are you still planning to do some shopping today?"

"I do have a few errands to run," Aletha replied, coming into the kitchen where Glenn was pouring water into the coffeemaker.

"Good," Glenn smiled. "I have an errand I'd like you to do for me."

The day got busier from there and Aletha forgot about the pictures. It wasn't until the next morning that it came to her that her prayer had been answered.

"My goodness! Would you look at that!" Aletha said aloud after lifting the flap at the bottom of the suitcase, finding the envelope of pictures underneath.

Aletha prayed about the little things. When she told the ladies at Friendship Bible Coffee that she had an answer to her prayer about finding some pictures she had mislaid, it surprised her that they would not assume she would pray for something like that. Praying for small concerns was common practice for her. Her husband Glenn affirmed that Aletha "prayed about little things in everyday life."

●●◆●●

"The instructions for the tabernacle and its furniture suggest that no detail of man's worship of God is too small for God's concern." –ALETHA JOICE

Burdens and Intercession

Aletha turned the page of the small book containing the list of missionaries she had committed to pray for during her personal time with God. The picture of Paul and Jan Stobbe reminded her of their request that people pray for their autistic son.

It must have been very painful to have to leave the mission field, *she thought.* That, combined with having an autistic son, seems like the greatest challenge and grief to bear.

"*That's tough!" she said aloud.*

With amazing swiftness, God spoke to her, "What's tough? I AM THE LORD!"

Oh, Lord, forgive me! *Aletha prayed.* Forgive me for judging that the Stobbes' situation is impossible to You. I praise You because You are able to heal this boy and/or improve his communication and self-help skills. I know whatever You allow will bring glory to Your Name through this family.

When Aletha finished her time of prayer, she went to her desk. Picking up the little stickers she had found, she dropped them into the envelope with the letter for Luke and Larissa she had finished the day before.

"I must remember to pick up a card for Dorothy's birthday," *she said to herself as she licked the envelope.*

Among the clippings of short verses or sayings on Aletha's bulletin board were various missionary picture-prayer cards, evidence of her heart for missions. "She always kept up to date on the missionaries," said Elaine Walrath, a good friend of Aletha's. "She had a missionary spirit even as a young person."

Missionaries knew that Aletha spent time in prayer for each of them, sometimes letting them know of specific prayers in letters. "She would write and say 'I was praying for you, so I'll write,'" explained Julie Siemens.

Aletha would use Scriptures, a verse and the reference, in her letters, putting something in that she felt would be useful to the missionary to whom she was writing. She would begin with 'I am praying for you that...' and then write in the Scripture quotation to complete the sentence. "We assumed that she prayed with our names inserted in the Scripture," commented Rita Mae

Braun. "That meant a lot to me. It was convincing evidence that, yes, she was spending time praying."

"She would send Scripture verses to me that she had prayed for me. I would look the verse up and see that she had sent something which met my need. For example, 'So, my son, throw yourself into this work...'[i] She was basically saying, 'Stick with it, God will honor you.' It was six weeks after she had prayed it for me when the letter arrived, but it arrived right when I needed to hear that message. It was an example of God's Spirit working among believers." –LYNN SCHELLENBERG[26]

One missionary couple, Trever and Joan Godard,[27] shared a special bond with Aletha because of her prayers.

"We did not share a friendship with Aletha Joice in the traditional sense of the word. However, we felt very close to her thanks to her commitment to loving us. For years, Aletha wrote notes of encouragement, Scripture verses, prayers, anecdotes, and happenings in the life of Parliament Community Church... We received them like a cool spring in the desert. Our call to ministry in Colombia, with many risks and sacrifices, [was] something that Aletha not only seemed to understand, but also sought to help carry us through. Her vigilant prayer on our behalf made a profound impact on our lives and, we are convinced, advanced the Kingdom of God in Colombia. Some have said that God called us to battle for His kingdom on the front lines. If that be true, Aletha was the messenger that ran ahead to the King, fell to her knees before Him, and pleaded for our victory and safety in the battle."

That safety in battle was profoundly illustrated in the lives of the Godard family in early November 1995, when they were living on an acreage overlooking the city of Cali, Colombia.

"The civil tension was mounting," wrote the Godards, "and it seemed that no family was untouched by violence. In spite of these circumstances, or perhaps because of them, Colombia was beginning to experience a spiritual awakening. People were hungry for God and our ministry of discipleship was growing. We have come to understand, however, that God's enemy doesn't readily surrender strongholds that he has had for generations. In order for us to gain territory for God, we needed intercessory prayer. Aletha's ear and heart were so attuned to God's voice that she knew what to pray before we even expressed our need. That particular November, she had been quite burdened for

---

[i] In reference to 2 Timothy 1:4 (MSG) .

us as she interceded. Each time she brought us to the Lord in prayer, she would weep. While Steve Klassen of Abbotsford, B.C. was at the church's missions conference, Aletha shared with him her burden for us. He encouraged her to continue her intercession and took seriously her concern by asking others to pray for us as well." –FROM A LETTER FROM TREVER AND JOAN GODARD (quoted with their permission)

Not only did Aletha write newsy letters, the people she corresponded with knew she prayed for them—that they were 'on her list.'

The Impact of Vigilant Prayer

The paper trembled in Aletha's hand as she read the Godard's account of what had happened in their home in Columbia:

> *Our family and discipleship team were assaulted in our home by six armed men. They pushed us into our children's bedroom. We knelt to pray and sing. The danger to our lives was very real, but we all felt an incredible sense of God's presence in that room. The Holy Spirit gave us words of courage, forgiveness, and love for our captors. When they finished looting the house, they tied our hands behind our backs. They tied Trever's hands as well and threw him face down on our son Silas' bed. With two guns pointed at his head, they spoke their intent to kill him. At the same moment, the man leading the assault rushed into the bedroom and told the other men with him that they were going to leave immediately. When the two men committed to killing Trever questioned their leader, he repeated that they were to leave without following the original plan. Instead the leader fired a blast of tear gas into the room as they all ran from the house, stealing our vehicle and other household valuables.*
>
> *Later, as we sat with our family and team, we talked, cried, and praised God for sparing our lives. The next day, Steve Klassen phoned and told us about you, our dear sister Aletha and the burden you had for us. Your sacrifice of sleep, time, and tears, in order that we might continue to fight the good fight for the Kingdom of God has been instrumental in sparing our lives."*

Tears running down her face, Aletha laid the letter down. Thankfulness filled her heart that she had spoken to Steve Klassen at the Missions Conference about the burden she was feeling for the Godards. How thankful she was that he had asked people in the churches to pray as well.

The above letter was quoted directly from a letter written by Trever and Joan Godard in response to the question of how they felt about Aletha's correspondence and prayers. The portions were reprinted with their permission.

At the time of this writing, the Godards have returned from Columbia and are serving at Bethany College in Hepburn, Saskatchewan.

"Oh God and King, please expand my opportunities and my impact in such a way that I touch more lives for your glory. Let me do more for you." –ALETHA JOICE

Daily

Aletha read the words of Scripture again: 'Love builds up.'

Lord, are you telling me that I have been talking too much and not letting you change her? That using the gift of my tongue won't do any good? But I've prayed so much for her.

The Lord's gentle rebuke came again. "Love builds up. Check on your motives. Why do you want me to change her?"

The truth of why she wanted the change was not easy to admit. It's not for her good, but so things will be easier for me. I'm concerned that my pride will take a beating, huh?

Aletha could almost see the slow smile and nod of her heavenly Father. "I love her. I want only the best for her."

And my tongue is a stumbling block?

This time there was silence. Aletha knew why—it was a rhetorical question.

Lord, *she prayed,* forgive me for tearing down instead of building up. It's tough on my ego to let you do the work, but keep my tongue in check. Help me to love and be silent.

Aletha closed her Bible and rose from her chair. Her time with the Lord today had not been easy, but deep down she knew her Lord also had her best interests in mind when He rebuked her and pointed her in the right direction.

Over the next months, Aletha found that letting the Lord work in someone's life without her help was tough on her tongue. She bit it a lot to keep from speaking.

Aletha spent time studying God's Word and praying on a daily basis. Her journals record many conversations with the Lord, the times when the Lord affirmed as well as the times when he gently rebuked. Her words, both of praise and petition during her personal time of Bible Study and prayer are interspersed with her thoughts on the passages of Scripture she was studying. She used other books to expand her understanding of the Scriptures, listing titles of books she wanted to go through in the future.

"Though Jesus gently rebuked Martha for being so busy with many things, He encouraged her to sit at His feet, as Mary was doing, and learn from Him. So often when I become frantically busy, I'm encouraged in my regular quiet times of reading the Bible and praying... then the undone housework, the demands of family or organizations, even churches, fall into their proper place of importance... and you know, the housework then seems to get done faster and easier, or I'm able to say 'no' to extra demands, or I'm able not to worry that the floor didn't get washed that week! That kind of release from pressure is encouraging to my physical health, my mental health, and to all those around me!" –ALETHA JOICE

Perhaps it was identifying with Martha's struggle that inspired Aletha when she wrote the puppet skit *Martha's Folly*[i]

---

[i] See Appendix 2: *Martha's Folly* for the complete skit written by Aletha.

Enriched by the time and effort put into sharing with others, the joy and power of the Lord in her life, Aletha committed herself completely to Him, willing to let Him use her, giving Him the glory.

TOP LEFT: Aletha, in the Leader Post announcement (photo courtesy of Betty Anderson). TOP RIGHT: Paul and Jane Stobbe, with their family in 2003. (back l-r) Jan, Andrew, Paul, and Aaron. (front l-r) Ben, Amy, and Brianna. MIDDLE: Trevor and Joan Godard with their children Silas, Kena, and Aaron. BOTTOM: The bulletin board above Aletha's desk.

"To win someone to You."

Soldiers

"Did you have a good time?" Aletha asked as Glenn came through the door carrying his skis in one hand and trying to juggle the door and his suitcase with the other.

"Great powder and a clear blue sky! I couldn't have had it better."

Aletha forced the smile to her face. Her bad news about the lump she had discovered could wait. Seeing his enthusiasm as he continued to tell her about the trip, Aletha was glad she had not told him before he left. She never wanted him to regret that trip.

Concern about the future filled Aletha's mind as she waited in the doctor's office. The lump in her breast was hard and hurt when she pressed it. She was still sure it would be cancerous. That would be tough.

"So what's tough? I am the Lord." Impressions from her quiet time a while back came to her mind. Now the Lord asked some new questions. "Is a lump too much for Me? Is surgery too much for Me? Is cancer too much for Me?" His answer followed immediately: "No, I am the Lord." Then a slightly tougher question, "Whatever the outcome of today's visit to the doctor and succeeding events, will you trust Me?"

Her answer was postponed as the doctor walked in and sat down at his desk. He opened the folder in his hand and gave Aletha the results of the tests. He went on to explain what kinds of things she could expect to happen as treatment progressed.

"Anti-nausea pills will help with the nausea, but it won't be a pleasant time. The chemotherapy gets any of the cancer cells we don't remove with surgery. They'll get their marching orders to clear out. Still, it won't be easy."

"That doctor wasn't kidding," Aletha groaned, as she sat in the rocker a few months later, holding her head. It felt like it was in a vice. "This definitely has not been easy. I eat a little bit and I throw it up. I toss and turn at night. I'm so tired. And now this. I faint and break my tooth out." Aletha coughed. Her throat still felt hot and constricted.

Then she smiled a bit, visualizing again as she had the day she got her results, the chemotherapy drugs as soldiers with little helmets chasing the cancer cells down her blood stream.

Aletha discovered the lump, later diagnosed as cancerous, in February of 1995. She had surgery in April, beginning chemotherapy treatments in early May. She became very ill with the treatments, but by the end of May, although her blood count was still low, she recorded in her journal going to church, a wedding reception, and putting in some bedding plants. At the beginning of June, another round of treatments brought illness again. In the months that followed, activities with God Squad, her family, and other ministries were interspersed with struggling to cope with the nausea and other side effects of chemotherapy.

During the time of her illness, Aletha made this entry: "Today I am thankful I have TIME to adore you." Although she was very ill, she used the time to study God's Word and apply it to her life.

"It is second nature to turn to God and leave the results in His hands." –ALETHA JOICE

Shaky Gratitude

"How are you feeling this morning?" Glenn asked as Aletha came into the kitchen where he was making toast before going to work.

"Nauseous," Aletha replied, looking up at the prism of colors the July sunshine was creating on the wall, reflecting off a cut glass dish on the counter.

"It's been a rough couple of months hasn't it?"

Aletha nodded. She sat down at the table and after Glenn had asked the Lord to bless the food she spoke again. "I'm like the Israelites. They were asking God to free them from bondage. I am asking him to free me from illness. I have been thinking about that Bible story, and God has been assuring me that He is able, not Aletha. He is able to free me from it. But there is another part to the request Moses makes for the people of Israel. He says, 'Let my people go so they can serve You.' I've realized if I ask the Lord to free me from illness, I need to be prepared to serve Him." Aletha paused, then added, "Right now, I have nothing I can serve with."

"But you will again when you're better," Glenn encouraged. "The Lord never asks us to do something without providing grace and strength to do it."

Tears came to Aletha's eyes as she considered the extra strain her illness had taken on Glenn. "He has had to provide lots of grace for you lately, hasn't He?" The miserable nights sleeping on that lawn chair mattress on the floor beside the bed so he wouldn't bump her in the night. What a loving sacrifice!

"I'm going to miss being in church so much this morning," Aletha said as Glenn went down the steps to the front door. "How I miss the fellowship, hearing the pastor preaching God's Word, the hymns, greeting friends."

Glenn looked up at her for a moment, then blew her a kiss and went out the door.

Aletha crossed the living room and sat down in the armchair. Oh, Lord, she prayed. Give a special blessing to Glenn this morning. Pour out Your Spirit on the service. I confess my gratefulness is shaky this morning concerning the trial you've sent me. Did I want to grow that badly? In any case, I lean on You. Don't let the ugliness of my illness distract me from a chance to grow closer to You.

The summer ahead looked discouraging because Aletha knew there would be more illness to come. In the middle of June, she settled on a promise from 2

Corinthians 9:8: "And God is able to make all grace abound to you, so that in all things at all times having all that you need, you will abound in every good work." She reworded part of it: "God, not Aletha, is able." Thus began a study on the word 'able,' which she felt would keep her learning and enduring throughout the summer.

On giving—"What I've given back of my treasures: my daughter and son, my husband, my home, my time. He has blessed me with peace and strength a hundred fold!" –ALETHA JOICE

Muffin?

Aletha stirred on the bed and Glenn jumped up from his makeshift bed on the floor. After a moment, Aletha heard sounds like chopping and tried to wake up enough to figure out what it was.

She had raised herself to a sitting position when Glenn came back into the bedroom, a plate in his hand. He came over to the side of the bed and handed it to Aletha. In the dim light, she could see there was something on the plate. Not wanting to hurt Glenn's feelings, Aletha reached over to take what he was offering her. A muffin! Well, why not try? Maybe in the darkness it would taste good. She took a tentative bite. It was good!

Aletha slowly chewed the first bite, then took another.

"Oh dear," she said, after she swallowed. "I'm going to get crumbs all over the bed."

"No problem, Madam." Glenn deepened his voice and stood stiffly beside the bed. "Just brush them onto the floor. The servants will be in to clean in the morning."

Aletha giggled. Glenn smiled. It was good to see her finding a little enjoyment, even if it was the middle of the night.

"What made you bring me a muffin in the middle of the night?" Aletha asked when she had finished the last of it.

"I asked you if there was something you wanted, and you said, 'Muffin,'" Glenn replied, sitting down on the side of the bed.

"I think I remember hearing you ask me that," Aletha said, grinning. "But I said, 'nothin.'"

Aletha and Glenn laughed together at the silliness of what had happened.

In an entry in one journal, Aletha refers to the story of Noah. "The flood covered all the earth. All living creatures died; all the righteous people were saved in the ark. God remembered Noah. He never forgot Noah.

"I believe God remembered Glenn and me, never forgot us through surgery and chemo months from April to August.

"Let us never forget our experiences. Let us remember to give God thanks. Let us remember to be of help to others. As Noah built an altar and the sacrifice pleased God, may our lives be a sweet-smelling aroma to God." –ALETHA JOICE

Aletha confessed to being unworthy and discouraged, yet each time, like the Psalmist David, she found things for which to praise the Lord amid the trials.

White Crown

Running her hand over the pink-white of her hairless skull, Aletha looked at herself in the mirror. The last of her hair had fallen out last week. She picked up the bandana she wore when she was going out. Funny how I didn't realize how much protection my hair was to my head until I didn't have any left, *she thought.*

They were going shopping for a wig this morning. She smiled as she mentally reviewed Glenn's silliness last night. "A flaming red head would suit my fancy," *he had teased.*

The idea of using the opportunity to have a different color of hair for a while passed through Aletha's mind, but it didn't linger. She hadn't really minded her white hair. After all, she was an older woman. Besides, it would be too many changes and people would just feel they had to comment about it. No, a wig as close to her own hair would be best. She didn't want to push aside the fact that she was ill, but she also didn't want to attract undue attention.

Aletha's hair was something people remembered about her. It seems to have been something that enhanced her personality.

"I met Aletha for the first time at Parliament Community Church. I was late [for my very first church service there], so Gavin, who had invited me but had to sing in the choir, asked Aletha to watch for me and meet me at the door. When I came in, I saw this white-haired lady. She was like an icon for me there in the church. That didn't change." –Doreen Butterfield

"Her looks—her beautiful hair. It was always well-groomed." –Irene Sotropa

"I think she would be the 'ideal Grandma'—gentle, tiny, silver grey hair. If they needed a Grandma for a play, she would be the one I would pick." –Nancy Jo (Russell) Ziegler

A verse of Scripture Aletha noted: *"White hair is a crown of glory and is seen most among the Godly"* (Proverbs 16:31, TLB).

A Blessing Indeed

"The malignant cells are in your bone marrow," the doctor said, looking at the report on her desk. Aletha moved her hand slowly along the arm of the same chair she had five years earlier, willing herself not to cry. "That leaves us with two options," the doctor continued. "Chemo or more hormone therapy. Chemo is out, because it would destroy your already low platelet count."

Aletha's heart lifted a little at the doctor's concluding sentence. Although it had been five years, the memories of the side effects of last time's chemo treatments were still very fresh in her mind. She would gladly try an option that would not make her so ill again.

Aletha and Glenn sat quietly in their chairs as they continued listening to the doctor's explanation about their choices.

"Arimedex is less apt to cause nausea, but will attack cancerous cells in the bone marrow."

The Arimedex seemed to work and the days after the visit to the doctor were full. Aletha thought about how well God Squad did with their performance at Promise Keepers. The arrangements for the taping session and the trip to Swift Current would still have to be worked out for next month, but she was thankful for the peace that the Lord was giving her.

A little over a month passed before Aletha again sat listening to the doctor.

"We're going to have to add another drug," she said. "I'd like to get that blood of yours in better shape."

But after tests a few days later, the news was not completely good. The hemoglobin was up, but the platelet count was down.

Aletha had been in remission when cancer returned in 2000, this time moving to her bone marrow. During this second round of illness and treatments, Aletha's journals contain fewer details of her illness. Instead, her entries are frequently about her walk with God. "Wanting nothing more, nothing less than what God wants for me. To be wholly immersed in what God is trying to do in me, through me, around me for His glory. Difficult to get my mind off treatment and progression of bone marrow cancer. To get beyond it... that would be a blessing indeed!"

Despite feet, legs, and abdomen being swollen because of fluid retention, her desire to bring glory to God with her life was uppermost in her thoughts. "Oh God and King, please expand my opportunities and my impact [to] all the health care personnel."

"The sun is shining," begins an entry in Aletha's journal. Adding a comment that her feet were not as swollen, she continues, "But we felt we should not go to church—snow and cold, but more importantly to be sensible and not set me back in any way. Also I have to think of Glenn, because he bears the brunt of getting me anyplace."

After a reference to Glenn preparing the meal and others in the family being there, Aletha concluded with praise to God. "Thank you God for letting us be together."

Silver Notes

"We decided we would all write notes of encouragement for you to put into your silver box." Aletha's guest handed Aletha a fat envelope.

"Please, sit down," Aletha invited. Dawna seated herself on the couch opposite her as Aletha opened the envelope and pulled out the pieces of paper. "I wish I could make some tea for you," she said, "but I just can't stay upright that long. I had a long stretch at the hospital today."

"I understand completely. Please, don't worry about it."

Aletha looked at the papers in her hand. Some were small notes trimmed with a floral border; others were longer on plain, unlined paper.

"I'll take time to read them later," Aletha said, putting the papers back in the envelope.

"That's fine," Dawna responded, noting Aletha's pale face and thinking she should not stay overly long. "Tell me something, where did you first find out about silver boxes?"

"The idea came from a book by Florence Litthauer called Silver Boxes. Our study was about encouraging others, so I thought this would be very appropriate. There are times in all of our lives that we need encouragement. It's good to get notes of encouragement at the time, but later we can go back to the box, reread them, and be lifted up again."

Dawna nodded. "I hope you will be around long enough to reread these many times," she said. "We've missed you at the women's Bible study."

"By the look of me, I'm a round all right," Aletha said, pointing to her swollen abdomen.

Dawna chuckled. "It amazes me that you haven't lost your sense of humor."

"In this family..." A smile crinkled the corners of her twinkling eyes. "Did I ever tell the story about skunk juice at a study?" she asked.

"If you did, I don't remember it."

"Around Christmas or New Year's one year, there were a number of leftover bits of juice in the fridge. I mixed them together and added ginger ale. It tasted fine, but each time our glass got close to our mouths, it smelled like a skunk. Thus the name skunk juice."

"I don't imagine you could make it again, either," Dawna said, "being that it was dribs and drops of so many different things."

Aletha laughed. "I like that—dribs and drops. They often teased me about it. Sometimes I fancied that just for fun, I'd like to try to replicate it, but as you said, there was no recipe."

●●◆●●

Aletha brought the concept of silver boxes and writing notes of encouragement to the ladies at a Bible Study at her church. She was very aware of how encouragement could return to the giver when it was needed. She recorded receiving this return of "neat, blessed encouragement" in her journal.

"I woke up about 2:00 a.m.—'encouraging word' thoughts were going through my mind—when it came to me that, of all of the encouragers I've had, the greatest has been Jesus Christ." –ALETHA JOICE

Tears and Love

The chatter around the room was pleasant in Aletha's ears as she contemplated all the things that had happened over the last few months. It was good to be here with those she loved on their grandson's birthday.

Aletha thought back to the sharing at the ladies' Bible Study brunch last week, to Julie's tears about the markings in her Bible and saying she felt she was holding a treasure. How blessed she had felt that Julie would hope to someday have one like it, all marked up with the things she had learned.

What a dear group of women. Someone told her that the week before there had been tears because she hadn't been present to recite the memory verse. A phrase from the book she was studying, about Jabez and his prayer about asking the Lord to bless him and enlarge his territory, brought a prayer of gratitude to her lips. Lord, thank you for enlarging my territory by the influence my teaching will have on others. They will go on to bring glory to You.

"Oh, boy!"

Aletha's attention was drawn back to the party.

"Thanks, Grandpa and Grandma!" Jake's delight at the gift she and Glenn had given him made her smile. He took the golf club topper from the package and went to get his club to try the 'gorilla' on it.

"Neat look," Aletha said when Jake showed the clothed club to her. "That should keep the club warm when you're out golfing. I'll have to come and watch you play sometime."

But I may never do it. Aletha pushed the thought aside before the sadness could seep in and dilute the joy of this day.

Aletha found it impossible to restrain the tears later as she gave each of her family a hug and told them she loved them as they left at the end of the afternoon. Jake stood aside while the adults all had a turn. At last, she reached out to him. As he came into her embrace, and she said, "I love you, Jake," he responded, "I love you, too, Grandma."

"Wow!" Aletha marveled. "A thirteen-year-old telling his grandmother he loved her. That was very special."

●●◆●●

Though she was very ill, Aletha's desire was still that she would have her 'territory,' the amount the Lord blessed her and the influence she was for Him, enlarged.

On one day, after the doctor had to use a tube to drain a buildup of excess fluid, a journal entry reflects Aletha's sense of humor. In the written prayer, she asks the Lord to enlarge her territory and then adds, "Not my stomach and abdomen! They've only gone down six inches."

Though in the night I do not sleep and in my legs there is no strength,
Though my platelets and red blood count fails
And there is no taste in my mouth for food,
Though Glenn has to cook and wash and massage my feet
And though the doctor orders more and more intimidating tests
"Yet I will rejoice... be joyful..."[i]

---

[i] A poem by Aletha, based on Habakkuk 3:17-18.

The Bonds of Friendship

Glenn hesitated, then went to the doorway and looked at Aletha lying on the couch, her eyes closed. So pale and swollen. He had told her friends several times already that she was too ill for a visit, but this time a dear friend of Aletha was in town, and only for a few days.

"Aletha?" Glenn spoke softly so that he wouldn't waken her if she were asleep. Aletha turned to look at him and smiled, encouraging him to continue. "Betty is in town. She and Vivian would like to come over and see you. Do you think you can handle that? I'll tell them to let me get you set up first."

Aletha nodded and closed her eyes again as Glenn went back to the phone.

The front bell chimed as Glenn finished tucking the blanket around Aletha's legs.

"Comfy?" he asked. Aletha nodded.

Going toward the stairs to answer the door, Glenn glanced back at Aletha. Her face was swollen, but to him it would always be beautiful. Her shiny white hair was like a halo.

"It's good to see you," Aletha said as the women stepped inside, her voice weak, but a smile of greeting on her face. "Please, sit down. I've asked Glenn to make some tea. Too bad Irene couldn't come, too."

The three long-time friends began to talk about their memories, how the sorrows and joys they shared had caused a strong bonding of friendship.

After they had chatted for a while, Betty noticed Aletha was quickly tiring, so she took out the devotional book she had brought along and began to read. When she finished, the friends held hands and prayed together.

Aletha and three women she had met and worked with in Christian Women's club became a very close quartet of friends, supporting and encouraging one another. "It was special—different than other friendships—there was a strong bond, a powerful spiritual bond. You use ordinary words to try to describe the friendship, but it wasn't ordinary." –VIVIAN NORBRATEN

"Our friendship grew over the years. We were the 'fearsome foursome.'" After saying that, Irene chuckled, then added, "Not really fearsome."

"She had a good sense of humor, was always fun... but had a serious side, too. I respected her, looked up to her—somewhat like a mentor. We mentored each other, appreciated each other. I miss her very much. But if you didn't grieve, it wouldn't be a good friendship." –IRENE SOTROPA

"When I think of Aletha, I feel gratitude for the privilege of having been a close friend of such a Godly and faithful friend. I look forward to being with her again when I, too, reach my Heavenly Home. Blessed be her memory!" –BETTY ANDERSON

"Lord, help me to always encourage when I open my mouth." –ALETHA JOICE

Mother of the Year

Aletha touched the spot where the doctor had pulled the tube from her stomach. It was very tender and sore. She had spent eight hours at the hospital today and they had removed four liters of fluid! That should help relieve the pressure.

"A letter for you, my dear," Glenn said, handing Aletha a long envelope. He sat down on the arm of the chair as she began opening the envelope, then got up again. "I think I'm going to make some waffles," he said, turning toward the kitchen.

Sometimes life seems so ordinary, *Aletha thought.* Making waffles, reading the mail. Yet so much has changed. Like Glenn making meals. It's good to know he will be able to do that on his own.

Aletha sat holding the folded letter, contemplating the struggles of the last few days and the blessing her family was to her through it all. She praised God for His presence, yet wondered how He was going to bless with all that had happened. The Lord's soft reminder came, "I am the God of Abraham. How I bless you is up to me."

Yes, heavenly Father, but like Job I still often question your motives. Yet I know I am to be dependent on you for the 'what, when, and where' of your blessing. It's difficult to get my mind off treatment and the progression of the cancer. To be wholly immersed in what You are trying to do in me, through me, and around me for your glory! It's like asking for supernatural favor!

"Lord," she prayed, "help me to get beyond it, to want nothing more, nothing less than what You want for me. That would be a blessing indeed!"

Aletha lifted the letter and, unfolding it, started reading.

> *Dear Aletha,*
>
> *"The Pregnancy Counseling Center is planning to have a tea on May 12 and its theme is 'Mother of the Year.' I (and a number of women at the church) would like to nominate you in the category of community service... because I want you to know how much you are loved and how much you have impact-ed the lives of people around you. I very much wanted to nomin-ate you as a way to honor you and all your work in our church.*

It is mostly a way to let you know that you have changed my life and the lives of people at our church.[i]

Wow! Wow!

"Glenn, come quick!" Glenn came around the living room door so quickly he almost fell.

"What's wrong? Are you okay?"

"I'm sorry. I didn't mean to alarm you," Aletha said, quickly. "But look at this!" Aletha handed Glenn the letter. "They want to nominate me for Mother of the Year in the community service category. Can you imagine? From motherless fourteen-year-old Aletha Rogers to Aletha Joice becoming a mother of the year? God is so gracious!"

"That's wonderful!" Glenn said after reading through the letter. He reached down to give Aletha a hug. She smiled up at him, and then sniffed. "Oh, my waffles!" Glenn exclaimed. "Guess this one will be downright crispy."

In the process of choosing Mother of the Year, all nominations[ii] go to a committee who then make their decision and notify the recipients of their award prior to a tea at which the awards are given out. No speaking is required by either the recipient or a proxy when the award is accepted.

Aletha's award, a picture entitled *Aspirations and Dreams*, had the inscription 'Mother of the Year Award—Community Service—Aletha Joice.' It was presented to Aletha at a High Tea, held at the Hotel Saskatchewan Ball Room. The artist of *Aspirations and Dreams* is Dwight Heinrichs.

---

[i] Quotations from the letter, written by Vicki Clarke, are used with her permission.

[ii] See Appendix 1: More Information, Just for the Fun of It—"Mother of the Year, Nomination and Award" for the letter Vicki presented to the committee.

Wheel Off!

Shelley pushed the wheelchair she was borrowing from work toward the van. Folding it up, she put it inside. A quick glance at her watch told her she had enough time to stop at the post office before going to pick Aletha up to go to High Tea at the Hotel Saskatchewan.

"I still can hardly believe it," Aletha said a little later as Shelley helped her into the wheelchair and they went into the doors of the ballroom. "Imagine, me being a Mother of the Year."

Later, as the program ended and she left the banquet with Shelley and Bette-Jean, Aletha was glad for the wheelchair, glad she would not have to walk all the way back to the van.

"I'm sorry this has been such a rough ride," Shelley said. The wheelchair had bounced over the edge of the lift in the hotel and now, as she wheeled Aletha through the parking lot, things definitely weren't any smoother.

After helping Aletha into the van, Shelley went around and loaded the chair into the back.

"Let's drop the chair off on the way home," Aletha suggested. "That way you can just go straight to your house without having to come back."

"You're sure you're not too tired?" Bette-Jean asked, concerned that the day would be too much.

"I'll be okay," Aletha answered, patting her hand and smiling.

After they pulled up in front of the care home, Bette-Jean and Shelley stepped off to take the wheelchair out of the van.

They lifted the wheelchair out and set it up on the sidewalk. Without warning, the big back wheel tipped over. It wobbled for a second and then lay still.

"The wheel came off!" Shelley exclaimed. "My goodness. I've never had that happen."

Picking up the wheel, they carried it and the rest of the chair into the care home.

"In all my years of work, I've never had a wheel come off a wheelchair," Shelley said as they brought the chair to maintenance. "We've taken so many walks with the residents without mishap."

"I'm so thankful Mom was not in the chair when the wheel came off," Bette-Jean added.

"The Lord was definitely watching over her."

●●◆●●

In an entry in her journal, Aletha records a conversation she had with God when she was seeking God's guidance about going to High Tea, the award banquet for Mother of the Year.

> ALETHA: Shall I plan to go to High Tea?'
> GOD: Yes.
> ALETHA: I guess that means, "Answer God's call
>   before one knows if one is feeling well or not."
> GOD: Yes.

Aletha added that she got up, planned to go, and "God gave strength and grace and joy!"

"Pray for a blessing, then expect it." –ALETHA JOICE

Last Cards

"Thank you so much for working so hard in The Light of the World *performance.*" *Aletha wrote slowly, her usual smooth letters looking shaky.* "*I appreciated your diligence and helpfulness in getting the stage packed up after it...*"

Her hand began to tremble, so Aletha put the pen down and leaned against the back of the chair.

How weak she had felt as she introduced the program yesterday. She was so glad Bette-Jean had been at her side to finish when she couldn't. How fitting that Bette-Jean, having been there at the very beginning of God Squad's history, had a part in the last hurrah.

What a job the puppeteers had done, she thought. Each of them had, as usual, put forth their best efforts. She glanced over at the bouquet they had given her after the performance and heard again the applause of the standing ovation.

Aletha shifted her legs, trying to make them more comfortable, and picked up the pen once more. She read what she had written, then added the last bit. "*...was over. Love, Aletha.*"

Aletha "sent letters to the puppeteers after the last performance. She was so weak, it used every ounce of energy she had to get it done." –DOREEN BUTTERFIELD

Aletha requisitioned words to write encouraging notes and letters to others. Words lent feet to her thoughts and ideas for Bible studies and speaking engagements. Many times, she reached for words to empty her feelings into her journals, and used them to converse with her Lord.

The following poem was found hiding in the words of one journal entry, clamoring to be set free:

Reluctant Trust[i]
Do you consider
what makes you reluctant

---

[i] The title and words in parentheses were added by the author.

to pray?
For me—it's choices, decisions,
wanting to get to the 'necessaries'
of the day
(instead of taking
important time to pray!)
Could be fear
of what He'll ask of us,
could be lack of trust
that He knows
what's best for us.

Triumphant Music

Aletha taped a little tab to the side of the page in her open journal.

"Memorial Service Plans for Aletha," she mused, looking at the words she had printed on the yellow-edged piece of paper.

Not many people have a chance to choose what will go into their funeral program, *she thought.* It seems kind of weird, yet I've left my life in the hands of the Lord, so why not my death? Why should it be weird to plan for something after my death, when I never considered it was weird to plan for something during my life?

"So what should I put in?" she asked herself aloud, writing 'Funeral Arrangements' at the top of the page. "My favorite songs, who should do solos, music, the sermon?"

She sat immersed in her deliberations for a moment and then began writing again, from time to time saying a word aloud as she wrote.

"Triumphant! That's what I want the trumpet music to be. And the congregation singing 'Joyful, Joyful! We Adore Thee' seems fitting. It will be what I'm doing. While they are singing praise to Him here, I will be with my Savior, joyfully adoring Him with the angels in heaven."

Aletha's desire to use the word 'triumphant' to describe the kind of trumpet music she wanted in her memorial service was appropriate not only because now she has triumphed over death—living with her Father in heaven—but she was victorious in life, dealing with and conquering sin through His grace.

Aletha had concluded that no matter how many days the Lord gave her, whether until 2005 or until she was eighty years old, she would plan to live each day as if it was the last. But she also seemed to have an insight that she would not live until she was eighty years old, that the Lord just wanted her to be willing if He would ask her to do it.

"Yes, Laverna," she wrote in one of her last journal entries, in response to a comment from a letter her friend had sent, "you may be right—God is calling me home. He's calling everyone home!"

Aletha Mary Joice passed away June 12, 2001. She had a passion for God and a love for the Scriptures, the church, and for her outreach ministry with God Squad puppeteers. Her life was a light for Jesus and she served Him faithfully in all her ministries. The memorial service for Aletha Joice took place at Parliament Community Church in Regina, June 21, 2001.

In her journal, Aletha asked the question, "What do I want to be remembered for?" After it, she listed her answers: "That I was faithful to God. That I loved Jesus. That I hungered for righteousness. That I influenced family and others to live wholeheartedly for God."

Her last journal entry was made Sunday, May 13, 2001. It was Mother's Day. Her handwriting was not the steady flowing script it had been in earlier journals, so the words, 'I'm thankful for my loving family,' were large, partially printed letters.

That family awaits the day when they know they will be reunited with her in her Home with the Father.

Memorial Service[i]

A framed picture of Aletha stood on a table at the front of the sanctuary, surrounded by a few of her favorite puppets, a fond reminder to those attending the service that the ministry of God Squad had been one of the dearest things in Aletha's life.

Pastor Phil Gunther's words, in his introductory remarks and prayer at the memorial service for Aletha Joice, reflected how her life had influenced those who knew her.

"I think Aletha genuinely lived the conviction of the apostle Paul who, in a letter to the Christians in the city of Philippi, said, 'For to me to live is Christ and to die is gain.'[ii] I believe Aletha lived that conviction, whatever the setting—among family or friends, neighbors, on tour with the God Squad puppeteers, or serving at church. Aletha challenged and encouraged others with her unwavering commitment to Jesus. He was the Light in her life.

"When Aletha first experienced the resurgence of cancer, she told me very clearly that she wanted us to pray that she would have a bold witness of Jesus in her life, whatever the outcome. Aletha was a light to others because Jesus, the true Light of the world, abided in her.

"This afternoon, I invite us to remember how Aletha touched our lives because she once walked here with us... to rejoice in the resurrection promise of the Christian church. Aletha did not grieve as those who have no hope. In fact, Aletha's hope was in the person of the Lord Jesus Christ, a hope that did not disappoint."

The pastor ended his opening remarks with a prayer that included words of thanks: "We give you thanks, our great God, for Aletha Mary Joice. We thank you for her life, thank you for her smile, her caring touch, her warm embrace. We thank you, Father, that through all circumstances she never failed to bring you glory. We thank you that she encouraged so many in their walk of faith."

He concluded the prayer by asking God to grant the family His grace and strength. He asked that the memorial service celebrating Aletha's life, and the

---

[i] See Appendix 3: Memorial Service" for excerpts from a transcript of the service.
[ii] Philippians 1:21 (NIV).

great hope of Jesus who promises eternal life, would be to the honor and glory of the heavenly Father.

The service included songs Aletha loved. The song leader lead the congregation in singing one Aletha had planned for her memorial service. The triumphant strains of *Joyful, Joyful We Adore Thee* were a prelude to the responsive reading from Psalm 121, which followed.

The harmony of a mixed quartet singing the words of the song *In His Presence* beautifully described what Aletha was experiencing right then in the presence of Jesus Christ—comfort, peace, and assurance, as well as a desire to know the Savior more.

A young mother, Julie Hornoi, affirmed the influence Aletha had on those around her, sharing how Aletha had touched her life, after which the congregation was again led in two of Aletha's favorite hymns, *He Giveth More Grace* and *There Is a Redeemer*.

In her presentation of the obituary, Aletha's daughter Bette-Jean stated, "This is a story of a woman who came to faith early in life and spent a lifetime developing that faith."

The pastor's concluding prayer again contained words of thanks: "Our heavenly Father, we give you unending thanks for welcoming Aletha home. We thank you that there is hope when our earthly tent folds. We thank you, Lord, for the... confidence and the trust she had in you despite the shadow of death. We pray that we would have the courage she had, to be beacons for the Light of the world. Lord, thank you for allowing us to have this celebration together. May your grace abound... this day and in the days to follow."

When the triumphant notes of Walter and Roxanne Andres' piano-saxophone duet of *The Lord's Prayer* faded, the song leader invited everyone to join in singing *Amazing Grace*.

After the last phrase ended, the organist continued softly playing more of Aletha's favorites. Appropriately, the title of the first postlude song, *To God Be the Glory*,[iii] reflected the focus Aletha wanted for her life.

[iii] A Fanny Crosby song.

Aletha, now with her heavenly Father, knows firsthand whether her prayer, that she be influential in winning someone to Him, was answered.

TOP: Parliament Community Church in Regina, the church Aletha was attending at the time of her death. MIDDLE LEFT: Aletha's "crown" of shiny white hair was noted by people who knew her (photo courtesy of Tilly Wiens). MIDDLE RIGHT: Aletha valued her friendship with Vivian Norbraten (left), Betty Anderson (to Aletha's right), and Irene Sotropa (far right), and they valued her (photo courtesy of Vivian Norbraten). BOTTOM: Aletha penned many thoughts in her journals. The one of the left was a Christmas gift from one of her puppeteers, and the one on the right was the last in which she made entries (photo used with permission of Glenn Joice).

EPILOGUE

The buildings on the farm where Aletha grew up are gone. The house where she jumped in her Granny's feather tick no longer stands on the yard. Buildings in the old town are falling apart, windows and doors sagging and weak. You could sit on the ground and talk of what had been there, lamenting the loss, or you could reminisce about the things that are gone and cherish the memories.

Aletha, as she was to those who knew her, is gone, too—no longer in the house. Her possessions are no longer being used. You could sit in front of the pictures of Aletha and lament about the hole she has left, or you could talk about what a blessing she was to those she touched in her lifetime.

We would like to keep the enjoyment of what happens in life and the people we know for a long time, but things change and those changes are not

The lot where Dr. Brown's house stood.

often easy. Glenn is creating space for new memories and for sharing fun times with his family, but the tears still shimmer in his eyes when he thinks of Aletha giggling about something.

Aletha has laid down the torch of being a blessing and encouragement to others. It wasn't easy when Aletha went to be with the Lord. Those who loved her had been blessed by her life, and would have liked to share many more years with her. But she has a strong, steady body now—one that doesn't change and weaken with illness or age. She is with her heavenly Father, her unchanging Savior, the Savior she so greatly desired people to know, the Father she wanted to hear say to her, as He had to His Son Jesus many years ago, "This is my daughter, whom I love, with her I am well pleased."[i]

---

[i] Aletha's paraphrase of the phrase in Matthew 3:17 (NIV).

MEMORIAL SUNDAY

Parliament Community Church, the congregation Aletha was part of at the time of her death, has been holding an annual Memorial Sunday. On this day, during the service, various people read a tribute to those who have died in the past year.

After a brief outline of her family history, describing her Christian walk and life of service, Walter and Arlene Schroeder[28] read the tribute for Aletha, in part the words which had been in the Mennonite Brethren Herald.

> "Aletha had a passion for God, as evidenced by her love for the Scriptures, the Church, and her outreach ministry, God Squad Puppeteers. Her life was a living testimony to being a light for Jesus. ... Aletha served faithfully and wholeheartedly in a number of the ministries at Parliament Community Church.
>
> "In her journal, Aletha penned these words: "What do I want to be remembered for? That I was faithful to God. That I loved Jesus. That I hungered for righteousness. That I influenced family and others to live wholeheartedly for God.""

Pastor Gunther's comments that day affirmed Aletha's confidence in her Savior's power over death. "Our Savior is not in the tomb. Aletha believed in that Savior and His power over death—His and hers. He arose to ascend to heaven and has raised her to eternal life."

"Aletha has now fought the good fight and finished the race. She kept the faith and has been graced with the crown of righteousness which our Father has awarded her. ...Our lives were immensely blessed by her faithful prayers and sweet words of encouragement." –TREVER AND JOAN GODARD

"I really miss her. She was a companion spirit. When she said she would pray for you, you could put that in the bank. She was there for you." –MARILYN DYCK

"I know that there will be days for all of us when tears will come at the thought of Aletha. But I also know that I will always be so thankful—happy to have had her with me on my journey. God bless you and surround you in many ways with His love and comfort." –VIVIAN NORBRATEN

INVITATION

In her testimony booklet, *My Confrontation with Life and Death*, Aletha wrote this:

> I am now well into my 'olden days.' Do I still dream? Yes! To stop, I think, is to be dead. Are high adventures still ahead? Yes, if I react positively to the question I ask myself, 'After I'm gone, will it have made any difference to anyone that I have passed his or her way?'
>
> I discovered early in life that the young do die. Now, by the simple and certain fact of aging, I am again confronted with death. How reassuring to know that it will be a home going—with a home prepared for me—a promise I read in God's Word. Therefore, I can press on in the race of life. I may not cross the finish line on the run—my back or my heart may give out! But I'll surely know the spring after winter, the sunrise after sunset, the prize which is life everlasting with Christ and loved ones who have gone before. That will be the highest adventure! That is the hope of the Christian. It can be yours, too!
>
> Jesus Christ, the One who holds the key to Life, says of Himself, 'I am the door...'[i] meaning He is the Way to eternal life—that He is waiting to be invited into our lives. He also says, 'Here I am, I stand at the door and knock. If anyone hears my voice and opens the door, I will come in.'[ii]
>
> If you haven't yet made this crucial choice, pray this simple prayer:

---

[i] John 10:9 (KJV).
[ii] Revelation 3:20 (NIV).

"God, I believe Your Words, 'For God so loved the world, that He gave His one and only Son, that whoever believes in Him shall not perish but have eternal life.'[iii] *Forgive my sins, especially the sin of ignoring You all my life. I want to know Your peace here in this troubled world and have assurance of life ever after—a quality of life both beyond my understanding and my wildest dreams. I give You my life and my fear of death. Thank you for taking me into Your family. I will seek help in learning to walk Your way. In the Name of Jesus I pray, Amen."*

My goal in writing this book, showing vignettes of Aletha's life, was twofold. First, so that others would want to know the Savior she trusted as their Savior. And secondly, so that those who know the Savior would desire to take up the torch of being a blessing and encouragement to others.

If you prayed with the words in the prayer Aletha wrote above, or used your own words to express your desire for eternal life with God, you now have eternal life. This is a gift from God, one that cannot be taken away.

[iii] John 3:16 (NIV).

BOOK TWO:

AND NOW GOD SQUAD JOYFULLY PRESENTS...

The stories of Aletha Joice and God Squad are parallel stories.
We've become acquainted with the lady behind the blue curtain.
Now let's find out what else went on behind the scenes.

CHAPTER ONE

SQUAD FORMATION

Was it a dream? Was it intrigue? Teen enthusiasm?

She was sixteen when those puppets stole her heart. Her name was Bette-Jean Joice.

Bette-Jean was at a church conference when she was first drawn to the little characters. Her brother Bob had gone on a band trip, so Glenn and Aletha told her that she could bring a friend and go along to the conference in Winona Lake, Indiana, to even things out. While they were at sessions, the girls were given the freedom to be in the apartment and to find their own entertainment.

Various church colleges did promotions at the conference, singing and doing other things to entertain. Some students formed a group called 'Free Spirit,' and chose to present puppet performances that year. Bette-Jean and Heather Miller, the friend she had brought along, discovered this form of entertainment. Intrigued, they followed the group everywhere they went.

"Mom, you have to see this!" was Bette-Jean's comment when she urged her mother to come and see what her excitement was about.

Unaware that they had found the seeds of what would become a twenty-seven year puppet ministry, the two teens decided they wanted to get some puppets of their own and create puppet shows. Glenn and Aletha agreed that they would purchase four puppets. But, realizing that sometimes teenage excitement and enthusiasm faded quickly, they included a condition—Bette-Jean and Heather had to do something with them. The 'doing something' meant not just playing with them.

Twenty-seven years later, those first four puppets, ordered at the conference, would still be 'coming alive' on the hands of puppeteers.

●●◈●●

Back home in Saskatchewan in 1974, Bette-Jean and Heather recruited more hands to work their puppets. Joined by Bob Joice and his friend Geoff Hiltz, there were now four people to bring these puppets to life.

But sometimes a play would require six characters. What to do? Why, just change clothes and voila, another character. But they had to change clothes fast and still keep the play going. These raw, male recruits needed to learn how to dress the puppets. "With the boys in the group," Bette-Jean commented with a smile, "we were teaching them how to play with dolls."

The teen enthusiasm didn't fade. The puppet troupe began performing at the local church. Now, when you have a group performing, you need a name for your group, right? But what to call it? The seed ideas began taking shape, one building on another.

Four is quad.

The puppets were being used to tell people about God.

There was a TV show at the time called *The Mod Squad*.

Squad was sort of like quad.

Use 'God' instead of 'Mod'... God Squad.

Yes! God Squad Puppeteers!

"I can't believe the name stuck," said Bette-Jean, now Mrs. Don Hand. "We named the group that sort of in jest."

Named in jest or not, God Squad had been born, and popularity grew. "People enjoyed the performances," said Heather Campbell,[29] the former puppeteer Heather Miller, now married and a mother herself. "It was amusing... unique at that time. We were one of the first puppet groups in Saskatchewan."

At first, the four puppeteers, Bette-Jean, Heather, Bob, and Geoff, performed mostly in their own church, the Sherwood Free Methodist in Regina, or at the church camp at Arlington Beach. But before long, the puppet performances proved attractive to people from other churches—in places like Avonlea, Weyburn, and Moose Jaw, to name a few. Although God Squad did not formally request bookings, they consented to come and perform when they were asked.

Thus road trips, the experience of which would be filled with memories, became part of puppeteering in God Squad.

So what was the attraction of God Squad, anyway? It's tough to know when you aren't in the audience, yet sometimes the puppeteers got a glimpse of what others saw. One such peek happened at Aldersgate College in Moose Jaw, where there was a large window off to the side. "When we were performing, we noticed the reflection of what we were doing in the window," said Bette-Jean. "We realized this was what the audience always saw and figured it wasn't bad."

Performing did not come without risks, however. It was time for the closing program at Arlington Beach Camp. Everything was set to go when a horrible discovery was made. The tape machine had eaten the master tape, which included all the music and voices for the performance! What to do? Fortunately, there was a back-up practice tape. The near disaster became a crucial learning experience. After that, God Squad always came prepared with a second tape. But like Murphy's Law, as far as Bette-Jean knew, it was never needed.

The conclusion? It's better to have your own sound system. But that goal would not be immediately achieved.

Three years later, God Squad was still performing, but as with any family, when teens begin to leave the nest, things begin to change. University classes were taking much of Bette-Jean's time, so God Squad performances were put aside and the puppet stage was empty for a while.

When Bette-Jean made the decision to attend college in Illinois the following year, her mother Aletha, behind-the-scenes advisor up to this point, began directing the troupe.

BOOT CAMP AND NEW RECRUITS

What was Aletha's vision for the potential of God Squad and the heights they could reach? What was on her mind in the early stages of the ministry? Bob, going to school locally, was still able to be in the group, but with Bette-Jean gone, God Squad was short a puppeteer. It was time to recruit new hands. So, along with a pie to a new family in church, Aletha brought information about God Squad and the opportunity it provided for their children. It was her first attempt at finding new recruits.

Presenting the opportunity to be part of God Squad was not always accomplished with the help of a pie. Over the years, young teens found out about God Squad in various ways—seeing the information about the ministry, watching the puppets perform in children's church or at an evening per-formance, having a sibling already in puppets, or overhearing a current puppeteer talking to a friend. In whatever way they learned about it, it sparked interest in joining the troupe, and many became part of God Squad.

Some potential recruits saw Aletha's church bulletin announcements about the need for puppeteers, along with details of a coming demonstration to intro-duce what God Squad was about. Bob Joice's adeptness at adding a touch of humor may have been a contributing factor in the attraction God Squad had for these new recruits.

Andrew Reddekopp,[30] a puppeteer for a number of years, described Bob's involvement in introducing God Squad to a youth group. "I remember he demonstrated how to do an entrance and an exit—the wrong and the right way. The wrong way was like an escalator, where you just 'slid' down; the right way was like the puppet was going down the stairs—a little bit at a time." Andrew chuckled as he remembered the short skit Bob had used to demonstrate the motion, which took place in a department store. After bringing the puppet correctly up the stairs, in view of the second floor, he murmured, "Hmm, lingerie."

Josh Bekker remembers the first performance he saw. "I remember the performance being in an old building," he said. "It looked like a fire hall." Playing that night was a variety show called 'Ticklish Reuben,[i] which had the church in an uproar. "It was so funny—mostly him (Reuben) laughing," explained the long-term puppeteer. Reuben, with his humorous sounding laugh, was always a favorite.

For some, the memory of going to a God Squad performance was one from childhood. "Long ago... very early on in my days," as Grant Sawatzky,[31] a recent puppeteer, put it. It was a memory that stayed in their minds until they were old enough to join.

Old enough was junior high age, but one young fellow found it hard to wait. He first saw the puppets perform when he was five years old. Right then, he knew it was his calling. "As soon as I'm old enough," Tyler Wood[32] told his mother, "I'm going to be one of those puppets."

He would often speak to Aletha, asking if he could do it. Each time she would explain that he would have to wait until he was twelve years old, the age when kids could join God Squad. "The day he turned twelve," said his mother Audrey, "he called her."

It has been said that 'seeing is believing,' but for many of the puppeteers the attraction was 'seeing and wanting'—wanting to be part of it. Attending performances in which a sibling was involved, and seeing a puppet 'come alive' when it came home to use for practicing was intriguing.

Jacqui Gagnon was a puppeteer with God Squad for several years and an avid fan of Aletha and puppeteering. This older sister's involvement gave younger sister Janelle,[33] a more recent puppeteer, a personal viewpoint. The group piqued Janelle's interest when they hung out at the Gagnon home. "They looked like they were having a lot of fun, always laughing and goofing around," remembers Janelle.

---

[i] *Ticklish Rueben* is a skit by Puppet Productions.

It seems one sibling was so eager to join that she worked at wearing Aletha down. Aletha had a rule that two siblings could not be in God Squad together. However, that didn't keep former God Squad puppeteer Mary Lou Sheppard[34] from trying to get Aletha's consent to join. Mary Lou's brother, Preston, was already in God Squad. "I was in grade six, about eleven years old," Mary Lou recalled. "I pestered Aletha about joining puppets... but she would keep saying I could when I was old enough. Finally she gave in, about a half-year before the minimum age, because I promised I would not fight with Preston."

Aletha made another exception to her rule of one sibling at a time. In the early days of her work with the puppets, she recruited siblings Tina and Kris Gowdy when the family moved to Regina. They stayed with the troupe for many years.

Maybe it was the eager desire of grade five and six young people to join God Squad, which in later years prompted Aletha to start a junior God Squad. For a short time, she taught them the skills of puppetry so they could get a taste of it, and later get into the older group. She held a practice one evening a week for the younger group, and another one for the regular group on a different evening. Presenting puppet skits for primary children at Children's Church gave these young puppeteers a taste of performing.

Puppetry was hard work, but for those who committed themselves to God Squad, it remained fun, providing a creative outlet and opportunity to learn about the techniques of puppetry. As a bonus, it brought about a sense of fulfillment, especially for those who found freedom of expression in performing behind a curtain. A puppeteer could hide, performing without facing the audience directly. "God Squad provided a place of belonging and a safe place to learn and experiment with my abilities," commented Kris Gowdy.[35]

Along with the opportunity for fun and learning, Aletha presented her expectation of commitment. How did the puppeteers feel about the commitment? Was it scary? Necessary? A little too much to expect? A good thing? The response to those questions varied from person to person.

Many of the puppeteers agreed that commitment was part of the involvement. They took the decision to be part of God Squad very seriously. "I tried to be at practices even when it was inconvenient," said Josh.

Some felt there was really no reason the commitment should be hard. After all, they did other things once a week as well. For a few, God Squad comprised their entire social life, so commitment to it was simply part of their life for a time. A few puppeteers found it hard, but they agreed it was still a good experience.

"Being there each week," said Tina, now Mrs. Cowie,[36] "really did help build up arm strength, and the consistency helped [me] to learn lines and positions. She [Aletha] had high standards, and that was good for us to learn."

Mary Lou affirmed the value of the commitment. "It was good personal discipline because you disciplined yourself to be dedicated to something."

Occasionally, the parents needed convincing to allow their child to join God Squad. Their concern was that the commitment would be more than their child could handle. "But once my parents saw the first show," said Jayne Werry,[37] long time puppeteer, "they were great with it."

What about the parents' commitment? The puppeteer's parents were involved in the commitment along with their child. In September, at the beginning of each God Squad year, Aletha would have a Parents Night. It was for the new recruits or those coming back to God Squad, along with their parents.

Always well-prepared, Aletha had a detailed agenda for the evening. Her list included plans to tell about the history of God Squad, to outline the purpose and general policies of the ministry, and a reminder to give out the policy statement for them to read. She planned for an explanation of how the finances were set up, the need and selection process for volunteers, and what she expected of the puppeteers. She was open to questions as she went along, wanting puppeteers and parents to be well-informed.

Parents Night included emphasis on the importance of the puppeteers' attendance at weekly practices. Aletha made parents aware that they needed to make a commitment to God Squad along with their child. She told them that if their child missed practices repeatedly, they would be asked to take their child out of the group.

Two items, information about performance schedules and care of puppets, were on the list as well. Time spent in prayer, dessert and coffee, and an opportunity to view the puppet practice area in the basement, ended the evening agenda.

How did parents feel about the commitment their children had to make to be at all the practices and work hard? They were happy about it. "You can't do it without commitment," agreed parents Gavin and Audrey Wood.

Most of the puppeteers were not able to drive themselves. They appreciated the support and encouragement of committed parents who took time to give them rides to practice each week, and to attend the performances. After puppeteers were old enough to drive themselves to practices, a family vehicle would often still be involved.

So what did you do if you lived across town and it didn't pay to go home between dropping your child off at practice and picking them up again when they were finished? Perhaps some leisurely grocery shopping in the hour and a half you had at your disposal. Leisurely, that is, until you came back to the stress of finding your puppeteer impatiently waiting because practice had been canceled that week. Even if puppeteers loved puppets, that didn't ensure they had a perfect memory!

Another thing having to do with commitment was also stressed to puppeteers and parents: the commitment to being considerate of others in the group by having washed feet, clean socks for practices and performances, and using deodorant. The puppeteers' proximity to each other behind the stage necessitated striving for a pleasant atmosphere.

Although Aletha desired commitment, she didn't nag about it—the choice was the puppeteers'. They knew Aletha wanted them to take puppeteering seriously. They couldn't make excuses like too much homework. She expected puppeteers to be at practices each week.

Aletha also expected puppeteers to be punctual, because it cut into practice time if they were late. She would wait to do the devotional if someone was late. "If we were late, we knew it bothered her," said Janelle, "but she didn't say anything because it was up to us. You didn't get a major part if you weren't committed to the discipline of being on time... It was more fun to be on time and be at practices."

Was Aletha disappointed when the puppeteers didn't show up for practice? "No," said husband Glenn. "She went with the flow. She often expressed surprise that they were able to perform at as many places as they did, because the puppeteers were involved in so many things like sports, school, and so on."

It required commitment to stay. In Glenn's view, the puppeteers "either liked it or they didn't." Part of that commitment was the love the young people had for Aletha herself, and her own commitment to being at God Squad practices. This was evident when she was undergoing chemotherapy. "Her body had swelled up a lot," said Aletha's friend Doreen Butterfield, "but she got Glenn to strap on her shoes and she went downstairs. She was uncomfortable, but still had the practice."

Many puppeteers made the decision to join God Squad. Some stayed a short time, a few months or a year, but a good number stayed throughout their junior high and high school years. Some puppeteers stayed on after high school or returned to help out after being away at college, and ended up staying in the troupe for an extra year or more. Even adulthood did not stop Bob Joice, one of the first four puppeteers. He was involved with working the puppets or helping behind the scenes until the last performance in 2001.

PAIN AND PERSEVERANCE

It was time consuming, hard work to prepare those delightful skits and mus-icals that God Squad brought to the puppet stage.

"The performance was short if you were timing it," commented Aletha's fellow library worker Kathleen Fisher[38], "but there was a lot more than what you saw at the front."

Arm and hand muscles sometimes protested. Try holding your arm up above your head, bending it forward ninety degrees at the wrist and moving your thumb against your fingers for a while. Not easy. Then try doing it with a puppet on your hand.

It took time to build up the muscles, "to get used to staying up in the air so long, and... continually moving a puppet's mouth," Tina remembered.

"Oh, it was tough!" was a more recent puppeteer's evaluation. She spoke of not having much strength in her arms, so she would repeat to herself, "I can do it, I can do it," over and over again.

"It was especially hard after Christmas and summer," said Jacqui Gagnon.[39] "Aletha always made us dig right in. I often supported my arm on my neighbor's shoulder."

When an arm got tired and began to ache, the natural tendency would be for the puppeteer to straighten the angle at which the wrist was bent. The result was that the puppet's head would tilt back, and the audience would see the 'neck and chin' view of the puppet. The puppeteer might not even be aware that they were lifting the head too much, so a reminder would be necessary. Sometimes puppeteers would need to be individually prompted to tilt their puppet's head down, but each member of the squad knew what a collective "heads-down" meant.

Aletha was conscious of the pain a puppeteer could feel, especially a new recruit, when first using a puppet. She tried to ease the discomfort and pain by giving new recruits older puppets to use. The mouths were less tight to work with, so they were easier to use until the puppeteer became used to having a puppet above their head. Aletha also gave new puppeteers short parts at first.

When it was not speaking during a scene, the puppeteers had permission to bring their puppet down, relax their arm and then come up again. For this, there was only one condition—the puppet was not to 'pop' back up, but instead, 'walk' back up. This reprieve, however, was only available during practices, not during performances. Aching arms or not, the show had to go on. Sometimes the main character would be up performing for a long stretch of time. Josh knew just how long it was, because his "arm was burning by the time [the performance] was over."

However, there were little ways available for puppeteers to get a brief rest for their arms while in the midst of a performance. When the play called for the character to turn around to face the back row of puppets, a puppeteer could let the mouth fall open for a few seconds.

It was especially hard to hold up especially large puppets for extended periods. With a head "about the size of a country mail box," according to Bob Joice, these larger puppets were heavy. The long mouths, extending well past the puppeteers' hand, were front heavy and hard to keep closed. They slid forward, especially when the puppeteers were tipping the head down, making eye contact with the audience.

Aletha would coordinate sketches to help give the puppeteers a break when using these large puppets. Like a lion puppet, for example. She would find places in songs where the puppeteer could shake it a bit, like a lion shakes his mane. By doing this action, the puppeteer could get the large-headed puppet further onto their hand again.

Each puppeteer felt and dealt with the pain in his or her own way. For some puppeteers, the pain never really went away. They learned to ignore it and continue anyway or, as Krista Bekker,[40] a more recent puppeteer, put it, "When your arm goes numb, you don't notice anymore." A routine activity, like playing the piano, helped loosen up tired, aching muscles for Krista.

Some still felt the soreness the next day, but others said their muscles adapted and they were not sore at all. Ongoing practice and exercise helped ease the pain and got arms accustomed to using the puppets. "It will get better," Aletha would assure the puppeteers. She would tell them to work through the cramps every day, sometimes recommending specific exercises, such as lifting weights.

SINGULAR DILIGENCE

Getting to know the songs in the skits helped the puppeteers improve their puppets' movements. Moving the mouth in coordination with the words being said or sung made the puppets more believable. After the puppeteers were familiar with the words the puppet was saying, they did not have to concentrate so much on the movement of the mouth. They could put more into interpreting the character of the puppet.

Aletha would send audio tapes home with the puppeteers. She encouraged them to practice in front of a mirror to see how they were doing with the puppet's movements, compared to what the character was saying.

"If you can see the eyes in the mirror, you are holding the puppet in a good position," she told them. That meant the puppet was facing forward, not tilted back and staring straight up at the ceiling. If the puppet's head tilted too far back, the audience could see into the top of its open mouth. It was a bit of a trick to open only the bottom part of the mouth, so a puppet looked authentic when it was 'speaking'.

Practice was the only way to learn coordination and authenticity. Aletha would let new recruits take a puppet home, where they had extra time to practice learning correct mouth and body movements.

Learning to use a puppet correctly took various forms. "I would sit in front of the TV or lip sync to songs on the radio," said Andrew Reddekopp.

Heather Miller took Aletha's instruction about working everyday seriously. "I would walk around the house with a puppet on my hand, and hold my arm up—practicing keeping my wrist in the right position."

The amounts of time spent practicing were as varied as the personalities of the puppeteers. Some teens must have been naturals at puppeteering, or caught on very quickly, as they admitted to not practicing very long. Others spent a half-hour to an hour each day of the week in addition to the time spent at puppet practice.

If you were supposed to be learning how to use a puppet, why not practice entertaining, too? Krista remembers riding in the back seat of the car and using the puppet to wave to people. Not only did she benefit from the practice, but it threw in some free advertising in the process.

The more experienced the puppeteers became, the more conscious they were of the puppets' movements. One puppeteer felt Glenn's comments helped a lot. "When you are talking," Glenn had told him, "you don't open your mouth for every syllable. You open it more when you emphasize something. Do the same thing with a puppet. That way, it doesn't just look like you're flapping your mouth all the time."

It did become easier and practice eventually paid off. The animation—how the puppet moved when it talked, if it faced the other characters at the right time, and whether it appeared above the top of the stage curtain correctly— became second nature.

How long does that second nature stay with you? While describing using a puppet, Mary Lou, definitely a veteran puppeteer, still unconsciously held up her arm as she spoke. She worked her fingers as if she were holding a puppet above the top of the curtain. When she realized she was doing it, she laughed at herself, then stopped.

THE BALANCE OF TOGETHERNESS

"Let's do it again from the part where..." or "Over and over until we get it right." Familiar practice phrases? Over and over could lead to frustration when the part just wouldn't come out right. Janelle remembers thinking, "Why can't we just get it and move on?" Doing it repeatedly meant practicing until they heard "Well done!"

However, those who loved being in puppetry looked forward to practicing. The boring or frustrating parts never outweighed the good ones. Part of the fun happened while waiting, often waiting a long time for their turn. "We had creative minds," Jacqui said, "and could make it interesting on the sides when we weren't doing a part." Sometimes they bounced around at the back in time to the music, or someone would provide entertainment, as one puppeteer did, by making the puppet he was working dance around.

The response to this on the side entertainment was likely what Glenn was referring to when he said, "You would hear the laughter downstairs and wonder if they ever practiced."

Aletha did her best to make it fun to be a puppeteer, and variety was one of the ways she did it. Each year, Aletha found different musicals, as well as short skits and songs, for the puppeteers to work on.

At times, Aletha would provide snacks after practice. What young person doesn't define snacks as part of the fun? They would often go out into the backyard or Glenn would come down and talk to them. If any guests were present, whether a visiting missionary or a recording technician, they were invited to join them.

Aletha allowed time for fun during practices. "She must have had room for fun," said Bob Joice. "She put up with Dave and me for years."

Nevertheless, there was a balance. Aletha kept the puppeteers focused. Spontaneous laughter, giggling, and jokes were part of the fun, but if they got too carried away during a practice, she would always bring them back under control.

"Sometimes she would threaten 'If you don't calm down, I'll have to separate you,'" said Jayne Werry. But the puppeteers would always heed her warning and settle down before she had to carry through.

"She was reasonable," another former puppeteer said. "Strict in a loving way. I was never offended by her saying, 'Stop fooling around and get back to work!'"

"Aletha ran the group with dedication and perfection," said Kris Gowdy in a letter. She would skillfully bring them back to the work that had to be done. It was "never in a harsh way," Kris added, "but in a 'this is what we are here for' fashion."

Aletha gave opportunity for creativity, to try something different. While practicing at home, the puppeteer would decide how the puppet would act, what they felt its personality should be for a scene. When they came to the joint practice, "they got input from the others as to how they felt the puppet should be portrayed—whether they agreed or disagreed, or if anything should be added," explained Mary Lou.

Although Aletha didn't always agree with him or her, if a puppeteer felt a certain puppet would work better for a certain character, she gave them the opportunity to try it. Then, if the way the puppeteer had thought the portrayal should happen turned out to be better, she was quick to acknowledge that.

Not all of it was easy. Bob and Shelley affirmed that Aletha put up with a lot with some groups, but she was very patient. Aletha could work with all kinds of kids. She appreciated all of them, no matter what they were like, and prayed for everyone in the group.

"She had lots of patience to put up with us at practices, me and Troy," Tyler Wood, an avid puppeteer, said. "We would be trying to make people laugh," he added, grinning at that point.

Observations of the balance of love and discipline Aletha achieved came from the puppeteers and those outside God Squad who knew her.

"In the God Squad context, she was a teacher. She always had her notebook open and would go through a page of notes, turn the page, and then go through the next one." –JAYNE WERRY (puppeteer)

"They respected her, did what she asked, tried their best, were eager to please her," –JIM SLOUGH[41] (recording technician)

"The kids were well-behaved. She had a great rapport with them." –IRENE SOTROPA (long-time friend)

DEEPER LESSONS

Aletha considered God Squad a ministry. Because her goal was to get them in the right mindset for that, one-third of the practice time each week was spent with a devotional. The other two-thirds was spent working with the puppets.

Aletha would remind the puppeteers that they weren't just entertaining, not just doing puppetry. They were telling people about Jesus; they were there to bring glory to God.

From their comments, it seems they had caught the purpose.

> "I think it was important that Aletha always had a devotional and we memorized verses that had to do with our performances. Her doing that... reminded us why we were performing—there was a bigger purpose." –TINA COWIE

> "It was God Squad, after all; not just a puppet group. It was good to keep sight of your purpose even though it was brought out in each play we did." –JAYNE WERRY

> "Her purpose in having devotions was to teach the young people for their later walk in life." –BOB JOICE

> "It was not about being at church, not about only having fun. For Aletha it was about God being as real in their lives as He was in hers." –JANELLE GAGNON

Devotions included spiritual lessons and prayer, often with chapters and verses from the Bible related to the story or skit being prepared right then. Aletha made sure the puppeteers knew what the content of the story was and what it was supposed to say.

Bob and Shelley Joice spoke of the time they were working on a play about David. Aletha read paragraphs and chapters from a book by Philip Keller, and Scriptures from the Bible about sheep and shepherds.

Aletha was aware that holding the attention of kids that age was not easy, so she told personal stories in the devotional time. "She would share examples from her life—[like] about her lamb Percy," commented Josh.

Bob and Shelley felt it was because of these stories from her childhood and teen years that the puppeteers got to know her as thoroughly as she got to know them.

TOP: The original four puppeteers. (l-r) Heather (Campbell) Miller, Bob Joice, Bette-Jean (Joice) Hand, and Geoff Hiltz with the first puppets (photo courtesy of Heather Miller; puppets by puppetproductions.com). BOTTOM: God Squad troupe, Christmas 1997 Clockwise from bottom right: Shelley Joice, Laura Barton, Jacqui Gagnon, Jennifer Ingram, Jayne Werry, Troy Dakiniewich, Tyler Wood, and Chuck Wright (photo courtesy of Gavin Wood).

CHAPTER TWO
A FAMILY AFFAIR

Like any ministry, the person who walks to the front of the stage and speaks to the audience has other people working alongside them. God Squad and Aletha Joice were known synonymously, but Aletha was not alone in her work.

GLENN

A familiar saying states that 'behind every good man is a good woman.' With Aletha, it was 'behind this good woman was a good man'—her husband Glenn. Glenn himself was very modest about his part in the ministry. However, if you heard the comments many people made, you would soon discover that he was indeed the good man behind this good woman.

What more emphatic way would there be to show that a man is supporting his wife's ministry efforts than to agree to having most of the available space in their basement devoted to God Squad? The stage, the puppets and other props, the lighting and sound equipment—all of it was collected in one basement, the Joices'. It showed an obvious dedication to the puppet ministry.

What about purchasing a van specifically for the ministry in which your wife is involved? One of the Joice vehicles was always big enough to transport all the equipment and puppeteers—at first a station wagon, and then later a van. Glenn looked after the vehicles, making sure they were reliable for road trips.

Right from the beginning, Glenn worked on many physical projects connected with the performances of God Squad, but he supported the ministry in more than this hands-on way. He was present at dress rehearsals, the last one or two practices before each performance, and was an encourager to all of the kids.

"He never criticized," said Heather Miller. "He critiqued. He did it in a humorous way. He was a complement to Aletha in what she did."

BOB AND SHELLEY

Two members of the Joice family who were a large part of God Squad's success were Bob and his wife Shelley. Aletha relied on them for many things. "We quarterbacked" was the phrase Bob used.

Bob and Shelley worked well together as puppeteers, and for that reason they were often part of the training sessions Aletha conducted with new recruits. In the later years, when Aletha had difficulty working the puppets, Bob and Shelley carried out the demonstrations of what God Squad was about.

When it was time to go to a performance, Bob and Shelley were often over at Glenn and Aletha's long before it was time to leave. They would be helping to load the equipment into the van.

Shelley was an excellent puppeteer and for many years her artistic talents went into making various puppets, puppet clothing and props, and painting scenes for stage backdrops.

The amount of time Glenn, Bob, and Shelley sacrificed for the ministry of God Squad would be impossible to measure. The amount of time spent digging out patterns for new puppets or helping prepare for road trips was never calculated, but these efforts demonstrated their strong commitment to this 'family affair.'

THE STAGE

The stage, or 'screen,' was a project Glenn worked on.

Initially, the stage consisted of six wood frames with a tan-colored cloth tacked to each. He put hinges on the frames so they could be folded accordion-style for transporting, and then set up in a U-shape for performances.

People had begun responding quite positively to the puppet performances, saying that they felt God Squad could do very well. The next step was ordering some books with puppet stage designs. The plan Aletha felt would be suitable for what they needed called for PVC pipe. This would make a light, portable stage, easily transported from performance to performance.

After Glenn had assembled the frame the first time, it stood solidly on its own, but when the curtain went on, the pipe came apart and down it came.

Heather, a puppeteer during this construction phase, remembers holding the frame while Glenn figured out what to do and Aletha giggled endlessly about it.

Glenn adapted by using numbered pins in the pipe to keep it together, and soon the second stage was born. Adorned with a new curtain, it once again hid the puppeteers behind its folds.

Despite adaptations, the puppeteers still had to be careful how they moved backstage. Bumping the vertical pole could result in the stage falling over. Therefore, they took care when assembling the stage. Assembling the horizontal and vertical supports incorrectly would cause it to lean forward too much or tip. During one performance, someone held the stage up until the play was finished.

Stage construction went through another phase. As God Squad took on more challenges and the skits became more complex, so also did the need for a more involved stage setup. Glenn found himself putting together a more advanced, two-tiered stage. This new stage sported deep, royal blue curtains and offered new possibilities.

BACKDROPS

The higher tier of the new two-level stage provided a place to hang backdrops. These were specific background scenes suited to the performance God Squad was presenting.

A scene of an inside room, the great outdoors, or the wall of a building were just a few of Shelley's artistic contributions. Each painted backdrop was signed and dated. Although some were suitable for more than one play, Shelley still painted numerous backdrops over the years.

The scenes for the backdrops were painted on cloth, so the fabric needed to be something that would not wrinkle and would absorb the acrylic paint. Usually a lightweight canvas or heavy cotton was chosen.

These backdrops were attached to the top edge of the upper tier of the stage and flung over to the front to change the background scene for the action. When the action of the play changed back to a previous scene, one or more of the backdrops were moved in reverse. For some performances, several layers of backdrops would be used. This necessitated coordinated timing for dropping new backdrops and bringing them back.

Reducing the work required for the number and variety of background scenes needed, called for ingenuity. Occasionally, a certain color of fabric was chosen to fit the need. A gray color, for instance, was suitable for a rock wall, on which Shelley would only have to paint the outlines and shading of the rocks.

Some backdrops were half the width of the back tier and thus less work to prepare. They could be hung over one side of the larger one to facilitate a change of scene. To give the feel of a wall, props would simply be set against a plain color backdrop. One backdrop for a 'royal' scene was purple velvet, made from an old set of drapes.

LIGHTING AND SOUND

In the early years, operating the sound for God Squad performances involved working a ghetto blaster,[i] or using the sound system where they were performing. Later it became a more complicated set up, involving speakers, amplifier, mixer, and tape player.

God Squad preferred to perform in a darkened room because, as Shelley explained, "the focus was on the puppets, not on whatever else was going on in the room or auditorium." If the light, perhaps coming through a window behind the stage, was very bright, the audience would see the shadows of the puppeteers and what they were doing behind the curtain. Spotlights helped to do away with that problem.

When it came time to set up the lighting for a performance, a great amount of work was involved. Portable spotlights fastened onto poles were assembled each time the stage was erected.

Bob was aware, too, of a fear the puppeteers had, that one of the curious children from the audience would grab a light standard or trip on a wire and pull something down. Thus, in addition to everything else that needed to be done in setting up for a performance, all the wires would be taped down.

These preparations took a great deal of time, so the Joice family was busy well ahead of any performance. Once everything was set up and the performance began, Glenn was the one at the controls of both the sound and lighting.

PROPS

When Aletha needed a moveable prop, she would describe to Glenn what she needed and he would figure out how to make it work. "I didn't really have artistic ability," said Glenn. "It was more mechanical. Aletha would tell me what she wanted and ask me to work it out."

---

[i] See Glossary for explanation of ghetto blaster.

That working out of the movements of non-puppet props took many hours in the garage jury-rigging, to use Bob Joice's word.

Glenn's biggest project was a prop for the musical *The Music Machine*. Music played and lights flashed when this marvelous machine came on stage. More about that big, colorful machine later.

FINANCING

God Squad was a noncommercial, nonprofit group, with voluntary donations providing the funds for the troupe. There were never any charges for performances. If anyone who wanted to book God Squad inquired about the cost of having them perform, they would be asked, "What would you pay to rent a thirty-minute film for your group?" It was suggested that they give accordingly, the amount being left up to the church or group making the booking.

The money from donations at performances went back into God Squad, but the offerings were not always enough to cover all of the expenses. Traveling expenses only came out of the donation when the amount was large enough. Most of the money went toward the purchase of more puppets or equipment for sound and lighting.

But when your heart is in ministry, you are not afraid to spend time and money on it. Such was the case with Glenn and Aletha. God Squad was often subsidized from their personal income. When God Squad first began, they paid the initial expenses for the purchase of the first four puppets. Over the years, their financial involvement included the provision of a vehicle and gasoline to take the puppeteers to venues where they were to perform.

Aletha's notes show a very careful record of costs for God Squad and received donations. She listed all the materials and supplies purchased each year—what, where, when, and how much—right down to pipe cleaners. Her notes also included comments about her research into the best prices of items they needed to purchase, and where they were available.

The amount of each donation, and to which performance it was connected, was recorded as well. Beside her list one year, Aletha made a notation about the total: "Does not include road expenses, gifts, wind-up, or bank charges," reflecting their personal contribution to God Squad's finances.

While Glenn and Aletha Joice's support of the God Squad ministry dipped into their own pocketbook, their donations of time, according to Bette-Jean's husband Don was like a part-time job.

This donation of time extended to Bob and Shelley, who often stopped by on performance day to help Glenn load the van. Year after year, stage components and props were just part of the many items transported to and from each performance. "They hauled everything up from the basement when they went, and when they came back, hauled it back down," recalled Bob Joice.

At times, the puppeteers were involved in bringing the equipment to a performance or taking it home. However, more often than not, Glenn and Bob were the ones loading and unloading the van. Some trips to performances required getting up quite early in the morning to get everything done.

THE 'EXTENDED' FAMILY

The voluntary work of the family and volunteers outside the family made it possible for God Squad to operate without a large budget or fundraising efforts. Volunteer tailors are one example. Although they did not make monetary donations, their work assisted the ministry financially by the giving of their time, and sometimes materials.

Mildred Peat and Doreen Smith, two friends of Aletha's, helped clothe the puppets. During a performance introduction, shortly after Mildred Peat went to be with the Lord, Aletha pointed out some of the puppet costumes Mildred had made. She expressed appreciation for Mildred's work and for her friendship.

"More than sewing, Mildred Peat was vitally interested in each young person involved in God Squad, prayed for us when we traveled and called to ask, 'How did it go?'... I miss her for more than costuming. When I've been poking my fingers with needles, I can hear her laugh, and when I've been slow figuring out how a sleeve should go or a backdrop fit on, I've missed her encouragement. We dedicate our performance tonight to Mildred Peat, whose life displayed 'love, joy, peace, patience, kindness, goodness, faithfulness, gentleness, and self-control,' the fruit of the Spirit of God."[ii]

[ii] Galatians 5:22-23 (NIV).

TOP: The flashing lights of the music machine were operated by its well-thought-out inner design (photo courtesy of Gavin Wood). BOTTOM: Behind the good woman and at her side. Glenn and Aletha, August 1998, at Christopher Lake.

CHAPTER THREE
BEHIND THE SCENES

BOOKINGS AND ADVERTISING

How did God Squad's performance bookings happen year after year? Was it a struggle to find people who were willing to let God Squad come to perform for their group? Aletha was not concerned about the number of performances they did each year; she left that up to God. That is not to say she didn't work at doing some advertising, though. She just didn't push to advertise God Squad.

How then did people know God Squad was ready to perform again when the new season came around? The troupe had become well-known, so groups familiar with the ministry often checked in to inquire whether they could book a performance. The requests came for Sunday School openings, Children's Church, or Vacation Bible Schools. Companies even called about scheduling puppet performances for the children at annual staff parties. Seniors centers and special care homes requested the troupe to entertain their residents.

Mary Lou remembers wondering about the seniors' response at one of the special care homes. "I wondered if they enjoyed the play," she said. "Could they see, hear, understand the jokes?" It was likely the staff heard positive responses from the seniors later, and so made future bookings.

Perhaps not everyone understood everything, but something was attracting people to book God Squad year after year. Maybe it was that hint of mystery, the sense that it might just be real, drawing the audience into the world of make-believe. "Even if," as Grant Sawatzky said in his ironic phrase, "you were old enough to know otherwise!"

When a performance was coming up, Aletha advertised with posters she placed on bulletin boards in churches and in public places such as community recreation centers. The posters would include a picture related to God Squad or a skit they were doing, along with Aletha's phone number. Wherever she left a poster, she gave permission to make copies or distribute the information.

When her local church made the booking, Aletha obtained assistance with a little more advertising. An extra invitation would go into each church mailbox for those in her church to invite their friends and neighbors. Shelley used her artistic talents to make a single, original invitation. She included drawings related to the upcoming performance. Aletha would write in the dates and other details, and then make photocopies to distribute. This mailbox insert involved folding more than a hundred invitations.

SUITED OR NOT?

Evaluation of the suitability of each skit, song, or musical Aletha was planning to use began long before practices started or performance dates were put on the calendar. Some were humorous, some more serious, but all were chosen to entertain. Aletha's primary desire was that they point the audience to the Savior, so she took a careful look at the materials she was thinking of having the puppeteers perform.

Aletha's precise, tabulated notes contained her observations about the variety of materials she had available in her tape library. She noted whether the songs were suitable for short skits or plays, and considered the suitability of the content of the musicals.

Aletha looked, for instance, at the pauses between songs in a prerecorded musical. If the pauses were too lengthy, she planned various ways to keep the interest of the audience. A little extra silliness by the puppet characters during an exit or entrance could cover a prolonged silence.

In prerecorded conversations, Aletha would note the quality of the narration between songs. She would note the value of the message a musical carried, and make comments about it: "Straight conversation, a little boring" or "Salvation explanation good."

Experience in both performing and practicing over the years enabled Aletha to look ahead and check for potential problems. One comment in her notes suggested that the musical itself was suitable, but she noted a potential difficulty. She proposed a solution with a reminder—"Attach Sampson's hair so it won't fall off," referring to the puppet who would play the character of Sampson.

When she was planning to compose a program of short skits, Aletha evaluated the individual songs in the same careful way she reviewed complete musicals. She used a variety of songs and would determine how each of them might fit into the whole program. A comment, such as "Fine by itself, but not following a Bible play," was one she might write down beside the name of a song.

The songs she chose for God Squad to perform often came from different tapes, and weren't always in sequence on any particular tape. She would record in her notes the title of the source tape, the side of the tape a particular song was on, and whether the voices were male or female, adult or child. She also noted details in the songs: "has clapping, long note ending, abrupt ending, slow, good swing." These in-depth notations helped Aletha decide how the puppets' movements corresponded to the songs. For example, if the last note was a long one, the puppet's mouth would have to remain open longer to appear to be holding the note, but not so if it ended abruptly.

When Aletha felt 'filler' would help the sequence of ideas flow from one song in a program to the next, she would work in narrations she had written. She planned creative lines or questions to introduce a song or to use in her comments when it was over.

Here are some examples:

> "It's time for a commercial, don't you think?" or "He's advertising the right thing, isn't he?" or "How did they spell...?"
>
> "You just saw that, as strong as Rocky was, he needed help, needed a Friend. You, too, have probably started something, thinking that you could handle it all by yourself. Then you got into a terrible fix and had to call for help." Then, with a touch of evangelism, she would conclude with, "You not only need human friends, you need Jesus, the best Friend."

Here is another example from a program she compiled, using songs in which the characters were all animals:

> "There are many birds and animals mentioned in the Bible. We hope that through them we've been able to remind you of the real life situations of the people of Bible times. People and their reactions haven't changed. The wonderful thing is that we have the Bible to tell us of failures and successes, and how, when God's ways are followed, our needs are met."

Time was a crucial element in a variety program. After tabulating the minutes each song on the list would take to perform, Aletha often added an extra song she wanted to prepare. This was in case the program of songs took less time than expected at the performance.

As she looked ahead to a performance, Aletha would evaluate the capabilities of the puppeteers. The decisions about which of them would work each puppet character were based on a variety of factors. How long a puppeteer had been with God Squad was one consideration. Some puppets were harder to work than others. The length of time a character would be up on stage required enough strength and endurance so that the puppet wouldn't falter. Some puppeteers had a natural musical ability, something that would enhance their portrayal of a character when they moved the puppet. Aletha would give out specific parts to fit that capability.

The role each puppeteer had was part of the whole performance, so, as Doreen Butterfield observed, Aletha "found suitable parts so each child who wanted to, could... be involved."

DETAILS, DETAILS...

After finding suitable material for the group, detailed work on characters and mood began.

Preparing for a play started with the list of characters needed to carry out the performance and which puppet would represent each character. This did not mean that each puppet corresponded to a single character; sometimes the play had several characters played by the same puppet. This required multiple costume changes and Aletha's notes indicate how she worked that out.

Beside the name of each puppet was a list of the clothing the puppet would need, and the sequence of changes required to portray the characters. For example, if the puppet named Chuck was to be four characters, the list might look like this: 'Begin with the basic white shirt, change to a Jewish top and a skull cap, then to a Chinese top, and finally an Arab costume and headdress.'

Often there wasn't much time for the procedure of preparing a puppet to portray the next character. Therefore, Aletha would instruct the puppeteers to make changes during moments when they were not on stage. One puppeteer might only have time to remove the original garment before needing to be back on stage, working his or her own puppet. Another puppeteer, in the moments he or she was not performing on stage, would be responsible for putting a different garment onto the puppet being prepared. In total, it would involve anywhere from five to six puppeteers to make all the necessary changes for a single puppet to portray several characters.

Changing clothing was not the only thing that changed when a puppet underwent a character transformation. Puppeteers also changed their mindset and the puppet's body language. "When you put one down and took another, mentally you went into the character you were picking up," Mary Lou pointed out.

Aletha had some examples of character portrayal instructions for the puppeteers in her notes, instructions to make movements such as, "Slow, sinewy... arms up like he's really somebody. Strut!" This would be to portray a character with a strong ego. Sadness could be achieved by hanging the puppet's head. One puppet's arm across another's shoulders expressed love. You would immediately recognize the regal personality of the character, when she instructed the puppeteers to bring the puppet "mincing in with fans" and then to "mince off"[i] in the postlude.

The mood was to some extent created by the music. However, how a puppet moved in time to that music enhanced what the song was saying. "Arms uplifted" was a way of showing praise to God. The instruction "Mouths shut together" after a long ending note was there to prevent breaking a solemn mood with an accidentally comical sequence of one puppet's mouth closing before the others.

The need for precision and detail in how the puppeteer worked the puppet in sync with the music was important for setting the mood and for realistic character portrayal. Aletha would tell the puppeteers that when they forgot about what they or the audience might be thinking, and tried to think as the puppet thought, they would bring the audience into the world of the puppet.

A SHORT PAUSE, BUT IT'S NOT INTERMISSION TIME

Remember earlier, when we talked about the need for 'filler' when the gaps between songs was quite long? Sometimes, the opposite happened, when two songs on a tape followed each other in quick succession. Puppeteers usually required extra time to get ready between songs. Aletha would make instructional notes specifically for the sound technician (the same faithful man named Glenn who was on lights). Her note would indicate when Glenn was to pause and start the tape. This would give the puppeteers the necessary time to pre-

---

[i] See Glossary for an explanation of mincing.

pare—change puppets, gather the props, or move them to new positions—for the next song.

Here are some examples of the characters' actions he wouldn't want to miss when they were his cue, telling him to pause the tape:

"When Sam nudges Luke."

"Tape off immediately after decree."

"Pause only... enough for trumpeters to move."

It meant keeping an eye on the performance at all times, sometimes using both hands, one to stop or start the tape and the other to dim the lights at the crucial moment. A wave from Aletha at the side of the curtain when they were ready would signal him that the tape could start again.

Glenn's job was not an easy one when the troupe was performing a variety show. His instructions then included which song was on which tape, and in what order he would need it in the program. He would need to change tapes quickly, all the while keeping an eye out for the signal from Aletha so he knew if they were also ready. Only occasionally would a second wave from Aletha be necessary to 'unpause' the action.

...AND MORE DETAILS!

Aletha's notes, regarding her planned instructions for the puppeteers, contained many tiny details, often in shortened form.

The puppeteer with a rooster character on his or hand hand had to be ready at just the right time. Therefore, shorthand hints, such as "Rooster crows," made the roster of instructions. The sequence of movements, when the lights came up or went out, was important, so "Leave arms around each other. Lights out" was on her list, too.

Hints for working with the puppets and props backstage were carefully laid out.

"Rods on well," was the instruction to be sure the rod that held the puppet's arm up was securely attached to the puppet.

"Puppet bodies well up... not crooked... hair fixed," told the puppeteers to check if the puppet was properly visible above the top edge of the curtain, and its hair was neat.

The phrase, "Get turned in first scene to talk, so back not to audience," was meant to remind the puppeteers to have the puppet they were using facing the right direction when it became visible above the curtain. This was so that the puppet would not look like he or she was speaking to a wall, for instance.

When she wrote, "Do not lean on stage—only appear to," though basically self-explanatory, was a reminder to the puppeteers working puppets in the front row. Since the stage was free-standing, too much pressure could result in it toppling.

It was important when a puppeteer wasn't working it that he or she place a puppet so it was ready for the next scene or action. "Remove sack cloth; leave him there," told the puppeteer to remove the costume of the puppet he or she had just worked and leave the puppet nearby for someone else to dress it in a new costume. If the puppet would not be used again in that skit, it would be placed in a box instead.

At times, the instruction included Aletha herself. "All up when ready! Wait for Aletha to get back to hold typewriter!" is an example of a time when Aletha would be introducing the skit beforehand. The action was to wait until Aletha had returned behind the curtain, ready to raise the prop, in this case a typewriter.

CUE ME!

With a long list of details and movements to memorize, what happened when loss of memory occurred due to performance jitters? Aletha prepared for that possibility, too.

Cue cards accompanied each performance preparation. These cue cards, filled with diagrams, reminded the puppeteers which of the puppets to use and where to position themselves. She diagramed the puppeteers' movements, from the front to the back tier of the stage, then listed them, using their initials.

The cue cards hung behind the curtains where the puppeteers could refer to them. Different cue cards hung on the curtain at practices than at performances. Preparation of these cards meant attention to little details and required much work. At practices, Aletha wrote out and diagramed the whole thing— which puppet to use, where each puppet should be. At performances, shortened cues showed when to be ready for the next movement. These diagrams had the puppeteer's names, and x's and arrows marking the movements for each scene.

Not all the puppeteers appreciated her thoroughness in drawing up the cue cards. "Her diagrams drove me nuts," said Bob Joice. "She would have directions for her directions, for her directions." He did concede, however, that it was just how he personally felt and that "the diagrams helped kids who were not concentrating."

Conversely, Aletha's organized plans left a good impression with Josh. "It was like being a professional puppeteer," he said.

Puppeteers like Janelle Gagnon, who felt she didn't really rely on the cue cards all that much, did concede that she checked them occasionally. "Just to make sure of the number of items before my turn came up again," said Janelle.

At the beginning of practicing a new play, those who followed the cue cards would check frequently. However, after practicing for a while, they had the movements of the skit memorized, so they only used the cue cards as a back-up.

Reliance on the cue cards was greater when the skit was complex. "We used them a lot more if we were performing lots of little songs and skits that had us changing a lot, and maybe we weren't as familiar with all the material," Tina explained.

Puppeteers who were more nervous used cue cards all the time. While they were not working a puppet or prop themselves, they would study the cards. They also checked what other puppeteers were to be doing, because sometimes they would need to pass a puppet to someone. This concern that others would benefit from you knowing what they were doing came from Aletha telling the puppeteers that they weren't just responsible for themselves, but for the whole group.

So why all the diagrams? Why cue cards?

"It was a method thing," was Shelley Joice's comment. "She planned and plotted. She was the most organized person I've ever known. As a former teacher, she laid out and organized everything."

Was Aletha concerned with perfection? It seems not. Bob and Shelley felt she allowed the non-gifted into the squad because of the ministry focus of God Squad. She saw potential, yet was easier on them because of the ministry focus. Thus the need for detailed cue cards.

Sometimes cue cards frustrated the better puppeteers, but Aletha expected kids to do as well as they could, to give a hundred percent. The cue cards ensured that all the puppeteers, no matter what their level of ability, could give their best. Most of the puppeteers felt they knew what to do by performance time. However, the presence of cue cards—knowing they could double check—seemed to give them all a sense of assurance, in one way or another.

PACK 'EM UP...

Every item they needed for a performance found a spot on the pages of Aletha's preparation notes. Backdrops, equipment for lighting, puppets, risers,[ii] blankets,

---

[ii] See Glossary for explanation of riser.

cue cards, knee pads, gloves, pins, glue, etc. When the time came to pack it all up, deciding what was going into the "Grandma" box,[iii] the red box, or the blue box was necessary. A list on each container detailed what was going inside. Boxes held the electrical equipment. Other boxes were for props and items like tape, scissors, and hairbrushes. Some boxes or suitcases were for the puppets. Even using the same puppet for numerous characters, fifteen to twenty characters might still be needed per performance. With a limit of only three or four puppets per container, several containers needed to be packed.

Aletha's lists, of what went into a particular box or suitcase in preparation for one performance, weren't necessarily the same as they would be for the next performance. A certain suitcase, holding miscellaneous supplies needed for one skit, might have puppets in it for another. Puppets packed into the brown suitcase for the performance last week might go into the red box this week.

Imagine a first-time puppeteer faced with the myriad details of packing all the supplies needed for a performance. Hearing the snatches of conversation, with all the instructions and questions being tossed back and forth, would have caused his or head to spin.

"There's the lighting and sound equipment. Be sure the lights box has all the lights, bulbs, poles, and bases—the tin suitcase can told extra cords, bulbs, extra lights, and screwdrivers. Check the sound box and be sure the tape deck, microphone, speakers, whoofer, outlet box, amp, and mixer are all there."

"Are the garments bags for costumes filled, and the curtain folded and ready for the suitcase? Oh, add pins and gloves to that suitcase."

"The light standards and larger props won't all fit in the boxes. They'll have to be carried separately."

"Have you counted rolls of carpet so the right numbers come along?"

"Are the kneepads in that box?"

"No room."

"Try the one with the kazoos."

"Roll the carpet tight, because you still need room for backdrops and stage frames in that big duffel bag. We'll need the proclamation sign and some blankets, too."

[iii] Boxes were identified with a name such as "Grandma," or by color. The contents were listed on the box, since then everyone knew that whatever went into the box would fit. The box would be neither too empty, wasting space, or too full, squashing the contents.

"Don't forget the extras—the backpack, elastics, the whistle, a shield, clipboard, pencil, and the long hat pins. Oh, and the kerchiefs, hanky, trumpets, moneybags, and flowers."

Then, as the containers moved out to the van, more instructions:

"Put that suitcase under the tire, the lights above right, and the prop box on top of the other suitcase. The larger risers will need to be stacked and—oh, put the low riser under the front seat. The two square rugs will fit under the back seat, and stand the thin carpet roll upright, back left. That will leave room for two sound pieces, left side, and the tin suitcase on the right."

I would venture to say that by the time it was all done, a new recruit would feel like sinking down against a wall and taking a deep breath to stop the whirling in their head.

Once preparations and practices were over, performance day would come. Before the performance, Aletha would give the puppeteers a concluding instruction. She told them they were not just there as a favor to whoever asked them to come, but to serve them. I wonder if anyone could disagree that the serving had started long before performance day, long before the house lights went down and the first puppet appeared over the blue curtain. Just preparing for a performance, with all the details and practice, was service already.

The audience has arrived and the show is about to begin.

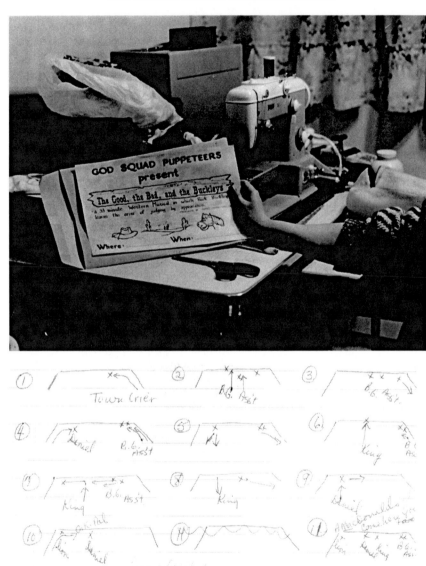

TOP: A poster Shelley drew up to advertise a God Squad performance of *The Good, the Bad, and the Buckleys*, a skit of Puppet Productions. BOTTOM: A sample of Aletha's detailed preparation work.

CHAPTER FOUR
ON WITH THE SHOW

INTRODUCTIONS

"We all like to laugh! However, there's a cruel kind of laughter... laughing at someone's disability, laughing at how they look, laughing at how they talk. But there's also a good kind of laughter. The Bible says the good kind is as good as medicine and easier to take!"

These lines in the notes Aletha made were part of what she was planning to use to introduce a God Squad performance.

Introductions were very much a part of a God Squad performance. While Bette-Jean was heading the troupe, she had done the introductions, but when Aletha began directing, the task was hers. Each introduction Aletha made to the audience included a bit of the history of God Squad, a brief description of the story they were about to see and a spiritual lesson a person could apply to their life. She assured everyone they should feel comfortable enough to laugh or clap. She explained that there would be a few short pauses, but to be patient, because the puppets would be right back each time.

If the presentation needed to be credited to an artist, Aletha was careful to do so. The introduction would acknowledge the artist and song title on the tape being used in the presentation.

An example from her preparation notes: "Because we know it's through Jesus we can have eternal life—have help to live here on earth, be able to really laugh because we're at peace with God and man—we can praise God... God Squad comes to praise Him with Gaither's song 'You're So Good to Me.'"

For the most part, God Squad did not write the musicals. They came from tapes designed for puppet shows. "You should know," Aletha would say in her introduction, "that our tape about Daniel is from Puppet Productions."

Not only would she give credit to musicians, singers, and professional production companies, but to others who had given of their abilities. For example, the people who made the puppets they had not purchased from a manufacturer.

At times, it was a plug for the local Bible bookstore where she had bought the tapes. After being told who had produced the recording she was using, she would inform the audience of the name of the store where they could get it. "On the other hand," she would add, "if you already have the tape and know the songs, we invite you to sing along!"

Aletha geared each introduction to the play being performed or series of songs being dramatized on that particular day. Some of her comments would be directed at the children, often asking them for a response, interacting with them. "Let's you and I do some funny things," she might say. "Let's stand and do what the flamingo does."

Some of Aletha's notes indicate she was directing her introductory comments to the adult part of the audience, more so than to children. The wording in such a case was a little above most children's heads. Here are a couple of examples.

> "The first song reviews some events in Bible times... and each time people learned that it is God who allows kingdoms or individuals to stand or fall..."

> "Our play about Daniel, while it exaggerates most blatantly, as most puppetry will do, does remind us how those in leadership, and we as individuals, become jealous. How our pride causes us to be tempted, by the chance to have greater power, and then do stupid things. But it also shows how Daniel's firm commitment to the one true God helped him to face evil calmly."

Just before Aletha completed her pre-performance introductions, she had a simple request about the privacy the puppets desired.

> "Our puppet friends like to be seen only when performing, so we ask you not to come backstage after the performance. It would be like going into their dressing room!"

After her request on behalf of the puppets, God Squad was presented to the audience. Aletha introduced each puppeteer by giving their name, saying which grade they were in, which school they attended, and how long they had been with God Squad. As each puppeteer was introduced, he or she would come up from their seat, go behind stage, and get ready to begin. The introduction of Glenn came with a touch of humor. "We're a group of teens and one long-ago teen... my husband Glenn, on sound."

When the last puppeteer was behind the stage, Aletha would say, "Lights! God Squad joyfully presents..." Here she would name the musical they were going to do, and then disappear behind the stage herself.

And the performance would begin!

PRECISION, PLEASE

"It was like the choreography for a dance," Josh said, talking about the movements involved in changing puppets during a performance and negotiating around the other puppeteers backstage. "Like dance steps, get the prop, be where you need to be. There wasn't much room, so you had to do the steps right."

Changes during a performance had to be precise. "You took one puppet off and grabbed another" was Andrew's description of their movements. "Each puppet was always supposed to be put at the exact same place... so you could reach for one, and know where it was."

It was tight back stage, especially in the corners. And hot! Lots of people! Puppets were lying both in readiness and in boxes, along with items the puppeteers would be using, stacked at the spot where they would need them. Two people might be flipping the backdrop over the stage while others were moving to new positions. There was a need to know exactly what was happening next, and where to go, so they didn't get in each other's way.

Success in making the movements go smoothly was aided by helping each other out. "If you finished with a puppet, you would pass it to someone next to you," said Janelle, "and move to the front where another puppet would be lying ready." There wasn't time to interact with others during a performance. However, moving risers into place for someone or delivering a reminder when they got distracted were some ways to help movements go well backstage.

Collisions did occasionally occur, so the puppeteers appreciated having a big stage. It was easier to move around when they did not have to be concerned about stepping on the toes of those already up performing. Or trying to catch a fellow puppeteer to prevent them from falling off the platform.

Were the puppeteers hampered by the 'dance steps' and tightness backstage? At first, some of them found crawling over legs to the front of the stage intimidating. Nevertheless, as they got to know each other better, they realized the closeness was part of the way it was done. Rather than a hindrance, they saw it as more interesting than always standing in one spot.

The fact that Aletha had planned it out reassured them that quick changes were done only out of necessity. They were confident that, although they didn't always succeed in practice, the show would go on and performances would work out well in the end.

TAKE A BOW

Aletha knew God Squad performances interested both the adults and the children in the audience. She was also aware that the message of salvation was a simple one—one that both a child and an adult could understand. She realized how effective the songs and skits were in telling about Jesus Christ.

It was for this reason that at the close of each performance, Aletha gave a summary of what happened in the characters' lives. She also gave the invitation to the audience to consider Jesus Christ as their Savior.

One example went like this: "You need electricity to light your homes, batteries for your car lights to light the road, flashlights to light a dark hole, spotlights to see puppets! More than all earth lights, we need Jesus—to show the Way for happy living here and the Way to everlasting life. Jesus said, 'I am the Light of the world. I am the Way, and the Truth and the Life.'[i] The Bible tells us that when we take Jesus as our Savior, we can help light or show the way for others to know Jesus. We can only do that [if] we have loads of His love to give away."

When the concluding remarks were over, it was time to take a bow. The puppeteers would quickly assemble in front of the stage. Together with Aletha, they would hold hands and bow. The applause of the audience brought unmistakable delight to the faces of the puppeteers.

...AND MOVE 'EM OUT!

When the laughter and applause died down, the show was over for the audience, but for the puppeteers, work remained to be done. The stage had to be dismantled and, along with the props and puppets, packed into those suitcases and labeled boxes, ready to load into the van for the trip home.

---

[i] John 8:12 and John 14:6 (NIV).

In the early days, there wasn't much to clean up. There were only a few puppets and a small, one-tiered stage. But Aletha was very organized in everything she did, and clean-up was no exception. "We functioned like a well-oiled machine," remembers Kris Gowdy. "We could set up and take down quickly. Everyone knew their responsibilities and what she expected."

As the ministry expanded and more involved skits were performed, there were extra puppets and props to pack. The more complex two-tiered stage, assembled and taken apart each time, and the more sophisticated equipment for lighting and sound, included more pieces to worry about. The amount of equipment to pack had increased, but each puppeteer still had a specific job. Some were assigned to take the back curtain off the pipe, roll it onto the cardboard tube, and put it into the cloth bag. Others helped with lighting or packing something else.

Before the first show of a specific play, practice time included learning how to pack the boxes. Each puppeteer practiced packing the box with their name on it, checking the contents against the list on the box according to the play they were doing.

Aletha taught the puppeteers to run a smooth clean-up time. The instructions were to pack up fast, but carefully. The puppets and equipment were expensive, and Aletha did not want anything to be broken. There were a number of performances of each skit, and gentle handling saved wear and tear.

Her emphasis on 'no dallying' helped keep the puppeteers focused on what they were doing. Although some felt it would have been easier to mingle and talk to the audience, they knew the puppets and equipment had to get put away so the young children didn't come backstage. Sometimes Aletha had to tell them to get back to work, confessed one long-term puppeteer, but each one knew his or her job, and were for the most part conscientious about getting it done.

Placing everything precisely in the van after a performance was not the final job. Upon arriving back at the Joices', the van needed unpacking and everything stowed in the basement once more.

"We had a chain gang at the house," Jacqui said of the unloading process. "We would form a line from the van to the basement, handing boxes to each other." It was a bit dangerous to be handing some things along while standing on the steps. If someone came with long poles, the puppeteers would just let that person past to carry them down. "Even so," Jacqui added, "we did a number on their walls over the years."

Was helping to set up before a performance and clean up afterwards a hardship? Done with a 'do-I-have-to' attitude? Not a bit. The puppeteers' opinion was that it was part of being in God Squad. It came with the territory.

They felt the part they had in helping was important. "Part of my job," said Tina, "was to help Glenn set up the lights, and I thought that was pretty important." One puppeteer went so far as to say that the work was fun, too!

The levels of willingness, from resignedness to enthusiasm, might have varied, but when asked about the puppeteers' willingness to help over the years, Glenn answered that some of them would have cleaned up even if he and Aletha hadn't been there.

Many of the puppeteers must have had confidence that Aletha had seen them take on responsibility well, and had noticed their commitment to helping while with God Squad. This was brought out later, when they applied for jobs and asked Aletha for references. "She filled out many forms the puppeteers gave her from employers," Glenn explained.

THANK YOU'S...

Thank you notes were written during the days following a performance. Aletha always strove to be gracious in whatever she did, and so it was important to her to acknowledge what people had done. She would thank people who had given monetary gifts to God Squad. She would also express her gratitude to the individuals who had invited the group to perform, thanking them for the opportunity.

Some notes of thanks went to the puppeteers, commending them for the way they did a part, or a good attitude they had shown. "Doing the piano," Aletha wrote in one note, "is a difficult part, but you did well... or "Your many parts took time to get synchronized and you got to them all."

She would thank them for their faithfulness and willingness, and often express how she felt about their participation. "Thanks for being a fun member of the group, being so cooperative" or "I appreciate your ability to take correction from me. I realize that I too have a lot yet to learn."

...AND EVALUATION

Always careful to do quality work, Aletha evaluated each God Squad performance. Every puppeteer was encouraged to do his or her best, even if some were not as competent as others. But if what they did detracted from her goal, she was not afraid to change things the next time.

The narrations she wrote were not exempt from the scrutiny. One comment in her notes was to herself: "Edit out the narration... put in brief introduction to the song."

Improvement of a performance was not limited to omitting elements completely. Sometimes they were merely small changes. Aletha recorded her plans in her notes with phrases like "Try confused exit" or "Try table farther over—other corner—so the chicken can get closer to the front when running across."

CHAPTER FIVE

THOSE PUPPETS WERE REAL CHARACTERS

IMAGINARY OR REAL?

"Puppets are just imaginary!" The irritated little voice was getting louder.

"No! They can talk!" a second voice, filled with determination, fired back.

"Well, yeah. But that's 'cause someone is talking for them."

"Yeah? Well, how come they can go up and down the stairs then, huh?"

"Somebody is making them." The second voice had taken on a touch of boredom.

"Who? Did their Mom make them?"

"No! They don't have a mother."

"Why?"

"Because they aren't real!" Exasperation was near.

"Are too!"

A silly, imaginary conversation? Perhaps. Still, are you absolutely sure the puppets weren't real? Children in the audience were convinced they *were* real. On occasion, some children in the front rows would shout at the puppets because of what they were doing onstage. Or they would become afraid because of the action.

What drew children into believing so strongly in the reality of the puppet leaning over the top of the blue curtain and asking questions of the audience? Try making a child doubt the reality of the puppets after what happened during one particular performance! On this unfortunate occasion, the stage was bumped. After seeing it nearly fall a few times, Glenn finally told the puppeteers to stop. A few held the curtain while he flipped the poles the right way around. The whole thing had to be lifted and turned because the pins had been put in from the wrong side.

Quick to respond, in the face of the unscheduled pause, some of the puppeteers pretended someone was wrecking their stage. They moved the puppets around in a frenzied way and with panicky voices asked each other, "What's going on? Who's wrecking our stage?"

Aletha seemed convinced there was a special something about those little characters. A kind of 'magic' that would be lost if the children came backstage after a performance and saw the lifeless look of the puppets lying around with their mouths open. It was for this reason that in her remarks she asked them not to go into the puppets' dressing room.

The puppeteers were in on the secret, too. If, after the show, someone would ask, "How did you do this or that?" the reply would be, "It's our secret." It was because they were never supposed to reveal things they did behind the stage. If someone would say, "Oh, that was so good," then ask, "Did you work such-and-such puppet?" the only response would be a shrug.

The children were eager to get behind stage after a performance and see those characters for themselves. The adults were likely a little more sophisticated about their interest in the puppets—"Pretending they thought the puppets were real" was Josh Bekker's view on it. "When invited to respond," Josh explained, "the adults didn't have a problem pretending, even if they were responding to a puppet." He felt that although the skits were directed at kids, the puppets interested all ages.

What captivated the adult's attention? Tina Cowie felt the adults enjoyed the puppets as much as the kids because "the adults could understand all the little jokes."

Was that 'special something' which kept the mystery alive just a phase kids went through, or was it more long lasting? The question comes to mind because of some of the former puppeteers' comments, even though they had been backstage, where you would think the evidence would be obvious.

"They were magical," Tina stated. "People listened to what the puppets were saying."

Another puppeteer commented that she wasn't sure 'who' had played the spider in a particular skit. She was really referring to which puppet played the part, but it seemed like the puppet had been so real to her young mind that now, as an adult woman with youngsters of her own, she still referred to that experience in terms of reality.

A STAR IS BORN

Who had a hand in creating these real, imaginary characters, the bodies that for a short time could weave a magic so strong that children believed the words they heard were really coming out of the puppets' mouths?

There were companies whose catalogues were filled with puppets to purchase—girls with braided orange hair and boys with a yellow mop. Curly topped mothers and a bald man, who might have lived next door. Pop groups, with green and pink hair. Bible characters and tuxedo-clad quartets. Farm animals, jungle tigers, and birds with multi-colored beaks.

So many from which to choose! Was it any wonder the arrival of the puppet catalogue was like getting a Christmas Wish Book? Aletha and Shelley shared a special delight in the arrival of each new puppet catalogue. "We would get all excited about the catalogue arriving!" Shelley said. "Mom and I would look at it together—all the new puppets they had, the materials, the paints."

Working new plays into their repertoire meant a constant need for puppets with different characteristics, like a special puppet to play an animal. They did order one or two puppets from the catalogues each year, but they were expensive. With costs of one to two hundred dollars each, buying them in large numbers would have stretched their financial resources too much.

The solution to saving money on the puppets they wanted was to purchase materials, totaling thirty to fifty dollars, instead of buying only ready-made puppets. The same creative daughter-in-law who painted backdrops also just happened to know how to sew.

"Aletha paid for the materials, and I volunteered time," Shelley explained. "Some of the time," she hastened to add, "she paid me to compensate for the thread and the time, especially if there was a deadline involved. It wasn't a huge amount."

The handmade puppets were created to meet the different needs for a performance. Improvising was part of the creativity. Shelley had the talent to improvise, and one fan of her work was her brother-in-law. "The ones Shelley made were always neat," said Don Hand.[42]

The characteristics of the puppets varied. Some were small enough to portray children, while others had larger heads, perhaps with a bushy beard, representative of a rough and tough character. Yet most of the puppet shapes were quite straightforward.

DRESS ME UP AND TAKE ME OUT... OF THE SUITCASE

Shelley's creativity in sewing extended to helping sew clothing for the puppets, but she shared this task with a couple of other volunteers. One of these seamstresses was Mildred Peat, the friend we spoke of earlier. The other was Doreen Smith,[43] another friend of Aletha's from the Free Methodist Church, the church the Joice family attended at the time.

Doreen did lots of sewing for her children, so when she bought fabric to sew for them, she would buy a bit extra which she could use for puppet garments. She also used scraps of cloth, not specifically planned for puppet clothes, which were left over from various projects.

The garments for the puppets were made using a child's pattern. "It was a basic pattern in size two and fit most puppets," Doreen explained. "The puppets were easy to fit—the arms were soft, no defined shoulders."

Puppet garments, however, had a unique requirement that children's clothing didn't. The sleeves on the garments had to be longer than usual so that when the puppet reached out a hand, the arm would not be revealed. Thus, the finished sleeves hung past the end of the hands. "With girl puppets," Doreen said, "I could use elastic and make a puffy sleeve, and thus it was longer. With guys I just made it longer, but you had to be careful not to overlap with the rods on the hands."

Aletha would give specific instructions regarding how the puppet she needed clothing for was going to be characterized in a skit. Doreen then knew when a garment needed extra sleeve length, for example. She would be told when one puppet was going to be used for more than one character, so Doreen made some clothes a bit bigger. The bigger garment would fit over another garment, so when a quick change was required, only one step—taking the top garment off—was needed, since the garment for a scene to follow was already on the puppet.

So what do you do when a puppet is complete, dressed in well-tailored garments, but still bald? A wig, of course! Using a wig easily changed puppet hair. The netting of adult wigs stretched easily over the puppet's head and held snugly in place, even when the puppet character swung in time to the music.

If you didn't have an appropriate wig, though, you could always improvise. "One puppet's head was covered with Styrofoam for curls," explained Shelley. "We used the Styrofoam peanuts they use for packing."

CHECK OUT THE NEWCOMERS

"There's a new puppet!"
"Hey, check it out!"
"Is it as easy to work with as this old one?"

The arrival of a new puppet at God Squad caused excitement for some of the puppeteers, while others, not as easily enthused, took it in stride.

What made the arrival of a new puppet exciting? For one thing, choosing a name for it. Why, you might ask, give the puppet a name before you knew what part it would have in a play? The question is puzzling unless you understand, as one puppeteer explained, that the puppets are actors. When a character was needed for a part, puppets could be referred to by name, rather than the character they were playing, because in the next play, the same puppet might be someone else. For example, a puppet named Sally might play Queen Isabelle in one story, and be Grandma Madeline in another. Calling the puppet Sally, rather than Isabelle or Madeline, cut down on confusion.

So how did the puppeteers decide what the puppets' names would be? Picking names out of a book might have been one way, but it was more fun to have a puppet named after you. When a puppet had blonde hair, naming it after a blonde-haired puppeteer seemed natural. "We would name the ones after ourselves that looked the most like us," explained Tyler Wood.

The arrival of new puppets included the task of working them in. "The puppets all worked a bit differently," Jayne recalled. "New puppets were more stiff, the cloth making up their mouths not yet stretched from moving up and down, so they were harder to use. Each puppet was a little different weight because of the way they were made. The arms worked differently, so your puppet affected your performance."

For some puppeteers, new was not necessarily better. One puppeteer felt the earlier puppets had more character—bald spots, stout middles, etc. The new ones were exciting when they came in, but had lost something for flashiness. Flashiness meant the puppets had more on them, so they were heavier as well.

However, the stiff and unused puppets became familiar and comfortable, so when faced with parting with some of the older models, the squad wasn't sure they could cope with it. "It will be all right," Aletha reassured them, after giving some puppets to a church group that was starting a puppet ministry of their own. "They were just a few old puppets."

Nevertheless, the puppeteers felt they would miss the old, easy-to-work faithfuls.

TENDER LOVING CARE

Bertha, Rosie, Jerry, and Joe, the puppets first purchased in 1974, were four of the old faithfuls who remained with God Squad. Puppets can't take care of themselves, yet these four were still in such good shape that twenty-seven years later they were still actively used for puppet performances.

Quite likely, it was because they had a good caregiver, someone who had their best interests at heart. Although Aletha allowed puppeteers to take a puppet home for practice purposes, when someone first joined God Squad, she had strict instructions as to the care of the puppet. It was not a toy. It was a performance instrument. Top quality performances meant keeping puppets in good condition.

Whenever the puppet was used, the puppeteer was to wear gloves. These were special, cotton gloves, worn to keep the moisture of sweaty hands away from the inside of the puppet. The discovery of what kind of damage sweaty hands could do to a puppet was made before the first four puppeteers began to do performances. The troupe had been practicing without gloves, and one day Aletha realized that the felt inside the puppets was peeling because of the puppeteers' sweaty hands

Each pair of gloves was initialed so that each puppeteer used the same pair while they were in God Squad. The gloves were passed on from year to year, so one pair saw many hands. One of the more recent puppeteers remembered his gloves bearing the initials of one of the earliest puppeteers.

Caring for the 'little characters' that had parts in God Squad skits and songs also meant gentle handling. They were not to be picked up by the nose or ears. "They were put in the suitcase right away after a performance... not dumped in unceremoniously," said Heather Miller.

There were a lot of puppets to take along, and to save space the puppets were placed in the containers with their mouths open, overlapping one with the other. At the same time, care was taken that noses and limbs were not bent in an awkward way, because they would remain 'deformed' when they were unpacked.

Because the puppets were very expensive to purchase, the puppeteers learned to treat them with respect. Aletha only trained a few of the puppeteers at a time to work with her in packing the puppets.

'REAL LIVE' PUPPETS

Not all the puppets could be packed in boxes. Sometimes the characters in a play were 'real live' puppets. Puppets who played piano and drums, frogs and monkeys who played trumpets. These puppets could play a tune because they were partially human... well, not really, but they were 'real live' puppets. Creating a 'real live' puppet could happen in several ways. Parts of the puppeteer's body, such as their arms, might become part of the puppet; their body from the waist up got in on the job, or the whole body was involved.

When a puppeteer's arms were part of the puppet, it took two people to operate them. One person knelt in front of another person; the one behind working the head of the puppet, and the one kneeling in front using their own hands and arms as if they belonged to the puppet. The person doing the hands would wear skin-colored gloves, with the same tones as the puppet's face.

Imagine what a task in coordination it must have been for the puppeteers to make this joint effort look like a single puppet was moving! Coordinating a set of human hands holding a drumstick or a keyboard, with another hand belonging to someone else moving the puppet's head, took some practice. Being a piano player himself, one puppeteer was at an advantage in being able to make it look very natural.

A quartet in one skit was a demonstration of the upper body being used to create 'live' puppets. Wearing oversized glasses, with fake eyes on the lenses, the foursome stood just behind the front tier of the stage. They dangled four sets of stuffed, cloth legs, which were attached to their waists, over the top of the front curtain. Four puppeteers made it look like four large puppets were sitting on the edge of the stage singing.

In an introduction to the song this quartet did, Aletha reminded people not to be lukewarm Christians, who tried to function all on their own. "If we desire to reflect God's glory," she said, "we must look continually into the face of Jesus, through prayer and reading of His word, the Bible, but also recognize the strength we gain from other Christians. The song is *Get Hot, Stay Hot.*" [i]

"I'm big," sang Goliath, another 'real live' puppet. Goliath was definitely a big puppet. He'd come out from behind the stage, swinging his huge club, dancing his way closer to the audience. His voice was big, too—deep and strong. The children would already have been laughing from the minute he stepped out, but before long, the toe-tapping rhythm was infecting everyone. At the conclusion of his song, Goliath returned to the puppet stage and interacted

---

[i] *Get Hot, Stay Hot* is a song from "Top Sing-Along-Songs" from One-Way Street , resources for Creative Ministry.

with the puppet who was playing David. When the stone from David's sling felled Goliath, his fall took up a lot of room backstage.

How was this 'real live' Goliath created? The basis of his giant-size costume, necessary to cover this giant-sized puppet, was an old, shortened, red dress from the thrift store. Other details of his costume caused a little humor. "It was a riot watching Goliath put on his 'legs'," Shelley recalled.

"I had to hurry," explained Josh, "so it became absurd, just because of that. A man in stockings is already funny, but the pantyhose was covered with yarn for hairy legs."

When his silver vinyl breastplate was in place, Goliath was impressive. Josh was one of two puppeteers who had the honor of being 'real live' Goliath in productions of the play, *David and Goliath*.[ii] Aletha picked the biggest person in the group to play the part.

So are you convinced? Were they real? One thing you do need to admit is that they certainly were real characters. No wonder the children laughed. No wonder the adults were intrigued! Each time a puppet played the part of a character in a play, either moving or delivering a funny line, someone was behind the curtain, performing the 'dance steps' just right.

UNPROCLAIMED, BUT WONDERFUL

"Want to shop for props at the prop shop?" Translated, that means, "Do you want to go shopping for the little extras which would be just right for a puppet skit, at the Fun House?"

Aletha made many trips to the Fun House, a little store in Regina that sold gags and costume items. She wanted to find just the right special little touches for a puppet skit. Cheap sunglasses, gag glasses (with large eye balls), wigs, out-of-season items like Halloween stuff in spring, hats, a rubber chicken—all unique purchases that couldn't be bought anywhere else. The soldier helmet for the 'real live' Goliath certainly fit this category.

Yet, despite finding things at the Fun House to fill specific needs for the skits, some props still had to be made. Once again, Shelley stepped forward and filled the need, designing and sewing, while Glenn used his ingenuity to get things mobile.

Let's take a closer look at some of the props and other supplies and how they were created to enhance the puppet skits.

[ii] *David and Goliath* is a skit from Fairhill Music.

- *Little Clucks:* Infant chickens, or baby chicks, were attached to the fingers of a glove, so the puppeteer could move them as if they were scurrying around.
- *Spider Web:* The largest spider web you've ever seen was one prop Glenn created. "I made circles of quarter-inch ropes, joined... with other ropes to form the web," he explained. "It was attached from the front stage to the back stage. Anthony in *Antshillvania*[iii] was caught in it."
- *High Flyers:* Glenn rigged up a system of rings and wires that allowed the puppeteer to buzz past with a bee, or flap the wings on a bird. These mechanisms enabled the puppeteer to 'fly' the prop across the stage. To work the flying motions of wings, Glenn attached two stiff wires to the tips of the wings. He attached the other end of these wires to a mechanism that slid up and down a third stiff wire, at the top of which he fastened the body. A puppeteer could move the prop back and forth across the stage in a gliding motion, meanwhile moving the sliding part up and down on the vertical wire. Thus the bird or bee appeared to be flying.
- *Fling the Sling and Ding the Giant:* When a boy is slaying a giant with a sling, he needs ammunition. Yet you don't want the ammunition to hurt anyone in real life. So why not paint Styrofoam peanuts to look like small rocks? That way, the giant Goliath lives to play the part another day.
- *Smell the Flowers:* A flower in the skit *David the Chosen One*[iv] had a similar mechanism, allowing the leaves to move back and forth in time to music. The flower appeared to be dancing. One of the 'high flyers,' the large bee we described a moment ago, buzzed back and forth around the flower, occasionally lighting on it as if gathering nectar.
- *Quiet as a Statue:* A Styrofoam head, the kind used to hold a wig, covered with Styrofoam 'peanuts' for hair, became a Roman statue for one play.

[iii] *Antshillvania* is a skit from Fairhill Music ©1981.
[iv] *David the Chosen One* is a skit by Puppet Productions.

- *Do a Little Slapstick, but Don't Slip on the Fall Out:* Slapstick comedy added to the fun of some skits. Picture, for example, this chase—a frenzied chicken, dashing back and forth across the stage, pursued by a butcher. Accompanied by appropriate background music, of course. That scene presented a need to have some 'feathers' flying. Again, Styrofoam peanuts came to the rescue. A puppeteer flung them into the air while the chase was going on. Only this time, there had to be a way to collect the peanuts so puppeteers wouldn't slip on them afterwards. The simple solution—let them fall into a receptacle.

A MACHINE PLAYS A SONG?

When Aletha chose to do the musical called *Music Machine,*[v] she wanted a music box with flashing lights, creating the illusion of something whirling around in a circular motion. Glenn knew what he needed to achieve the effect, but didn't know how to put it together.

It was time to ask for advice. Gavin, a family friend, was mechanically inclined, so Glenn asked him if he thought the idea he had was possible. Gavin felt using a small motor, geared to a slow speed, and switches, causing lights to go on and off so fast they appeared to be in motion, would work. An auto supply company ordered the small motor for them. Glenn also recruited another friend, Harvey Smith, an electrical engineer, to help assemble and install the electrical equipment for the machine.

Inside the large, bright red and yellow machine, a tape played when someone dropped coins into the funnel. A handle on the outside turned on the sounds the machine made.

Although time to get ready was limited, they were successful. Gavin said he "was a little concerned that it might all fall apart when they first used it, but it traveled all over for many performances." The machine and its music were a great success!

---

[v] *Music Machine* is a skit from Bird Wing Music ©1977.

"PROP MANUFACTURER RETIRES FROM ACTIVE DUTY"

What is Glenn using his garage for these days? How does this successful prop manufacturer spend his time now that his creations, those wonderful moveable gadgets, are no longer in demand?

Glenn has parked his vehicle inside the garage instead of in front of the door. He has spent time redesigning the basement. Part of it is set up for a grow light and some plants. He renovated the puppet practice area, making room for a pool table for family and friends who come to his house.

Did the changes happen as the result of being relieved that the basement could finally be used for other things than God Squad?

"No," said Glenn. "It was Aletha's ministry, but my heart was included in the support I gave her in that work."

"It was Mom's passion," noted Bette-Jean, "not Dad's, but he was in there, helping build things and was patient with Mom doing it."

TOP: After more than twenty years, the first four puppets were still being used in performances (puppets by puppetproductions.com). MIDDLE LEFT: The butterfly prop, created by Shelley Joice with a mechanism by Glenn Joice (photo courtesy of Tina Cowie). MIDDLE RIGHT: Glenn Joice in his home in Regina, taken in 2002. BOTTOM: 'Real live' puppets singing *Get Hot, Stay Hot* from the musical *You Are the Light of the World*, a project by One-Way Street (photo courtesy of Tilly Wiens).

CHAPTER SIX
ABOVE AND BEYOND THE CALL OF DUTY

ENTHUSIASM AND SHARING

Being the director of God Squad was fulfilling and exciting for Aletha. "It was like she was involved in a career" was Irene Sotropa's comparison.

For most of the years Aletha worked with God Squad, she was behind the curtain working alongside the puppeteers. In the first years, she would handle a puppet herself as well as showing them which puppet, instrument, or prop to use. Often she would hand puppets to them if a transition had to be handled quickly. She didn't handle the puppets as much herself in later years, but was still helping behind the curtain.

Her excitement about her puppet ministry spilled over into conversations at church committee meetings. Aletha would speak of those who had been in God Squad previously, and those who were currently in the troupe. Personally involved in the lives of the teens in God Squad, she had friendships with, and prayed for, the puppeteers.

"It seems it was always on her mind; it was important to her," said Kathleen Fisher.

Aletha's enthusiasm went beyond teaching puppetry and performing skits. She loved to share God Squad's ministry in more ways than just with the audience. Aletha's sharing included sharing the puppets themselves.

Missions and missionaries had a big corner in Aletha's heart, and missionaries were among those with whom she shared the ministry. Missionary Lynn Schellenberg was invited to come to a puppet practice when she was home on furlough. She was "impressed with the encouragement Aletha gave the children to try things, be an individual, yet fit into the scheme of things." Lynn was often busy with her itinerary on Sundays, the day God Squad usually performed. The opportunity to go to their practices made her feel like God Squad was conducting a performance especially for her.

Aletha lent some puppets to missionaries Garry and Rita Mae Braun to use for Children's Church during itinerary trips. They had asked specifically for one with a darker face, having been missionaries to Africa.

Aletha was very protective of the puppets. She rarely allowed puppets to go home with the puppeteers, other than an older puppet sent home with new recruits to use for practicing. However, because she had a deeper involvement with the lives of the youth in her puppet ministry, she did make a few exceptions.

The puppets had become experienced travelers, going to and from God Squad performances. It wouldn't have seemed strange for them to be packed into a suitcase when Aletha lent a few to one puppeteer. He wanted to do a performance for the children at a family gathering. Getting packed up and traveling was old hat for both the puppets and this puppeteer.

The puppets took a longer, international journey when they traveled with a church youth group on a missions trip to Mexico. Along with the loan of the puppets, Aletha gave the youth some help in preparing for the performances they would do in Mexico. The usual three to four months of weekly training became a few one-hour sessions during Sunday School. This training would not have been easy to accomplish in the shorter length of time.

Another year, puppets were loaned to the youth, who were headed to California on a missions trip. The eight young people took turns working the five puppets. Their success was due in part to following the hints Aletha gave them on how to operate the puppets. She spent a couple of hours with them on Saturdays before they left to teach them some basic skills. Before they began, an adult who went with the youth had asked, "How hard could this be?" but was surprised at how much hard work it was.

Aletha took a possessive pride in the puppets—how they would look, whether they were used properly while they were away—but on the other hand, along with her loan, she gave assurance of her prayers. The prayers were for the team and the effect the puppet performances would have on the audience. After they returned, Bobby Jo Stenzil, a sponsor on one missions trip, noted that "Aletha made a point of asking how the trip had gone, how the people had responded, and how the team had done."

FRIENDSHIPS WITH THE TROUPES

Friendships were an important part of Aletha's life, and they were not reserved for her peers, adults only. "I think Aletha had a soft spot for Josh," Doreen Butterfield commented. Whether or not that was true, Aletha did value Josh as a friend, and he her.

"It might have seemed a bit odd to ask her to do the toast at our wedding," Josh commented, "but I wanted someone who was a speechmaker, who would do a clean, professional job. She knew me better than any other people except those who knew me longer, like my parents and my family."

Josh was interested to know what impression he had made on her. "It was not vanity," he said, "but because I recognized her as a wise person, and knew she would pick out traits I should work on. I knew I would appreciate the advice she would have for me."

Assuming it was true that Josh had a special spot in Aletha's heart, when you talked to other God Squad alumni you would discover that, if he did, he was not the only one. "Out of the God Squad context, she was a good friend," Jayne Werry affirmed. "She would have me over for supper sometimes. She wrote letters when I was in England."

Her closeness to Aletha caused Jayne deep sorrow when, while she was still in England, her parents told her of Aletha's death. A sorrow, she said, which had been hard to contain at the public email cafe[i] where she received the news. Jayne was scheduled to be back on the Thursday of the same week, so was able to attend the memorial service.

Aletha went all the way to Ontario to give a tribute to Tina Cowie at her wedding reception. "Aletha made a big impact on my life," Tina commented. "Not only through God Squad, but Aletha and Glenn adopted me as their niece, and I still refer to them as Aunt Aletha and Uncle Glenn. She continued writing me up to her death. They always remembered me at my birthday and Christmas."

As is true of all friendships, some are closer than others. Some last a long time, others are remembered a long time. The closer or longer friendships Aletha had with some puppeteers weren't on account of her feeling they were somehow more special. Every one of the God Squad members had a place in her heart.

"Aletha thought the world of the kids... loved them all," affirmed Doreen Butterfield.

---

[i] See Glossary for explanation of email café.

For some, the friendships formed with Aletha while they were in God Squad extended into their adult years and had a long-lasting influence on their lives.

BE NOT AFRAID

Was Aletha's involvement with God Squad without its fears? A comment in some Bible study preparation notes shows that she did not experience less fear than any other person. She wrote about experiencing the kind of dreams she had read about in a book by Lawrence J. Crabb Jr. and Dan B. Allender, called *Encouragement, The Key to Caring*. The authors said they suspected that "fears pushed out of our minds will occasionally surface in our dreams."

"I have been directing and working in our puppet group since 1974," she wrote in a journal entry, "yet each year, before our first performance, I will inevitably have this dream... when we're supposed to be setting up, kids don't show or they keep taking off from setting up, and half the stage frame is missing. We start to perform and our stage starts to shrink—until we're virtually lying on the floor working our puppets—then totally exposed! It seems that we fear not measuring up to the task, or that inadequate preparation will lead to unacceptable performance!"

Despite having fears about performances, the continued success of God Squad and its popularity with both children and adults, suggests she conquered those fears.

MARTHA'S FOLLY INTRODUCED

Writing introductions and filler narrations were part of the preparations Aletha made for each performance, but she also had a dream of one day writing her own puppet plays. That dream came true when her troupe performed a play she had written herself, *Martha's Folly*, in 1999. She had researched and worked at writing it for several years. Bob and Shelley Joice listed things she did while she was preparing the play. She talked to a rabbi, got a Jewish 'hat' for props, found out details about the Jewish traditions. The Jewish community was happy to share details with her.

When the play was ready for rehearsals, the puppeteers went through the Bible story it was based on during their devotional time. Aletha also shared the things she had learned about Jewish traditions with the puppeteers.

Despite all of her own hard work and preparation, the glory went to God. "She was very humble about saying she had written it," said Jared Goertzen,[44] one voiceover[ii] for the play.

Much work went into creating a truly Jewish atmosphere for the performance of the play, including the music from a tape produced by Jews for Jesus.[iii] The play, in its entirety, is included in the appendix.

[ii] See Glossary for explanation of voiceover.
[iii] Jews for Jesus is an organization that reaches out to Jewish people with the gospel. They also create musical recordings, some of which were used in Aletha's production of *Martha's Folly*.

CHAPTER SEVEN

THE LAST PERFORMANCE

"I think the last God Squad performance, *You are the Light of the World*, was the most memorable for me," said Audrey Wood. "It was very fitting. The light of the world was what Aletha was, what she wanted to portray." Long time friends of Glenn and Aletha, Audrey and her husband Gavin, were both at the very first and last performance God Squad presented.

The members of God Squad wanted the last performance to be a good one, to "go out with a bang," asserted Janelle Gagnon. They wanted it to be one that people would remember.

And a memorable performance it was, rewarded by a standing ovation. People gave the ovation for the performance, but in a great part it was for Aletha, who, although suffering from bone marrow cancer, was there to see her troupe perform. Fittingly, when Aletha became too weak to continue with the introduction, her daughter Bette-Jean, an original puppeteer, finished it for her.

Tears came to many people's eyes that night when Aletha accepted a beautiful bouquet of roses from the hands of a puppeteer involved in the performance. Glenn stood close to her side, and many people came to speak with Aletha after the performance.

A short news item appeared in the Mennonite Brethren Herald about the event:

> "God Squad, a puppet ministry at Parliament Community
> Church in Regina, presented the musical, *You are the Light of the
> World*[i], on Sunday, May 6, 2001, challenging the audience to be
> 'on fire' for Jesus Christ. Aletha Joice, long time director of the

---

[i] *You Are the Light of the World* is a production of One-Way Street, resources for Creative Ministry.

ministry, was present for the performance despite struggling with a recurrence of cancer. Behind the curtain seven young people, Janelle Gagnon, Jared Wiens, Grant Sawatzky, Jon Schroeder, Ryan and Tim Friesen and Krista Bekker, operated the colorful puppets. Since its beginning in 1974, the puppet ministry has entertained people of all ages."[ii]

After the performance was over, Aletha went home to rest. But not for long! Over the next few days, she used up many ounces of energy to write each of those puppeteers a thank you note.

The note Aletha wrote to Jared Wiens showed again the value she placed on the young people in God Squad, and her ever-ready encouragement. "It's been a great pleasure and fun to work with you in God Squad. You've been like a son watching out for me, helping wherever you could and yet not neglecting your puppetry! So any time you want to call me Grandma Joice, that'd be fun! Thank you for your loyalty, faithfulness, and respectfulness at all times. You listened carefully to and took directions well, but still used your own initiative, which I enjoyed."

She was very weak, but as always, she wanted to cheer for each of the young people she held so dear. She commended them for their efforts in what she called "the last hurrah."

[ii] Quoted in part from the July 13, 2001 issue, with permission from the Mennonite Brethren Herald.

CHAPTER EIGHT
A FUTURE FOR GOD SQUAD?

The puppets no longer 'dance' on someone's hand. They are sitting on a long shelf watching ping-pong, maybe a little afraid of getting hit with balls. Do you suppose they long to move again, to hear again the laughter and shouts of children?

Are there any willing hands in the next generation of the Joice family? Anyone expecting that God Squad would continue to be part of family activities? Dreams or plans for God Squad in the future?

GOD SQUAD IN THE NEXT GENERATION?

"I will feel guilty if they aren't used," Bette-Jean commented, when asked whether she had plans for the puppets. "But I haven't decided how to use them." After a pause she began talking about some ideas she had considered. "Maybe a drama club at school; teaching puppetry as an art form. I could have the grade eight students learn a fairy tale and do it for the younger kids. Or use the heart, lung and brain puppets to teach about health."

"I wouldn't want it to stay that way though," Bette-Jean continued. "That wouldn't be a ministry. I would like to direct a kid's puppet group, but not right now. If I was not working full-time, I could do it. Also, travel into town each time is too cumbersome. I would like a place in town where the stuff could stay, and we could meet there as well. Logistically, it is not possible right now.

"I am okay with being patient as to what happens. Puppetry is good for kids, those who are non-musical for example, or who don't like to be up front, face to face with an audience. They can be a comedian by having the puppet do things, get people to laugh, but not be up there and be seen by the audience."

Shelley still loves puppets and remains interested in doing puppetry in some way. Along with Jayne Werry, Shelley is a member of a local puppet guild, attending workshops, discussing puppetry, and getting advice. Sometimes Shelley brings puppets she has made and gets comments on them. For the present, Shelley has become involved in other ventures. "I'm more into the black-light puppetry now," she said. "I'm also working with making miniature dolls."

Bob Joice still has an interest in continuing puppetry in some way, but having arthritis means that it will have to be a different style. Holding the kind of puppet that requires lifting his arms over his head is painful. "You have to consider that your whole household is organized around it," Bob said. He feels continuing with a group of puppets and puppeteers, such as God Squad was, would take that kind of commitment. He also feels his focus in puppetry would be different. His style of involvement with the puppeteers would not be as deep as Aletha's was with God Squad. His emphasis would be more on the training part of puppeteering.

Much of Jake's future is yet to be revealed. However, age fourteen at the time of writing, Aletha's grandson isn't at all sure puppetry is something he would want to do. Having grown up with it, part of him wanted to get involved, but another part didn't. "When I started the year," Jake commented, "I wanted to go. But then later in the year, I felt I didn't really want to [but] since I had started, my parents pushed me. When you are in the audience it seems so smooth, but backstage it's chaos most of the time. I'd still like to see it around. The productions every year were enjoyable. I still might want to be part of it someday, but I'm not sure," Jake concluded.

END OF AN ERA AND SEEDS OF IMPACT

So it seems an era has ended. God Squad puppets sit on a shelf in a recreation room covered with a white sheet, while ping-pong balls fly around them. Is it a sad thought? Not really. All it would take are a few hands to slip inside those little characters to bring them to life again. Neither is there sadness in the effects the ministry of God Squad has had on people's lives.

What were those effects? Were there any commitments to Christ because of a performance? Were there any conversions within the troupe because of the devotionals Aletha shared at each practice? What purpose did the ministry serve?

God Squad was good for self-esteem, giving young performers confidence about performing, especially those who were too timid to perform without the protective shield of the curtain. It was a place to develop friendships. Working and having fun together lent itself to a closeness puppeteers didn't often find in other friendships. God Squad was entertainment, but at the same time a ministry to others. It was hard work, demanding strong commitment. A learning experience for developing and perfecting life skills. It taught concepts of serving, and inspired ministry in the puppeteers' lives. In short, in some way, it affected all those who were involved.

Perhaps we can best summarize it with a comment made by an older man who came up to Aletha after a performance. He thanked her for coming, then posed the rhetorical question: "There's more than one way to present the gospel, isn't there?"

Seeds of the gospel, the good news of salvation through Christ, presented in many places by God Squad, are still being watered. The alumni, scattered all over the country, still remember what it was like, and some specifically continue to share Jesus with a puppet ministry or have a dream of doing so.

Only the Heavenly Father knows the complete impact. But we do know that young lives were influenced and nurtured by the example of a steadfast and faithful worker named Aletha Joice, the woman behind the blue curtain.

BOOK THREE:

A MEMORY BOOK

Everything that happens in our lives has a place in our memory—either as something we can access from time to time, or as an inconsequential item, not worth cataloguing. This section of the story about Aletha Joice and God Squad is from that accessible store of memories, of those involved in God Squad and people who saw the performances.

Some memories are prompted from seeing a snapshot of a puppet or a performance, while others are there simply because they happened. These don't need any prompting to bring them forward. Some memories are unique, others similar to those shared by someone else, but all are special.

CHAPTER ONE
THE ALUMNI REMEMBER

The puppeteers, now God Squad alumni, have many still poignant memories to share about their time in the troupe. Some already adults, the alumni look back with fondness, remembering the effect being in God Squad had on their lives.

THE INFLUENCE OF A LIVING EXAMPLE

The memories about the influence Aletha had on their lives, by her example, predominated the former puppeteers' comments. She not only cared about their ability and performance, but for them as young people.

"Aletha was a good example of servanthood," Andrew asserted. "I appreciated the effort she put into everything she did—the devotionals, the practices. It showed she was doing it for the Lord. That was her reason for everything she did. It was good quality because she was doing it for God."

Some of the influence was more personal, when the young person came from a family that was friends with the Joices, for example. "It's hard to separate that from the influence being a puppeteer had on my life," said Heather, when speaking of this effect. "We got together every Christmas and New Year's for years. The influence was more socially."

Often the impression you have of what a person is like influences you to behave in the same way. Perhaps the collection of memories the puppeteers have of what Aletha was like will someday influence them to emulate her in their own lives.

"Very nice, gentle and caring. Always willing to help out or provide encouragement. Didn't easily get frustrated with the stress of teaching puppets." –TREVOR FRIESEN[45]

"Gentle, quiet, laughed with the rest. A love for God." –JANELLE GAGNON

"We were fifty-five years apart, yet she understood what kind of things a kid of thirteen found humorous." –JOSH BEKKER

"One thing that stood out to me... was her patience. If someone wasn't getting a part quite right, she would teach them the best she could, and just help them along the way." –GRANT SAWATZKY

"She was a Godly person and one of her goals in life, that I saw clearly, was to please God and to furnish teens with skills to present the gospel." –RYAN FRIESEN[46]

"She provided an excellent role model for me to follow... one that could be applied to everyday life. I knew that her willingness to serve Jesus was a daily, hourly, by the minute endeavor. Not only through God's work that we did through puppetry, but through all the other groups she was involved with and her extreme commitment to prayer. I also appreciated the way she corrected and taught us. She was always positive, and when she told us to do things differently, it was always with patience." –JARED WIENS[47]

"God Squad was like a little care group... There was so much coming at me in high school. It was like being in church, with other Christians who were there for the same reason you were. Aletha was a Christian leader... [and] would read the Scripture and explain it, let us ask questions. It prepared me for Bible School, to learn to think for myself. You have to know for yourself what you believe." –LAURA BARTON[48]

AUTOMATIC EVANGELISM

Being a puppeteer in God Squad was sometimes helpful in being a witness to friends.

"It gave me a boldness to be different," said Josh. "Grade nine and ten students are mostly close-minded. If friends asked and I had to say, 'I can't go to a movie because I have puppet practice,' I'd have to explain what puppets was about. Telling them about God Squad—that it was a church group going around telling Bible stories—was automatic evangelism, because of the Christian meaning."

"It opened doors," affirmed his sister Krista. Often friends would ask Krista what she was doing on the weekend, so she would say, "A God Squad performance—want to come watch?"

"It was a... perfect chance to show God's love or get a message across to the little kids without boring them." –TREVOR FRIESEN

CONCEPTS LEARNED

The puppeteers learned more than just how to use puppets. They talked about having found out what was required for a successful ministry, the reason for the methods Aletha used, and why she stressed the importance of preparation. Their conclusion was that Aletha was very professional about the way she did things.

They spoke of learning the concepts of teamwork and helping each other.

"It helped me work in a group other than school and sports," Tyler stated. "To get along, help each other. It taught me to work with people better."

"Aletha reminded me, several years after the fact, of a trip to Avonlea, Saskatchewan," recalled Kris Gowdy. "It was raining buckets when we arrived at the church. My sister Tina did not have adequate shoes to navigate the water-soaked path to the church, so I piggybacked her into the building. Aletha thought that was a great expression of an older brother's consideration for his sister. I probably didn't do it naturally. Maybe serving on God Squad brought the best out of us."

FRIENDSHIPS FORGED

When a young person was new in town, joining God Squad was a way to get to know people and meet new friends. Some friendships made in God Squad were long-lasting, while others lasted only for the duration of the years the puppeteer was part of the group.

For the early puppeteers, a crossover occurred between their youth group and God Squad. Bob and Shelley Joice, key members of God Squad, were the youth leaders at their church when Kris was involved with God Squad. They saw each other several times a week because of their involvement in youth,

Sunday School, church, God Squad, and other social activities. "We were a close-knit group," Kris commented in a letter.

One person the alumni puppeteers considered a friend when talking about friendships in God Squad was Bob Joice. "[He was] older, but not my parents' age," Josh said, adding a comment about his memory of Bob telling stories about his youth group involvement while God Squad was on road trips.

Some former puppeteers who forged friendships in God Squad still share common memories of inside jokes and laughter. "Not long ago," Jacqui Gagnon related, "some of us had a reunion. We laughed and laughed about things we remembered."

CHAPTER TWO

FAVORITE THINGS... OR NOT

What were their favorite things to remember? Favorite songs, skits, puppets, or favorite characters? Favorite experiences... and some not so favorite? What did they remember about practices and performances, the places they went and what they did?

Let's look at some favorite memories of the former puppeteers and see why the memories had merit.

FAVORITE PUPPETS... UM... CHARACTERS?

Keep in mind that a favorite puppet is not the same as a favorite character. The reasons for the choices the alumni made about their favorite puppet varied almost as much as the shape and size of the puppets they chose.

One of the reasons for a puppeteer's choice of a favorite puppet was its weight. A lighter puppet was favored because controlling the mouth was not as tiring, since there was less weight on the arm.

Loyalty did not appear to be a determining factor in the choice. When new puppets arrived, a new favorite might be chosen.

For some, a bit of a foreign touch had appeal.

"My favorite?" mused Krista. "Tony, a Hispanic-type puppet with black hair—he wore a bright green shirt."

"The human arm puppets always intrigued me," said Tim Friesen,[49] "because I could never figure out how the mouth and both arms could operate at the same time." Despite figuring out the mystery by being a puppeteer, the intrigue was still sustained.

"Priscilla," Jacqui stated quickly. She explained that she didn't use the puppet herself, but felt the puppeteer working Priscilla had a knack for bringing out her personality.

Another puppet with a touch of personality was Granny, the puppet with wire rim glasses and gray hair in a bun. This was the favorite of the oldest puppeteer, the one who served the longest, Aletha Joice. Perhaps it reminded her of her own Granny.

Working a puppet themselves, or watching someone else using it, dictated some favorite characters. Take note that now the choices are of characters, the part a puppet played. There was Arno in the musical *Arno's Adventure*.[i] "He was the lead character," said Tyler, explaining the reason for his choice, "so I could be up a lot." The character Selfish, in the same play, was one that came to Jayne's mind. "I liked the way the puppet worked with the song. I liked to play that part best."

Although Josh was a good singer himself, did he for some reason identify with someone who sang off-key? "I liked the monks practicing singing," said Josh. "Brother Maynod was an outsider who came to join the monks. He was a terrible singer. The others told him to back up repeatedly, and eventually, when he was in the closet they said, 'Now shut the door.'" At this point in relating his memory, Josh paused, then smiled, and added, "Click."

The list of favorites went on. And the winner? The lions.

"The lions were cool," said Tina, of the big, full-maned puppets. Particularly cool was the lion in *Daniel in the Lions' Den*,[ii] with his deep voice and the funny way he talked. Whenever something came into conversation to which they could reply with the phrase, "I didn't know that," some puppeteers would imitate his deep-voiced way of saying the line.

Aside from puppets or characters, many props that added a little something extra, a touch of humor, or visual interest were on the list of favorite things. The colorful worm remained in several puppeteers' minds. "On doctor sticks,[iii] so you could move it along the top edge of the curtain," related Jacqui.

Talking about their favorite puppets, characters, and props led to remembering favorite skits and happenings in them. Although Tina's vote for favorite character was in *Theodore Chattermouse*[iv] she also liked the short skit *Bernie the Bike Breaker*[v]. She thought it was a "neat" musical.

---

[i] *Arno's Adventure* is a skit by Puppet Productions.
[ii] *Daniel in the Lion's Den* is a skit by Puppet Productions.
[iii] See Glossary for explanation of doctor sticks.
[iv] *Theodore Chattermouse* is a skit by Puppet Productions.
[v] *Bernie the Bike Breaker* is a skit by Puppet Productions.

"The skits we thought were funny were the most fun," Andrew said. "Like *Daniel in the Lions' Den*—ah, yes, the lion's deep voice." Once again, a smile accompanied this memory.

"One skit had something about a jack-in-the-box," Josh explained. "It was something about going to a restaurant. The lion was hungry and made the comment that the jack-in-the-box was too far away to go and get burgers. Some puppeteers didn't know what this jack-in-the-box was, so Aletha explained to them that Jack-in-the-Box was a restaurant in the United States. Most kids watching wouldn't know either... but they didn't need to know in order to enjoy the skit. They just enjoyed it."

FUN AND FOCUS

Practice, the place where much of a puppeteer's career time was spent, had its own unique memories. For a few, practices invoked no feeling at all. They were not overly enthused, but at the same time understood the importance of practice. Some found practicing pleasant, a place to learn about the technique of puppeteering.

Because the performances went by quickly, the puppeteers didn't have a chance to interact with each other. It was for this reason that many felt the practices were the most enjoyable. Sometimes just the trip to practices each week was part of the fun. Especially when the person you carpooled with didn't have time to finish supper, and so polished off the last bites of a pork chop en route to the Joices' house.

The memories of the devotional time Aletha had at each practice, and what it meant to the puppeteers, varied. Although not something they dreaded, for some puppeteers it was just part of God Squad practices. They didn't feel it made a particular impression on them. For others, the meaning was deeper. They saw the purpose it had for the group, and realized the effect it had on them personally.

The devotional time created a common bond, a togetherness. It provided a focus to what they were doing and helped them remember it was not just puppetry for its own sake, but that they were doing it **to** praise God.

One group of God Squad puppeteers memorized Psalm 1. "It took us a long time," admitted one of them. Nevertheless, it was a memory that would last. At an anniversary many years later, someone read from Psalm 1. Jacqui Gagnon, one of several alumni in attendance, said they had looked at each other at that point, because they recognized the Psalm.

PERFORMING FEARS

Memories of bringing their puppet character to life in God Squad was assoc-iated with some fears the puppeteers experienced occasionally. One of their worst fears, and the one mentioned most often, was of stumbling and going through the front curtain. Another, related to that, was tripping over or falling off a riser and into the wall. Interpreted, 'wall' means the curtain that created the back tier of the puppet stage.

Perhaps because it had happened once, they mentioned fears of the tape player eating a performance tape.

REMEMBERING THE GOOD, THE BAD, AND... THE UGLY?

God Squad was not limited to performing under the relative safety of a roof. Although they preferred setting up the stage indoors, on one occasion the outside wall of a church building was all they had. The risk of rain didn't deter the people, so the performance went ahead.

A performance at the Cornwall Shopping Centre in downtown Regina made them even more uncomfortable. The stage was set up in a large, open area on the first floor. This area, surrounded by the second floor balcony, allowed the audience to stand and watch from a vantage point above the stage. It made the puppeteers a little uneasy, since people could see behind the curtain. It was the one exception Aletha made to her rule that no one was to see what went on backstage. Perhaps her longing to have the puppet ministry be a witness for Jesus Christ overrode her fear that the "magic would be gone."

Exception or not, to know that people could see them from above was unnerving for the puppeteers. Although they didn't think about it when they were actually performing, it was embarrassing while they waited for their turn to work a puppet again. "It just didn't seem right—people looking down from up above. It wasn't supposed to be that way," said Tyler.

Did the puppeteers have a favorite spot to perform? Not many of them did. Although they would become comfortable at places they went to more than once, they didn't return to one place often enough to make it a favorite. There were places, however, which for various reasons stood out in the puppeteers' minds. For instance, the churches in Moose Jaw would get together and put on a community fair. Going there held the additional attraction of being able to participate in the carnival.

Parliament Community Church in Regina was Krista's vote. "It felt more like a performance because the lights were off," she explained. The sanctuary there had only two narrow windows. The windows were covered, so the only illumination was the spotlights focusing on the puppets.

Did going to different places cause difficulties with performances? Not really. It just created a need to make adjustments to the varied physical setups from place to place.

A higher stage presented a challenge for the puppeteers. When the puppet stage was set up at Parliament Community, "it was quite far back and high," said Josh, "so the puppets had to be tilted down more to face the audience."

One church, Prince of Peace Lutheran in Regina, where God Squad held performances a number of years in a row, had quite a small stage. They made an adjustment for the troupe by setting up an extension at the front of the stage.

From time to time, God Squad had to be ready for some unusual circumstances. One such performance was in a newly built church. Construction was not complete by performance day, so the show was slated for the gym area. The troupe was faced with gyproc dust and an unfinished, cold cement floor. The brick block walls had openings in them, but no doors, and it was a cool, windy day. They strung cords all over to plug in the lighting. They placed blankets on the floor, both to set up the puppet stage and on which to lay the puppets down, so they wouldn't get dusty.

"You never knew what you might have to deal with," Shelley said, when talking about the situation. "Sometimes you had to improvise."

But the show went on.

CHAPTER THREE

HIT THE TRAIL

ROAD TRIPS

"Road trips were fun!" was the phrase used by the puppeteers to describe how they felt about going to other venues to perform.

As the early popularity of God Squad grew and more people became acquainted with this quality entertainment, God Squad began traveling farther afield. The trips had started with other Free Methodist churches nearby. Places like Avonlea, Eyebrow, and Moose Jaw were just the beginning. According to Don Hand, "There wasn't a Free Methodist church in Saskatchewan that had not had God Squad there."

At the beginning, Glenn and Aletha felt Bette-Jean was not quite old enough to take the puppeteers on the road by herself. Two people, Humbert Sealy, a youth leader in the Free Methodist church at the time, and an older brother of one puppeteer, accompanied them.

There were many road trips over the years, many miles covered to travel to communities across Saskatchewan—west to Moose Jaw and Swift Current, south to Avonlea, southeast to Weyburn, Estevan, Wawota and Manor, northwest to Eyebrow, northeast to Melville and Yorkton, north to Saskatoon, Melfort, Prince Albert and Spiritwood. The miles stretched to Alberta— Camrose, Edmonton, and Calgary—and even to Roblin, Manitoba.

Overnight accommodations, when they were on the road, were in peoples' homes. In this way, the young puppeteers got to know people from all over.

Did everyone get along, riding in the confined spaces of the van, covering several hundred miles at a time? Not always. Some groups enjoyed each other's company more than other groups. Sometimes one member of the group pestered another, but the verdict remained—road trips were still fun!

There were various reasons for that conclusion.

"It was good to see different places."

"There was lots of joking around."

"I liked to travel."

"Snacks on the way."

The reasons varied, but the one reason the puppeteers had in common was practicing the spoken lines and singing the songs from the skits along the way. By the end of the practice time for each skit, and performing the same one several times, they had the lines and songs so thoroughly memorized that they could work through the whole musical in the van.

There was no formality about the way they decided who would say what lines. They just shouted out the lines they knew—some lines were the ones for their puppet, some were others' lines. If one person didn't remember a line, another would just jump in and help.

Aletha often traveled in the same vehicle as the puppeteers. It was only on the last few trips, when she was battling cancer, that she and Glenn traveled separately in a car. If you ventured comment, you'd likely say she missed the camaraderie of traveling with her troupe.

It could have been this shared camaraderie that got Bob, still a new driver, stopped for speeding on a trip back home. Or then again, as the story goes, maybe not.

Glenn glanced into the rearview mirror of the station wagon. A half-mile back, he noticed a red flashing light coming up behind Bob. Glenn slowed and, pulling onto the shoulder, stopped. Then, realizing he had the registration for the car Bob was driving, he began backing up.

Bob's eyes darted to the speedometer when he noticed the red light of the police car.

"Oh boy," he whispered to himself, obediently slowing the car and stopping on the shoulder.

The police officer came up to the car, waited for Bob to roll down the window and then shone his flashlight around inside.

"Close to home?" the officer asked.

"Ten miles."

"Let's see your driver's licence, son."

"Yes, sir." Bob reached into his pocket for his wallet and the newly acquired license.

"*You realize you were speeding, don't you?*" *the officer asked, shining his flashlight onto Bob's license.*

Bob nodded.

Looking up as Glenn's station wagon stopped nearby, the officer asked another question. He listened to Bob's answer, then handed Bob's license back and walked over to the station wagon.

Glenn lowered the driver's window and looked up at the police officer.

"*Could I see your driver's licence, sir?*" *the officer asked Glenn.*

Glenn extracted the small paper from his wallet and handed it to the officer.

"*Do you realize you were driving rather erratically? Back and forth between sixty and seventy miles an hour is a bit fast, especially with the road conditions tonight.*"

Glenn groaned inwardly, not even sure exactly how fast he had been going. He immediately resigned himself to paying for two speeding tickets, but hopefully not too large.

"*Bob is your son?*" *the officer asked, handing the license back to Glenn and switching off his flashlight.*

"*Yes, sir,*" *Glenn answered.*

"*You should be setting a better example for him.*"

Glenn nodded, puzzled. He hadn't said anything about Bob being his son.

"*Stay within the speed limit the rest of the trip.*"

Glenn looked up at the police officer. "*I will. Thank you*"

Amazing, Glenn thought as he drove away. He didn't even give me a written warning.

When they arrived home, Glenn got out of the station wagon and walked down the driveway to the other car. Bob, still sitting behind the wheel, and the puppeteers all wore big smiles.

"*What did the police officer say to you?*" *Bob asked.*

As Glenn related the officer's words, the smiles got bigger.

"*I wondered how he knew you were my son,*" *Glenn added.*

"*He asked me if I was traveling with the car ahead,*" *Bob answered.* "*I said, 'Yes, that's my Dad. I'm trying to keep up with him.'*"

In all the years God Squad traveled, the only time the police stopped them was on that memorable trip back from Melfort.

CHAPTER FOUR
MODEL FOR A DREAM

MINISTRY IN THE MAKING

What kind of influence did being in God Squad puppet ministry have on the lives of the young people involved? Which experiences, both at the time they were puppeteers and as they grew older and left those experiences behind, drew them to want to continue being a puppeteer into their adult years? What gave some puppeteers the desire to someday affect people's lives with puppet ministry, as theirs had been while in God Squad?

The desire to have a puppet ministry of their own, a seed planted during the years of God Squad puppeteering, was not fulfilled for all of the former puppeteers who dreamed of it. For one puppeteer, circumstances such as a transient youth group and the cost of the puppets left the dream just that—a dream. The small church they attended was unable to support them in the venture.

Another member of the God Squad alumni is performing in a small way, using puppets in kids club at his church. Yet the desire is there to expand into a larger ministry, perhaps someday to have other kids performing with him, thus fulfilling his dream to once again be part of a puppet ministry.

Other alumni saw their dream become a reality while they were still young. God Squad impacted brother and sister Kris and Tina so greatly that when their parents moved away from Regina, they purchased their own puppets. They invested in one boy and one girl puppet. Purchased at about $100 each, it was a fairly large investment for the two young people.

The two of them began doing skits and songs for Sunday School openings and other events. However, more requests began coming in, so the ministry took off. Kris and Tina continued to build up their equipment and puppets. "Puppet ministry became quite important to both Tina and I," Kris affirmed.

Eventually, when their family ended up back in Oshawa, Ontario, they started a puppet ministry with teens in their church. They directed their own full puppet team called Raised Hands for three years, performing locally and traveling, just as they had in God Squad.

The siblings modeled the group as closely as they could after God Squad. "We tried to have the same high standard with Raised Hands," wrote Tina, "as Aletha had instilled with God Squad."

"It was a great opportunity for us to invest in teens and for us to develop as leaders," said Kris.

After a few years, with Tina married and Kris having returned to school, it became difficult to continue. Still, the dream was hard to release. It was only a few years ago that they sold their equipment and puppets.

"It was very difficult to part with them," said Tina.

At the time of this writing, thirty-three year old Kris is attending a small Wesleyan Bible College in Sussex, New Brunswick. He attributes some of his confidence to having been a puppeteer. "It was a really good experience for me. I was a teenager who didn't have a lot of confidence back then. God Squad provided me a place of belonging and a safe place to learn and experiment with my abilities."

Kris also spoke of the quality of leadership Aletha's dedication and structure taught them as young people in God Squad. "We got the job done very well because of her leadership. She had to have believed in us and loved us for who we were, because she wouldn't have put all the work into God Squad if she hadn't. Now that I am involved in youth ministry, I see the value of significant adult leaders, mentors, and role models that are needed for youth to... look up to. God Squad provided me with significant learning and equipping opportunities. As teens, we didn't realize what we were learning, but we did learn, I am sure."

CHAPTER FIVE
ALL CHOICE SEATS

THE AUDIENCE RESPONSE

Once the puppets were put away and the music had stopped, what stayed in people's minds? What thoughts did people who had been in the audience go home with after the curtain came down and the stage was empty? What were their memories of God Squad performances?

First impressions were not necessarily the impressions that remained later. Bobby Jo's question, "What will be so great about this?" changed to a new conclusion that "it drew every child and adult in some way, affected everybody." The responses varied from "I don't remember much... I just knew it was something inspirational for our children" to an immediate response about a specific skit or puppet.

Looking back, people realized that the impact was different for the children, the teens, and the adults. Children saw puppets in a play. The older ones got the full impact of the message, the principles and the moral issues being conveyed. The humor, however, appealed to all ages. "If you looked out at the audience, the adults were enjoying it as much as the kids," affirmed Elaine Wiens,[50] a member of one of Aletha's Bible study groups. "She worked [humor] in, yet there was a lesson," commented Garry Braun, former missionary to Africa.

Gavin Wood remembered enjoying the quartet of dark puppets—"Fellows who would throw their heads way back to sing"—in *Music Machine*, which God Squad performed in 1980 and then again a few years ago. Gavin and his wife Audrey, parents of a puppeteer, family friends of the Joices', and loyal fans were at both performances.

Although specific memories were not always clear, as the following quotes show, the audience was aware of several things: Aletha's thoroughness in making sure the puppeteers were well-trained, the amount of work involved in putting on a puppet production, and the strength of the ministry.

"I realized the incredible amount of work involved," said Garry Braun. "In the preparations—making the puppets—and into the practice... hours and hours with the God Squad kids on their particular roles."

Kathleen Fisher felt "God Squad was high quality for youngsters to be doing."

"It was a strong ministry," said Doreen Butterfield, "presented in a light-hearted way, but there was a lot of work and discipline involved. [Aletha] was strict, but it was good, there was a strong message in the performances."

> "It was always well done—not haphazard—good quality." –JIM SLOUGH
>
> "The plays were all good. It was amazing how they got puppets to do things." –ELAINE WIENS

People not only attended performances, but were fans of God Squad, following the ministry, aware of what was happening with the troupe. "We enjoyed the productions immensely," stated Dr. Wayne Hindmarsh in a letter about his memories of God Squad. "This was truly a successful outreach ministry," affirmed the former grade four student of Aletha's, now a professor.

There were those who saw the opportunity God Squad had for ministry, and prayed for them. One missionary noted that when she received the church bulletin and saw an announcement about a performance, she prayed for God Squad.

The thought of having fans would have tickled Aletha. Yet, with her feelings about how important prayer was to any venture in life, she would have been happy for prayers on their behalf.

CHAPTER SIX
FROM OUR SPOT BACKSTAGE

FROM THE PUPPETEERS' PERSPECTIVE

Knowing from behind the stage what the response of the audience was to a performance was hard, but for the puppeteers it was a unique perspective. Just as they were performing without being seen, so too they performed without seeing their audience. Until a performance was over, that is, but even then feedback was limited because the puppeteers were putting away the equipment.

There were, however, comments and questions people asked at performances, from which the puppeteers drew a few general conclusions about the audience. It was clear to them that puppet groups were not operating in many places. It was a novelty; few people knew very much about God Squad.

Most of the time, adults came to the front and spoke to the puppeteers after a performance. They commented on how much they had enjoyed the performance, telling the puppeteers they had done a good job.

Although the puppeteers didn't get a lot of comments from children after a show, children who had been at a performance later remembered the puppets talking to them. Krista remembers children, who had been sitting in the front row, telling her later while she was babysitting about the "crazy things the puppets used to do."

HUMOR AND LAUGHTER

Was there a "most remembered" perception the puppeteers had of the audience? One phrase they used to answer that question, more than any other, was "the laughter." The puppeteers enjoyed a few laughs at the humorous material when they began a new skit. However, after working with it the first two or three times, the skit became so familiar, they stopped thinking of it as funny. Not, that is, until they heard the laughter of the audience, of a "whole mess of people," as one puppeteer put it.

The humor they shared at practices, the camaraderie backstage, or the fun of trying something new that didn't work couldn't happen at a performance. So the laughter of the audience gauged for them how the show was going.

At the same time, it came as a surprise to the puppeteers when the audience didn't find it as funny as they had when they first began working on the play during practice. One puppeteer felt the explanation was that sometimes the puppeteers had inside jokes about which the audience didn't know.

Trying to gauge success by the response of the audience was difficult at times. Josh particularly remembers being at one senior's home in Regina. "There was less laughter and groaning about the performance," he said.

At one of the earlier performances at Arlington, the original puppeteers, hearing the laughter during a show, realized that there were lots of people in the audience. They were backstage, however, and didn't know until later that there had been three hundred people sharing in the laughter. Puppeteers who worked the puppets in the years that followed, also heard the laughter of many audiences. And it wasn't only the laughter of children they heard. "Even the adults got right into it," was Janelle Gagnon's perception.

CHAPTER SEVEN

THE LAST TROUPE REMEMBERS...
AND CONTEMPLATES

They were the last troupe Aletha directed, the last ones working the characters at the last performance of God Squad. They had found out about God Squad in much the same way as the puppeteers before them and had felt some of the same feelings of intrigue and desire to be a puppeteer. They worked with the same diligence to perform well and enjoyed the response of the audiences.

But for the last troupe, the memories also included a poignancy the earlier troupes hadn't experienced. They were looking into a future where God Squad no longer existed, a future without the woman behind the blue curtain.

Here are some memories from that unique perspective.

TROUPE MEMORIES

Grant Sawatzky felt a bit sad, but he realized that "everyone has a plan that's laid out for his or her life. Aletha's involved touching many, many kids over a lifetime through the puppet performances. Her job was done, and done well." Grant's observation about Aletha's illness, and that she would not live much longer, reflected her determination. "You could barely tell that she was sick," he said. "Aletha was as cheery as ever."

Tim Friesen remembers the request to be the one to give her flowers at what turned out to be the last performance. "I was really hoping she could make it," he said. "I kind of prepared myself for the possibility she might not. I know she is in heaven and that is a good thought."

"At first I just thought that she would get better," Ryan Friesen began. "But as she got sicker, I started to realize that might not be God's plan... This hit me pretty hard... I didn't want God Squad to end. During the last practices, I focused on doing a good job and not on the fact that God Squad might end. My response to her death was sadness—for the family, the end of God Squad—but happiness that she did not have to suffer anymore, and that she is now singing, maybe even leading a heavenly puppet group, with the angels in heaven."

Ryan concluded that Aletha was a Godly person. "One of her goals in life, that I saw clearly, was to please God and to furnish teens with skills to present the gospel."

Did any of them have a desire to be involved in God Squad in the future, should it be operating again, and the opportunity presented itself? Trevor Friesen's comment, "It probably wouldn't be the same without Aletha," would mirror that of many other former puppeteers.

What was their response when they realized God Squad might not continue as it had, or no longer exist at all? "It had always been there. It was a ministry," Janelle observed. "But," she hastened to add, "we still have memories.

I can use what I have learned, both the technique and the spiritual lessons, in the rest of my life, and therefore it continues."

In response to the question of how she felt about the news of Aletha's illness and eventual death, she said, "It was tough at first, but she always had a smile. God showed me that she went to be with Him. She loved Him so much, so how much more of a blessing could her death be?"

LEFT: The last troupe after their last performance at Parliament Community Church in Regina. Clockwise from Aletha: Janelle Gagnon, Jaren Wiens, Grant Sawatzky, Jon Schroeder, Ryan Friesen, Krista Bekker, and Tim Friesen.

A WALL OF MEMORIES

The hallway walls in the home Glenn and Aletha shared is a photo gallery. Many pictures hang there, including pictures of Aletha as a child, pictures of their wedding day, and of their family. Photos stretch across both sides of the hallway.

Creating a photo gallery of all the people Aletha shared her life with and all the milestones in the story of God Squad, would need a long stretch of space. The pictures are spread across the country.

The wall of photos on the following pages, cannot possibly hold all there is. Nevertheless, by looking into the gallery, you will find a visual glimpse of some milestones and memories.

Thank you to all the people who consented to the loan of pictures from their albums, graciously entrusting me with them.

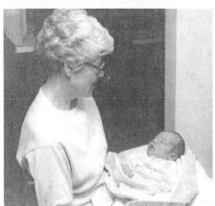

TOP: The family at Bob and Shelley's wedding, July 31, 1982. (l-r) Glenn, Aletha, Bob, Shelley, Bette-Jean, and Don. BOTTOM LEFT & RIGHT: Aletha and Glenn take turns holding one-week-old grandson Jake.

TOP: Bob joined father Glenn (right) and two family friends, Gavin Wood (left) and Doug Reimche (second from left), in a male quartet as a teen. The quartet is seen here in 1969, singing at Canadian Bible College. MIDDLE LEFT: Jake Joice, at age two, unwrapping his gift a little bit at a time. MIDDLE RIGHT: "Can I help study?" BOTTOM: A slightly older looking quartet in 2003 (photo courtesy of Gavin Wood).

TOP: The extended Joice family. (back l-r) Siblings Cliff, Dorothy, Ken, and Franklin. (front l-r) Aletha's father Walter, Aletha, and her mother Elizabeth. BOTTOM LEFT: A photo of Franklin, from the locket he gave to Aletha. BOTTOM RIGHT: Aletha's parents, Walter and Elizabeth, pictured here on their wedding day.

TOP LEFT: Garry and Rita Mae Braun, missionaries to Mali under Gospel Missionary Union, with their children Luke, Larissa, and Joel. TOP RIGHT: Missionaries to Kentucky, Scott and Julie Siemens, with daughters Kelsey and Rachel. MIDDLE: Richard and Hazel Funk, missionaries to Austria. BOTTOM: Tim and Carolyn Gartke, missionaries to Lithuania, with their children Trenton, Nathaniel, Trina, and Amy.

TOP: Donna Stenzil, missionary with Heart to Heart Ministries (from her prayer card). BOTTOM LEFT: Lynn Schellenberg, missionary to Liberia with Sudan Interior Mission (from her prayer card). BOTTOM RIGHT: Josh Bekker poses in front of the Mayan ruins he visited on a trip to a rain forest in November 2000, while teaching in Guatemala (photo courtesy of Josh Bekker).

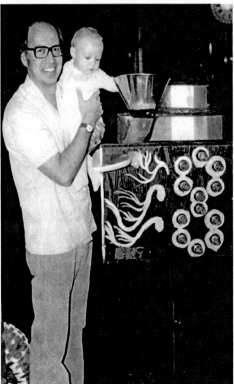

TOP: A casual shot of God Squad. (l-r) Shelley Joice, Jayne Werry, Troy Dakin-iewich, Aletha Joice, Tyler Wood, Glenn Joice, and Jackie Gagnon (photo courtesy of Jayne Werry). LEFT: Already interested in what went on with puppets, a young Tyler Wood is seen here with Glenn Joice, checking out the Music Machine (photo courtesy of Gavin Wood). ABOVE: Glenn proudly looking on and lending his strength at the last performance (photo courtesy of Tilly Wiens).

TOP: A sleepover under the stars? Jayne Weary with puppet (photo courtesy of Jayne Werry). ABOVE: "Say, why don't you come? God Squad is going to be performing." ABOVE RIGHT: A colorful toucan bird, created by Shelley Joice. RIGHT: Puppet characters Anthony and Dragonfly, from *Antsillvania*. BOTTOM: Granny gets a kiss from Grandpa. All featured puppets, excepting the toucan, are from puppetproductions.com.

APPENDICES:

THE CURTAIN IS ALMOST DOWN

Questions never end, curiosity is never completely satisfied, and the gleaning of information can go on into the wide expanse of knowledge. As the book unfolded, there seemed to be unanswered questions. I became curious about more things, and began to wish I had space in the story to share more information about some of the items about which I was writing.

This appendix was designed to have a little fun with a few more answers, have more curiosity satisfied, and find some information to fill your cups of facts.

APPENDIX ONE
MORE INFORMATION, JUST FOR THE FUN OF IT

CABLE CHAIR (Cable Swing): Because he was a handy type of person, Glenn Joice felt Aletha's father might have been the one who constructed the cable chair. The details of its operation described in the story are from Glenn's description of how he remembered it operating.

ABOVE: A sketch to show the concept of the cable chair system across the river.

CRAZY QUILTS: What was crazy about a quilt? Why was it called a crazy quilt? Using the term to refer to a random, irregular pattern in needlework occurred as early as 1878. Various reasons for why the use of the term began have been brought forward.

Perhaps it was the odd shapes of the fabric patches used to make up the design. "Pieces were 'crazed'—irregularly broken up—in the same way as is a 'crazed' shine... the glaze cracked in an irregular pattern... Although crazy patch work or crazy quilting was the term by which the style eventually became known, it is also referred to as puzzle patchwork, Japanese patchwork, or mosaic patchwork."[i]

Whatever the reason for its name, the crazy quilt has become known as the oldest American quilt pattern. Crazy quilts are made by sewing together odd shaped pieces—circles, triangles, squares, ovals, distorted rectangle shapes, etc.—either on their own or onto a backing or foundation patch until it is covered. "The resulting blocks are then sewn together to create... the desired pattern."[ii]

Sometimes the scraps were trimmed and the raw edges folded under and "held in place by a row of fancy hand-sewn embroidery stitches."[iii]

Quilt makers filled the quilts with cotton or wool. They could purchase the cotton in prepared batts (a smooth even layer), sold by the yard in the same way as fabric. The wool often came from the sheep in a farmer's own flock. It was cleaned and either used loose or made into a batt.

The completion of the quilt included quilting or tying. Quilting was done by stitching through the layers of the quilt either in a random way, or by following a specific pattern, such as concentric circles, for example. The heavier wool quilts were tied rather than quilted because of the thickness involved, especially if they were made with heavier fabrics. Some quilts, especially more elaborate ones, were filled with less batting so the needle could better penetrate the material.[iv]

Certain patterns and materials were used during certain years. Originally, during the 1800s, crazy quilts were made as a practical way to keep warm. Then, at the turn of the century, crazy quilting became "the most economical method of using scraps of material,"[v] reaching the height of its popularity around 1884. Some women had more leisure time in these years and they began making

---

[i] McMorris, Penny, "Crazy Quilts", E.P. Dutton, Inc. p. 10.
[ii] McKenry, Ruth, "Quilts and Other Bed Coverings in the Canadian Tradition", Van Norstrand Reinhold Ltd. Toronto 1979 p. 89.
[iii] McMorris p.10.
[iv] McKendry from information from pp. 95-97.
[v] McKendry p. 38.

fancier crazy quilts, using silks and velvets and outlining the patches with orna-mental stitches. These more elaborate quilts were not stuffed, and became light-weight summer quilts or throws.

The sources of the fabric scraps differed. The farm women used scraps of cloth from worn clothing, or the long missing necktie or pieces of a vest, while the wealthy women could afford new materials.

Because department stores recognized that fabric scraps were in demand, competition grew. Some firms began to offer free fabric samples and scraps from the manufacture of clothing, thankful not to have to waste the cloth. Others off-ered kits that included patterns, instructions for assembly, and the scrap pieces already cut.

The best way of dating quilts is to compare the fabric samples of material used in clothing with the scraps of cloth used for quilting. "Even though women did save scraps of cloth for quilting, the contents of the rag bag were under heavy demand..."[vi]

The making of crazy quilts has outlasted the changing favor with which it was viewed over the years. "Because very few people slept alone, single beds were scarce. Almost the only ones to be found were very narrow and intended for the hired help who slept in the kitchen, in the back hall or over the back kitchen. Any sleeping quarters were considered good enough for the unfort-unate hired hand. One theory often held was that he would not linger too long in the mornings if he was sufficiently uncomfortable. This attitude continued into the late 1930s when, not surprisingly, hired men became hard to get. Old quilts were kept long after they were considered too shabby even for the child-ren's beds and passed on to the hired man. We can thank him for the survival of many tattered old quilts that are historically interesting despite their cond-ition."[vii]

EWES, LAMBS, AND PERCY: We don't know if the little lamb Aletha raised was a rejected twin or an orphan. However, Percy was very tiny when she brought him home in the basket of her bike carrier.

Perhaps the farmer Aletha got the lamb from didn't want to bother bottle-feeding the lamb or finding an adoptive mother for it because of the time involved. For whatever reason, he gave it to Aletha to raise.

The writers of *An Introduction to Keeping Sheep* describe an alternative the farmer might have had. "Sometimes a ewe which has given birth to twins will reject one for no apparent reason," say authors Jane Upton and Dennis Soden.

[vi] McKendry p. 118.
[vii] McKendry p. 40.

They describe a method of getting a ewe to accept a second lamb when she gave birth to twins. "If both lambs are strong and active, tie the ewe to a corner of the pen using a halter, and after a few days she will usually accept both lambs. Try taking both lambs away for about half an hour. When they are returned she will usually be so pleased to see them that she allows both of them to suckle her."[viii]

Whatever the reasons behind Percy being given to Aletha, she loved him. She continued to love him as an adult sheep and thus the protest about the bull fighting her brothers did with him.

It is interesting that the reason her brothers were able to teach the lamb to 'butt' was that sheep will run at their goal head down and eyes closed. It was because of this tendency that the boys could step aside just as Percy came running and the full grown sheep would hit the air or something other than he intended—at times, even an unsuspecting visitor.

FEATHER TICK: A feather tick, like the one Aletha jumped into, was a traditional bed people made while still in their European homelands. Although they were unable to bring their feather beds with them, because of the difficulty in handling them aboard a ship, they brought the idea.

"As soon as a settler was able to, he gathered a few geese to supply him with feathers for his bed."[ix]

Competing with the wild animals for his geese, however, made it difficult to acquire enough feathers in a short time. Supplementing it with other feathers didn't work, as they tended to lump together and the tick would become hard. If the down feathers were plucked while the goose was alive, so it could grow more, gaining those feathers could also be hard on the goose. Fortunately, usually the goose was dead before the feathers were plucked.

When the feathers had been gathered and picked over, the poor quality feathers were discarded and the usable ones were hung to dry. The bag of feathers needed to dry for about a year before using them, or they would smell. Because it was so time-consuming to collect enough feathers for a feather tick, goose down was worth a considerable amount of money.

When the feathers were dry, they were stuffed into ticking, a bag made of densely woven cotton or coarse linen tow. To prevent the feathers from poking out of the ticking, the inside of the bag was sometimes rubbed with homemade brown soap. Another method of keeping the feathers contained was to make a thin muslin inner bag to contain the feathers, with an outer covering of a calico

---

[viii] *An Introduction to Keeping Sheep*, Upton & Soden p. 71.
[ix] McKendry p. 46 .

print. This method had the added advantage of being able to wash the cover without the fuss of washing the tick with the feathers inside.

Washing the feather tick could be done, but was a lot of work. The tick was scrubbed and hung on the line, where its position had to be changed frequently and rubbed between the hands to fluff up the feathers while it was drying.

Having a goose feather tick was highly desirable because of its luxurious comfort, "but a certain amount of affluence and hard work was necessary to obtain one. Unless such a bed is actually slept upon, it is difficult to relate just how voluptuous it feels."[x]

You might be faced with a severe temptation to go over and jump into the feather tick at the Lower Fort Garry Museum in Selkirk, Manitoba. After listening to the guide tell you how difficult it was to fluff it up, resisting would be in order. Try to fathom how a little girl like Aletha could fluff up such a huge feather mattress.

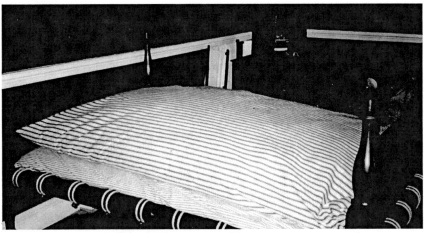

ABOVE: A feather tick (photo courtesy of the Lower Fort Gary National Historic Site museum in Selkirk, Manitoba).

FILM PROJECTION: In the days when Aletha was teaching, preparing to show an educational film to a class was not as simple as it is today. A teacher can now roll in a TV and DVD player both on the same stand, plug them in, insert a movie and push play. But back then, a teacher projected reeled movies onto a collapsible screen. This meant the teacher would need to bring in a table for the projector, the heavy projector itself, the screen, the container with the reeled

---

[x] McKendry p. 50.

film, and an empty reel of the same size. It might mean more than one trip unless a volunteer was recruited to help.

Once everything was in the room, the set up process began—and quite a process it was.

The screen was rolled up like a window blind and housed in a metal canister, which in turn was attached at its center to a telescoping rod. The rod was the upper portion of a folding tripod. When the tripod was unfolded, the canister was still parallel to the telescoping rod, held in a vertical position by... Suffice it to say, this was only part of the set up.

Bringing an extra table into the classroom for the film projector, the next piece of equipment, often necessitated moving students' desks aside to make room for it. The heavy film projector was set up on the table, and the teacher would begin the process of threading the celluloid film. Threading started from the full reel, hung on one extended arm of the projector. It progressed through a series of rollers and guides, going through all of them in the right sequence. After passing the projection lamp, the film reached the empty reel hanging on another arm on the opposite side of the projector. Just looking at a picture of the number of rollers the film would thread through gives one an idea how complicated it would be to get the sequence correct to exhibit the film.

When all was in readiness, the trial run began—switching on the projector to see if it was working. Often the film would 'wobble' and/or the picture would be blurry. This meant finding out what the problem was and trying to get it

ABOVE: Film projector (photo courtesy of the Antique Mall in Regina, Saskatchewan).

working properly before the class arrived. If you had been a little late getting started, trying to get things up and running while they fidgeted and talked could be cumbersome.

All things working well during the trial run didn't mean they would continue to do so throughout the movie. Sometimes the film came off a roller or broke and the teacher would have to stop the movie. He or she would need to make the necessary adjustments or repair, while keeping an eye on a now restless class, often moaning and groaning about the delay.

How delighted the teachers in those days would have been, I am sure, to be able to show a movie to a class with the mostly untroubled ease teachers do now.

GASOLINE IRON: "Flame throwing monster" was the phrase Aletha might have used to describe her feelings about the gasoline iron she had to learn to use for ironing clothes after her mother died. The expertise needed to use this appliance was much more involved than reaching over, putting the plug into the wall, and switching on an electric iron. The gasoline iron was just that—powered by gasoline.

A small round tank at one end of the iron held the fuel. An air pump on the tank built up pressure so that when the valve was opened fuel released into the base of the iron where it could be ignited with a match. Using the iron resulted in fuel consumption, depleting the air pressure. This would necessitate pumping it up periodically, to keep the iron lit.

Opening the valve and holding a match up to the side of the iron as the gas was coming out was tricky. If too much fuel came out before it was lit, flames would shoot out. When too little fuel flowed, the iron would light but then go out, and the process had to start over.

The iron sat on a metal stand on the ironing board, keeping the heat away from the ironing board cover. Care was always taken that no one bumped the iron while it was ignited and in use.

The iron had no temperature settings for different kinds of material. Ironing began with low heat tolerance fabrics, while the iron was still relatively cool, moving on to more heat-resistant fabrics like cotton. It was too great a risk to place the iron on the middle of a garment to start ironing it. Instead, a spot at the bottom edge of a garment, such as a shirttail, was tested first. If, before the ironing was completed, the iron seemed to be getting too hot, it was turned off in between to cool it down. The ironing could commence only after the iron was cool enough to be lit again.

ABOVE: Gasoline iron (photo courtesy of the Antique Mall in Regina, Saskatchewan).

HAND PUPPETRY: Do they really walk and talk? How do these little characters imply such a reality that the children in the audience are drawn into their make believe world, responding by talking to them during a puppet skit?

Nancy Cole, in her book about the history and methods of puppetry, explains a bit of the mystery behind a puppet's lifelike effect. She feels it is "their ability to be more human in the course of a short performance than most human beings manage to be throughout an entire life time."[xi]

She comments that when a puppet character has left the impression of being real, it is a measure of success. "Audiences often succumb to the point of view of puppets, and follow their advice simply because empathy is complete and identification strong. Puppets, after all, are people we believe in..."[xii]

But there is more to it than just the character, who after all is lifeless when not on stage. Credit must go to the operator. Nancy explains why. "For however brief a time, however simple the stage, the set of puppets, or the technical effects, the ability of the puppeteer to lead his audience to set aside their disbelief and enter into the world of his performance is the definition of his excellence."[xiii]

How does that proficiency, that ability to entice the audience to participate in the world of the puppet, happen? Practice, practice, practice. You must come to know the puppet so well that it becomes part of you. Nancy quotes Jim Henson's viewpoint: "The only way a puppeteer becomes proficient... is by

---

[xi] *Puppet Theatre in Performance* by Nancy H. Cole, p. 10.
[xii] Cole p. 10
[xiii] Cole p. 20

spending... literally days in front of the mirror, watching your characters act and react, listen, think, and do all those tiny little things that a person does... There are so many mechanics involved in puppeteering that all of those mechanics have to be totally automatic before you can give a real performance."[xiv]

But how 'alive' would puppets be without that other crucial factor—the audience? "Puppets, to be at their best," says Nancy, "require live audiences to respond to... the dynamics of people and puppets in direct communication. The thrill of audience participation achieves no greater success than when an audience of children speak to a puppet hero villain in unison, a concert of voices cheering and booing but controlled completely by the small figure on stage..."[xv]

"[The puppet] appears to live, and yet he has no other life after the performance. We can talk to him, love him, hate him, participate in his schemes, and since the puppet is not alive to reprimand us after the performance—nor can he 'tell on us'—we are utterly free to enter [his] world."[xvi]

"LITTLE SASK"[xvii]: The Little Saskatchewan River runs south from Riding Mountain National Park and enters the Assiniboine about fifteen kilometers west of Brandon, Manitoba, near the Grand Valley Campsite and Water Slides, though these were most certainly not part of the landscape as Aletha knew it when she was a child living on the ranch.

The river then passes through Minnedosa and Rapid City, Manitoba. As it approaches the Assiniboine Valley, it begins a rather sharp descent, providing rapids in the early summer. Although fast and unpredictable in spring, it is usually a small and harmless stream. It would have been this lazy stream that Aletha floated down in the summer.

One can see the river by looking across the valley a few miles northwest of Kirkan's Bridge, which spans the Assiniboine ten kilometers west of Brandon. Access is just east of the town of Rivers, Manitoba.

MOTHER OF THE YEAR—NOMINATION AND AWARD: This nomination of Aletha Joice for Mother of the Year in the Community Service category was originally written and presented to the Pregnancy Counseling Center by Vicki Clarke. It has been edited for this book, and appears here in its shortened form, with Vicki's permission.

[xiv] Cole quoting Jim Henson, creator of the Muppets, New York City, May 3, 1977, p. 22.
[xv] Cole p. 10.
[xvi] Cole p. 20.
[xvii] Information about the Little Saskatchewan River was gleaned from Wikipedia. Drainage area information was obtained from the Environment Canada website.

Vicki is a young mother of two boys. Vicki, having also had cancer and experienced the loss of a child before full-term, was encouraged by Aletha during these times of difficulty. Vicki is involved with the Pregnancy Counseling Center in Regina.

Aletha attends Parliament Community Church, is married to Glenn, and has two children and one grandchild.

Aletha Joice has been involved with volunteer groups in our church, many of which impact people outside the church. She demonstrates a variety of talents in our church library, as a Bible study leader, in committee work, and with God Squad puppeteering.

Aletha touches and is involved in the lives of people of all ages, bringing the spirit of mentoring to all of her community service.

Aletha began God Squad, a puppet troupe that performs biblically based puppet shows. Over the years, the puppet group has performed and traveled to various communities and cities.

Last fall, Aletha began training a group of junior teens for God Squad in her home where they learned not only about puppeteering, but also about God, commitment, and discipline. She wants the teens to learn how to love the community service they do and why it is important. She has a gift for instilling leadership qualities in young people.

When planning Bible studies and mission events, she takes her responsibilities seriously and begins preparations months in advance. Her ideas span not only age, but levels of Christian maturity.

It is the spirit that Aletha has when she serves, however, that is the main reason that I, and others, would like to nominate her. She looks to uplift and has a genuine and transparent care for others. When looking at missions material for children, her concern is for how and what they learn and that it be pertinent for their lives today and in the future. People spoke of her interest in those she touches in her service as being deep, personal, pure and right. We feel cared for by Aletha and at the same time edified and challenged to be more for God. Words people used to describe her included "dedicated", "intelligent", "a consistent witness", "selfless", "well read", "optimistic", "a soft heart for missions", "turns the focus from herself to others" and "definitely a Godly woman".

When I think of a truly Godly mother, I think of one who communicates love and care for her children (in this case people who have been touched by Aletha) today, grants a vision to draw closer to God, and enables them to love and serve others for God in the future. One woman said it beautifully when she said, "Aletha is like a grandmother to many." We who have had the privilege of feeling mentored by Aletha would like to rise up and call her blessed!

Strength and dignity are her clothing, and she smiles at the future.
She opens her mouth in wisdom, and the teaching
of kindness is on her tongue.
Her children rise up and bless her.
A woman who fears the Lord, she shall be praised.
−PROVERBS 31:25-26,28,30 (NASB).

LEFT: A photo of the pencil drawing by Dwight Heinrichs, titled Aspirations and Dreams, that Aletha received as her Mother of the Year award. Photo taken with the kind permission of Glenn Joice, and used for this book with the permission of the artist. The artist based his title on the idea of the aspirations a mother has for her child, and the dreams of the child in her arms. Permission for use of the photo of the drawing was also kindly granted by the mother, Dorothy Scolnik.

OUNGRE: Oungre is the small Saskatchewan town near where Aletha lived for the first seven years of her life. Aletha's husband Glenn had spoken about Oungre and the possibility that Dr. Brown's house, where Aletha was born, might still be standing. A writer's curiosity craves satisfaction, so on April 14,

Photos from the present, so you can picture the Oungre post office (TOP) and store (BOTTOM) of the past. Perhaps they still serve as inspiration for an artist who enjoys painting the rustic.

2002, Glenn graciously consented to guide my husband Dave and I to Oungre and show us around town.

On the way to Oungre, Glenn also gave us a verbal tour, commenting on the surrounding area, some buildings, and other things we observed on the way:

1. Big Beaver, Bengough, East Poplar, and Coronach were Glenn's areas when they were living in Weyburn and Glenn was with the Department of Social Services.
2. The hills in the distance, called the Rolling Hills.
3. "The black soil was very good for producing good crops," Glenn told us, quickly amending and adding, "Along with rain."
4. Foster's Grove, which is now a regional park. The family had reunions there when they lived at Oungre.
5. A school where Glenn and Aletha had attended a Sunday School picnic while in Weyburn.

6. The many oil pumping rigs, which some call 'donkeys' but Glenn referred to as 'oil jacks'. There were a high number in that area.

When we arrived at Oungre, Glenn pointed out the house he thought had been Dr. Brown's. The lady sitting in the yard was currently living there, but the house had belonged to her grandfather. Dr. Brown's had been next door, but had been torn down about three years earlier. She pointed out a house across the street that had been the hospital.

The village of Oungre has about twenty people living in it now. Several dilapidated buildings, one of which was the general store and another the post office, still stand along the main street. Coming into town, you pass Lyndale School, the new village school where about seventy students currently attend, now mostly from the surrounding villages and rural area. It was a rural school called Knoxville School, which Aletha attended.

All that is left of the house Dr. Brown used for his practice, when Aletha was born, is an overgrown sidewalk leading from the street. Through an opening in the hedge, one can see what would have been the front yard. The grass has grown over and through the old sidewalk so much that it looks like a hard gravel path.

PRAIRIE FARMER: If you like trivia, read on...

The *Prairie Farmer* magazine was first published in 1841 for rural America. The magazine also purchased air time on the radio station WLS, owned by Sears Roebuck. Many *Prairie Farmer* editors gave livestock and produce reports or weather updates on WLS.

In 1928, Sears Roebuck sold WLS to ABC for $250,000. Prairie Farmer was the majority stockholder in ABC, with twelve hundred of the twenty-five hundred shares, worth $100 each.

The magazine later purchased all the shares, and after the sale moved the studios to *Prairie Farmer* headquarters in Chicago.[xviii]

SUPERINTENDENT VISITING SCHOOLS: Most teachers felt a level of tension that was not a part of a regular school day when a superintendent, hired by the Department of Education, came to pay a visit. This person often sat at the back of the classroom, observing and taking notes. Aletha experienced the same apprehension many teachers did—what would the superintendent's report say

---

[xviii] The *Prairie Farmer* now has a website at www.prairiefarmer.com, where you can check the weather (if you live in the United States, that is).

about her teaching? The personal touch was absent, as the report went directly to the Department of Education. Little or no interaction went on between the superintendent and the teacher during this visit.

The procedure of a superintendent, visiting the schools to observe, was in place for about forty to fifty years. The task of evaluations changed around 1980, when each school division began having its own superintendent. The principal of each school began to have more input, and the local school board, rather than the Department of Education, became responsible for hiring teachers.

Aletha had stopped teaching by this time.

APPENDIX TWO

MARTHA'S FOLLY

The following puppet skit, written by Aletha Joice, is based on Luke 10:38-42.

Some phrases Jesus speaks are from Bible passages in Matthew 8:20, Matthew 23:37, and Luke 12:24,27 (NIV).

Choreography was added to her script for this publication, based on a video of the skit. The words of the songs are used with permission of the writers.

MARTHA'S FOLLY

People Characters:
Mary
Hannah, the maid
Disciples—Peter, James, John
Martha
Cook
3 would-be followers of Jesus
Lazarus
Jesus

Animal Characters:
three large chickens
several chicks
rooster
black cat
small mouse

Props: Sun, cloud, feathers, rubber chicken, sign with 'Two hours later' on it, sign with 'One hour later' on it, puppet-size flute and violin, bowl for chicken feed, bowl with vegetable pieces, extra vegetable pieces, Styrofoam 'feathers', small table with candle and bowl of fruit, larger table with place settings and food, dish with desert (honey puffs)

Backdrops (background scenes painted on cloth):
Some scenes for the skit are needed more than once, so the backdrops are attached in layers and changed as required (see 'Sequence of Backdrop Changes'). Puppeteers use gloves while changing backdrop scenes.
Backdrops required for use in the skit:

- #1: Outdoors—Mary, Martha, and Lazarus' home; hills with plowed fields in the distance, bushes in the foreground.
- #2: Kitchen—Mary, Martha, and Lazarus' home; a wall with a shelf and a window (no scene visible outside the window).

#3: Solid blue cloth (for scene going back to events which happened in the past).

#4: Outdoors—hillside pasture with grass, flowers, and sheep.

#5: Dining room—plain wall with a window where a neighboring house is visible through it.

#6: City—view seen from the rooftop of Mary, Martha, and Lazarus' home.

Sequence of Backdrop Changes:

- Backdrops #1, #5, and #6 are hanging in place over the front of the top tier of the stage, with #6 at the bottom, #5 over it, and the outdoor scene #1 visible, when skit begins.
- Backdrop #2 (kitchen) is put over the front.
- Backdrop #3 (solid blue) is put over the front.
- Backdrop #3 (solid blue) is brought back, again revealing backdrop #2 (kitchen scene). #3 is removed and #4 attached.
- Backdrop #4 (pasture) is put over the front as Mary and Martha work.
- Backdrops #4 and #2 (pasture and kitchen) are brought back, revealing backdrop #5 (dining room).
- Backdrop #5 is brought back, revealing #6.

(U) and (L) indicate which tier (upper/lower) of the puppet stage the action is happening.

THE WOMAN BEHIND THE BLUE CURTAIN

Scene 1: *Outdoors (yard) at Mary, Martha, and Lazarus' home.*
(U): Sun comes up. Rooster enters, moves around to several spots with some pecking motion, then stops and crows several times. Rooster exits. Cloud moves over the sun. Sun and cloud exit. Action begins on lower tier.
(L): Chickens enter, making poultry sounds. Begin scurrying around as Mary enters and begins to feed them. When Mary is finished, she and chickens exit. Mary and one large chicken re-enter.

Mary sings Avinu Malkenu.[i]

Mary: *(singing)*
> Avinu, Malkenu, Maker of all things
> Ruling o'er the works of Your hand;
> You loved us so
> You sent Your Son.

Mary hugs chicken, which has come up beside her as she is singing.

To take our sin and shame
Our Father in heaven, holy is Your name.

(U): Trio (one female and two male) enter; one male has a flute and the other a violin.
(L): Mary and the chicken turn to face the trio.

(U): Trio sings Avinu Malkenu through once, then female exits. Male with flute plays first two lines of Avinu Malkenu, then exits. Male with violin plays last three lines and then exits.

(L): Mary and the chicken turn back as Martha and Hannah enter, joining Mary in the yard. The large chickens enter and move around, doing pecking motions as Mary and Martha talk.

Martha: Mary, Jesus is coming today. Also Peter, James, and John!
Mary: Today! Isn't that wonderful?
Martha: *(speaking faster as she thinks of all the things which need to be done)* Yes, and I'm cleaning house and baking bread. *(turning to Hannah)* Hannah, take this down.

---

[i] Words and music © Michael Ledner 1992 International Copyright Secured, All Rights Reserved. Used by permission.

Hannah writes; sounds of pen scratching on paper are heard.

Martha: We're going to have chicken soup with matzah balls, roasted chicken, chopped liver, cucumber and yogurt salad... *(Martha pauses)* with honey puffs for dessert. *(Martha sighs)* But I'm still sewing up that new tablecloth, so *(Martha points to Mary)* you'll just have to catch and kill the plumpest chicken out here.

Mary: Oh, no, I can't. Call Lazarus or Cook!

Martha: *(shaking her head)* You know Lazarus went to buy sheep from Bartholomew, and he took Cook with him.

Mary: Oh... well, Hannah, you do it.

Hannah: That's not my job, ma'am.

Martha: *(shaking her head)* Hannah has to finish the cleaning... Now, *please* get that chicken! It'll have to be cleaned, plucked, and roasted by 5:00 o clock. *(Martha turns to leave)* Come along, Hannah.

Martha and Hannah exit. Mary watches the chickens start to eat again.

Mary: *(sighing and laying head on arms on stage front)* I hate this job.

Mary starts to sneak up on a chicken.

Mary: Here chicky, chicky, nice chicky...

Mary catches a chicken and holds it lovingly.

Mary: Oh no, it's you, Pet. I'm sure you're much too skinny.

Mary gently lets chicken go; starts stalking the next chicken—it keeps walking too, just out of reach, increasing its speed and squawking as Mary increases hers. Mary pounces on it and holds it tightly. The chicken squawks loudly.

Mary: Oh dear, poor chicky... I'm sure you're too skinny, too... I'll just accidentally let you go...

Martha enters.

Martha: *(speaking sternly)* Mary... hurry up.

Martha grabs chicken Mary has just let go.

Mary: Oh Martha, the poor thing... I can't kill it... nor watch.

Mary exits stage left; running.

Martha: *(calling after her)* You'll be glad enough to see it when it's roasted!

Martha exits stage right, carrying the chicken.

(L): Loud, fast Jewish-style piano and violin music, playing parts of introduction to Behold. *'Feathers' flying, Martha with back to audience plucks chicken fast and furiously. She slows down, then after finishing faces audience and sings* Behold.[ii]

Martha: *(singing)*
     Pour and drink the living water
     From the well that's never running dry
     For the Lord has become my strength and my song
     He also has become my salvation.

(U): Trio enters.

Trio: *(singing)*
     For the Lord has become my strength and my song
     He also has become my salvation.

Music fades as trio exits.

Backdrop change: to #2 (kitchen)

[ii] © Lillenas (The Copyright Company) 1975.

Scene 2: *Kitchen of Mary, Martha, and Lazarus' house.*
(L): Martha enters.

Martha: *(Plops chicken on table)* Hannah.

Hannah enters.

Martha: Please clean this chicken and get it in the oven, then come and help me
with these vegetables. *(Martha hands chicken to Hannah)*
Hannah: Yes ma'am. *(Hannah exits carrying chicken)*

Martha begins preparing vegetables hurriedly, then slows.

Martha: *(aloud, to herself)* Jesus, Peter, James, and John *do* need a good meal and a
place to rest away from the crowds.

Mary peeks into the room, then enters.

Mary: Is it done?
Martha: *(speaking shortly)* Of course not! Hannah is just preparing it for the oven!

Mary slowly comes further into the room.

Mary: No... I meant... it... it... well... it's not... squawking anymore?
Martha: *(more tenderly)* No, Mary, it's out of its misery. *(leans close to Mary)* I didn't
like killing it, either. Please forget about it and help me with these
vegetables. Hope Cook gets back in time to make the dessert.
Mary: Yes, Martha. *(Mary begins helping Martha)* I'm sorry.

*Hannah enters and holds a bowl. Mary and Martha continue cutting and putting pieces in the
bowl. Hannah exits with the bowl of vegetables.*
Mary and Martha turn to audience and sing Morning Star.[iii]

Mary and Martha: *(singing, with choir harmony back up)*
Hallelujah, Hallelujah. (repeat five times)

[iii] Words of *Morning Star* by Stuart Dauerman © 1989 Used by permission.

Mary and Martha 'ahh' during the verse as choir sings, then sing along with the Hallelujah's.
      Take heed to the word of the Lord (echo Hallelujah, Hallelu)
      It's like a light that shines in the dark (echo Hallelujah, Hallelu)
      Until the dawning of the day
      When the shadows flee away.
      And the morning star arises in our hearts
      Till the morning star arises in our hearts
      Hallelujah, Hallelujah... (repeat five times)

(U): One member of male trio enters stage center.
(L): Mary and Martha turn to face male singer.

      Male trio member: *(singing, with choir singing echos)*
      Take heed to the word of the Lord (echo Hallelujah, Hallelu)
      It's like a light that shines in the dark (echo Hallelujah, Hallelu)
      Until the dawning of the day
      When the shadows flee away.
      And the morning star arises in our hearts
      Till the morning star arises in our hearts
      Hallelujah, Hallelujah... (repeat five times)

(U): Male trio member exits.
(L): Mary and Martha face the audience.

Mary and Martha: *(singing, with choir back up)*
      Hallelujah, Hallelujah.
      (Fading) Hallelujah, Hallelujah.

(L): Mary and Martha exit.

(U): Sign "Two hours later" moves across stage left to stage right.
(L): A knock sounds at the door. Mary enters stage right, runs across to stage left and exits.

Mary: *(off stage)* Come in, come in.

Mary enters stage left, moving to stage center and turning to Peter, James, and John as they enter stage left behind her.

300

Mary: Oh, is Jesus not with you?

Peter: He'll be along shortly. He wanted us to come ahead, so as not to keep you waiting. If it's all right, he wants us to eat, then go on to prepare our next appointment.

Mary: Of course. *(calling)* Hannah!

(U): Hannah enters.

(L): Disciples look up at Hannah.

Mary: *(looking up at Hannah)* Hannah, tell Martha the disciples will eat now.

Hannah: *(looking at disciples)* Yes, ma'am. It will just be a few minutes, ma'am.

Hannah exits.

Mary: It must be exciting to be with Jesus. Do you have any better idea when He'll set up His Kingdom?

Peter: Oh, any time now. You should have seen Him feed five thousand people from just five loaves of bread and *(emphatically)* two fish. *(pausing)* No one would worry about starving under His leadership.

James: Nor get sick and die. Why, He could give people in His cabinet authority to go out and heal, just as He did us. Wouldn't it be great for a cabinet member's campaign speech? To be able to say, *(James lowers his voice and speaks in slower, firm tones)* 'Jesus sent me out yesterday, and I healed all the sick people in Bethany!' *(with expression of great satisfaction)* Uh-huh!

John: And He *did* say He'd be *betrayed*. But don't worry. We think He must have meant that He'd have enemies. The chief priests will always be against Jesus.

James: We were talking about His Kingdom and the high government jobs that would be open. We'd like to apply.

Cat enters. Mary picks it up and begins to pet it in her arms.

Peter: Yeah. Mary, would you believe that James and John had the nerve to ask for the very top positions?

James and John cover their faces with their hands and lower their heads, embarrassed.

Peter: And they were real sneaky, too. They got their mother to ask for them.

Mary: Surely *you*, Jesus' disciples, didn't quarrel, did you?

Peter: Not for long. Do you know what Jesus did? He picked up the nearest child, like this...

Peter takes cat from Mary. Cat meows.

Peter: ...and said, 'Whoever, welcomes this little child in My Name welcomes me; and whoever welcomes me, welcomes the One who sent me. For he who is least among you all—He is the greatest.'

Peter lets the cat go. Cat exits.

Mary: I always knew Jesus wouldn't pick favorites. Sounds to me like everyone would want to be part of His Kingdom.

John: I don't know, Mary. Listen to what He said to some men who wanted to follow Him.

Disciples and Mary exit.

Backdrop change: to #3 (solid blue)

Offstage: Harp plays mysterious type of music, showing the scene coming next is a memory of something past.

Scene 3: *Along a road.*

(U): Jesus enters, stage center. A man appears at stage left and speaks to Jesus.

First man: I will follow you, wherever you go.

Jesus: I don't have a permanent home. Do you want to wander, all your life? The foxes have holes and the birds have nests, but I don't know where I'm going to sleep next.

First man bows his head, then turns away, and leaves. Second man enters stage right.

Jesus: *(turning to speak to second man)* Follow me.

Second Man: But my father is elderly and not well. Please let me take care of him until he dies, and *then* I'll follow you.

Jesus: There'll be plenty of other people around to care for your father. I need you to proclaim the Kingdom of God.

Second man hangs his head, then turns and leaves. Third man enters stage right.

Third man: *(eagerly)* I will follow you, Lord, but first let me go and say goodbye to my family.

Jesus: If you become entangled again in your family's needs and activities, you'll never have time to serve God. Have you ever watched a man plowing in his field? As long as he looks ahead, his plow moves straight. But if he looks back, the plow goes crooked and he seldom gets straightened out again.

Third man listens with astonishment, then turns abruptly and leaves. Jesus exits slowly.

Offstage: Music—introduction to We've Been Approved by God.

(U): Three disciples enter stage left.

(L): Mary and Martha enter stage right; a mouse enters stage left.

***Disciples, Martha, and Mary sing* We've Been Approved by God.[iv]

(U): The disciples stay stage left as the first four lines of the song are sung.

[iv]Words adapted from Scripture, 1 Thessalonians 2:4.Words and music © Michael Ledner 1994 International Copyright Secured, All Rights Reserved. Used by permission.

(L): The mouse moves across the stage bobbing body and head in time to the music as the song is sung, occasionally 'crawling' along the stage rail (top) or clapping with the beat.

Disciples, Martha, and Mary: *(singing)* We've been approved by God
(L): Mary and Martha move toward stage right with two bounces, in time to the beat of the music.

Disciples, Martha, and Mary: *(singing)* to be entrusted
(L): Mary and Martha bounce back again, crowding the mouse, who has to move over.

Disciples, Martha, and Mary: *(singing)* with the Good News
(L): Mary and Martha bounce back to stage right, where they stop.

Disciples, Martha, and Mary: *(singing)* of Ye-shu-a HaMashiach.

(U): Disciples move from stage left to stage right in bouncing motion, keeping time to the music as they sing the four lines again. They only cross the stage once.
(L): Mary and Martha bounce as before but now to stage left first, then right, and left again, in time to the beat of the music as the lines are repeated.

Disciples, Martha, and Mary: *(singing)*
       We've been approved by God to be entrusted
       with the Good News of Ye-shu-a HaMashiach.

During the singing of the next group of lines:
(U): the disciples move back to stage left in bouncing motion, keeping time to the music.
(L): Mary and Martha remain stage left, occasionally raising their arms as they sing.

Disciples, Martha, and Mary: *(singing)*
       So the words that we speak
       are not to please men but to please our God;
       He examines our hearts
       and He alone is worthy of our praise.

While the music plays the first four lines again:
(U): The disciples move to stage left, then back to stage right, doing high kicks and shouting 'Hey!' while keeping time with the music.

(L): Mary and Martha each raise one arm and, while linking the other, dance in a circle, keeping time to the music.

The mouse exits quickly (scared away) at first 'Hey!'

When the song is finished, the disciples, Mary, and Martha exit.

Backdrop change: Blue backdrop is removed, revealing #2 (kitchen) again.

Scene 4: *The kitchen.*

Disciples and Mary enter stage left.

Mary: Seems to me you really need to listen to Jesus and what He says about His Kingdom.

James: Sometimes we just want to get away from all the crowds—and plan the constitution of Jesus' future government.

Martha enters stage right.

John: Right now, James, we need to get going to find shelter before dark.

Peter: *(facing John)* Yes, let's Go. *(turning to Mary and Martha)* Thanks for the delicious meal.

Mary and Martha. Greet Lazarus for us. Goodbye.

Martha and Mary: *(together)* Goodbye.

Disciples exit.

Martha: *(sounding a little miffed)* Would you believe they ate all the fresh bread?

Mary: Martha, they were hungry... and they *do* love your bread.

Martha: *(somewhat appeased)* Yes, I'm glad they do but... *(looks out of the window)* There's Lazarus and Cook coming now. Let's hurry and clean up. Maybe I'll have time to bake more.

Mary and Martha begin cleaning. Quick piccolo music.

Backdrop change: to #4 (pasture) as they work.

Music fades as Mary and Martha finish working, and exit.

Scene 5: *Pasture with sheep.*
Clarinet and oboe music, up and fade.
(U): Lazarus and Cook enter with three sheep ahead of them.

Sheep: Baaa. Baaa. Baaa.
Lazarus: *(to Cook)* That was a good day at the market. We made good buys, thanks to your guidance.
Sheep: Baaa. Baaa.
Cook: *(petting a sheep)* Yeah. I'm glad that Martha said she could spare me today.
Sheep: Baaa. Baaa.
Lazarus: I'll look after these sheep. I've a feeling that Martha will expect you right away. *(Lazarus chuckles)*
Cook: *(with a meaningful nod)* Yes, I expect so!

Low cello music up and fade as Lazarus and Cook exit two different directions.

Backdrop change: to #5 (dining room).

Scene 6: *The dining room of Mary, Martha, and Lazarus' home.*
(L): A knock sounds at the door. Mary enters stage right and runs to stage left.
(U): Hannah enters.

(L): Mary: Oh Jesus, welcome!

Mary enters stage left, then moves stage center as Jesus enters stage left.

Mary: *(looking up at Hannah)* Hannah, bring water and towels for the Master.

(U): Hannah exits.
(L): Hannah re-enters near Jesus with a water jar and towels.

Jesus: Thank you, Hannah. That will feel so good.

Jesus holds his foot up; sound of water running is heard as Hannah pours water.

Jesus: The roads are very dusty and hot.

Hannah hands Jesus' towel. Jesus begins drying his foot.

Martha: *(calling from stage right)* Jesus, is that you?

Martha enters stage right. Table rises stage right, near her.

Martha: Dinner is nearly ready.
Jesus: Thank you, Martha.

Jesus holds his second foot up; sound of water is heard as Hannah pours water. Hannah hands Jesus a towel. Jesus rubs his foot dry. Mary, Jesus, and maid exit stage left.

Martha turns to small table set with candle and fruit, admiring it.
Martha: I'm glad I finished this new tablecloth... and these new candles are exquisite. Jesus will enjoy this luscious, fresh fruit. Now if I can just get that bread baked in time and keep that chicken warm. Sure could have used Lazarus' and Cook's help today.

Martha exits. Table is lowered.

(U): *Sign with "One hour later" moves across stage.*
(L): *Large table is raised. Jesus, Mary, and Martha are seated at table finishing eating.*
Music plays as action begins, then fades.

Martha rises and begins clearing the table. Noise of dishes clattering is heard. Jesus hands Martha his plate. Mary and Jesus remain seated at the table.

Mary: There's a cool breeze coming in now. We'll just take our time; no need to rush dessert.
Jesus: That was a wonderful meal, Martha. Come back and sit with Mary and me.
Martha: I'll clear the table while the tea is steeping, Jesus. *(then, aside to Mary)* You *could* help.

More noise of dishes clattering, as Martha continues clearing the table.

Mary: Please. Leave the dishes on the table until later. Jesus has to go soon and I want to hear the latest on His kingdom.
Martha: Well, that's all very good *but (pauses while looking at and leaning toward Mary)* someone needs to watch the tea and *(pause)* I *(slight pause)* can do that while I'm cleaning the table.

Martha goes back and forth clearing the table. Jesus continues talking to Mary.

Jesus: Therefore I tell you, do not worry about your life; what you will eat or drink. Is not life more important than food? Look at the birds of the air. They do not sow or reap, yet your heavenly Father feeds them. Are you not much more valuable than they? Who of you by worrying can add a single hour to his life?

Martha: *(bringing dessert to the table)* Jesus, here is your favorite dessert—honey puffs.

Jesus: Thank you, Martha. That looks delicious.

Jesus leans back a bit as Martha places the plate in front of him.

Jesus: Bring Mary's and yours and sit down and eat with us. *(turns to Mary)* Mary, it is costly to...

Martha begins to leave, then returns, interrupting.

Martha: The tea is ready. *(aside to Mary)* Mary, you *could* bring it in.
Mary: *(ignoring Martha)* What was that Jesus—about cost?

Martha turns away, shaking her head in frustration, then turns back again and speaks.

Martha: *(angrily)* Lord, don't you care that my sister has left me to do all the work by myself?

Jesus begins moving toward Martha.

Martha: *(gesturing and becoming more emphatic as she goes along)* I killed the chicken, plucked, cleaned, and cooked it. I baked bread... twice! I sewed that new tablecloth, ran to the orchard for the fresh fruit, and even cleaned the foot-washing basin. And now, while I'm serving, Mary just sits here and listens to you. *(with tears in her voice)* Tell her to help me!

Martha leans over, her head on her arms on stage front, crying.

Jesus: *(going over to Martha and touching her shoulder)* Martha, Martha, you are worried and upset about many things, but only one thing is needed.

Martha turns toward Jesus.

Jesus: Mary has chosen the way to learn about the Kingdom of God.

Jesus returns to the table beside Mary. Martha alternates between hanging her head and looking toward Mary and Jesus, appearing to be thinking while Jesus speaks.

Jesus: And why do you worry about clothes? Consider how the lilies grow. They do not labor or spin. Yes, God clothes the grass of the field which is here today, and tomorrow is gone. Will he not much more clothe you, oh you of little faith?

Martha turns toward audience.

Martha: (*as if to herself*) Well, so what if they don't get their tea when it is best?

Martha stands there a bit longer, turns, and goes back toward table.

Martha: May I join you?

Jesus: Martha, (*pointing to chair*) this chair has been waiting just for you.

Martha sits.

Jesus: Now, where was I? Do not worry about saying, 'What shall we eat or what shall we drink,' but seek first God's Kingdom and his righteousness and all these things will be given to you as well. Therefore do not worry about tomorrow.

Martha: (*nodding*) I think I see what you mean. I'm sorry, Mary, for pushing you to help me, and forgive me, Jesus, for thinking the perfect dinner is the most important thing in life.

A knock sounds at the door. Martha rises and goes to look out of the window.

Martha: (*excitedly*) Our other guests have arrived! (*turning back from the window*) Let's join them on the rooftop and celebrate God's love together.

Mary and Jesus rise. Mary, Martha, and Jesus exit. Table is lowered.

Music up and then fades into introduction for concluding song.

Backdrop change: to #6 (city seen from the roof).

Scene 7: *The rooftop.*
(U): Peter, James, and John enter stage left.
(L): Mary and Martha enter stage center, followed by one large chicken.

All sing, King of Glory.[v]

(U): The disciples remain standing stage left, swaying with the beat as they sing.
(L): Mary, Martha, and the chicken sway with the beat. Mary and Martha occasionally raise their arms as they sing.

All: *(singing)*
>The earth is the Lord's in all its fullness
>The world and they who dwell therein
>Lift up your heads you gates and ancient doors
>That the King of Glory may come in.

(more quickly)
>Lift up your heads you gates and ancient doors
>That the King of Glory may come in.

(faster)
>Who is this King of Glory strong and mighty?
>Y'shua our Salvation, it is He!
>Who is this King of Glory? He's the Lord of Hosts.
>Y'shua HaMashiach, it is He!

Music plays part of song just sung, while the characters move back and forth across the stage doing high kicks in time to the beat and shouting 'Yo!' and 'Hey!' ending at stage left as the musical repeat finishes. They sing the next lines stage left, moving with the beat.

All: *(singing quite fast)*
>The King of Glory will come through the Eastern Gate
>Y'shua our Salvation, it is He!
>He will rule upon His Throne forevermore
>Y'shua HaMashiach, it is He!

He will rule upon His Throne forevermore
Y'shua HaMashiach, King of Glory it is He! *(all raise their arms)*

When the song is complete, all bow and exit.

The End.

APPENDIX THREE
MEMORIAL SERVICE

The following are excerpts from a transcription of the memorial service.

"I am going to stop here just for a moment because, although Aletha's text says 'I'm going to read it to you,' there are no verses written here because we know she did it from memory.

"That [ability to quote Scripture] was her gift to me. And so I would like to recite those verses." (Julie recited the Scripture from Luke 21:1-4.)

     —JULIE HORNOI, a woman who had been Aletha's prayer partner, reading
          from a talk Aletha had given at a ladies' meeting.

"Recently Mom had begun to study the small book *The Prayer of Jabez* by Bruce Wilkinson. This prayer is found in 1 Chronicles 4:9-10 and it reads like this, *'Oh, that you would bless me indeed and enlarge my territory. That your hand would be with me and that you would keep me from evil, that I may not cause pain. So God granted Jabez what he requested.'*"

"Mom highlighted these words, the prayer, in her little book and then personalized some of them in her journal. *'O that you would bless me indeed... lots. I want nothing more, nothing less than what God wants for me. I want to be wholly immersed in what God is trying to do in me, through me and around me for His Glory!'*"

"Mom's last puppet play was entitled *You are the Light of the World.* She was a light, and she would be saying to each of us, 'Go and light your world.'"

     —BETTE-JEAN HAND, Aletha's daughter, from a tribute.

•• ◆ ••

"I still remember Aletha giving me notes of encouragement as the pastor here at Parliament. She was very faithful in that and I've kept them. I remember one that really struck me as she was telling me how she prayed for me throughout the week. For each day there was a certain thing that she prayed for in my life—for my ministry as a pastor, my role as a father, my role as a husband, for my wife, and for my children. I've never forgotten that, and I hope that torch is passed on because it certainly has been a strength in my life."

"In Randy Alcorn's novel *Deadline*, he tells a story of a slave who tried to outrun death. He couldn't. The writer of the Old Testament book of Ecclesiastes records for us the brevity of life and the surety of death. He writes like this: *'There's a time for everything. A season for every activity under heaven: a time to be born, and a time to die.[i] ...Man's fate is like that of animals, the same fate awaits them both. As one dies so dies the other. ... All go to the same place. All come from dust, and to dust all return. ...[ii] Death is the destiny of every person. The living should take this to heart.[iii]*

"I don't know about you, but that sounds mighty depressing to me, if that's all there is to this life and life after death. I would be overwhelmingly steeped in despair if that was all there was. It's not that the writer of Ecclesiastes has told us something that isn't true. There will come a time for us to die. We can't outrun it. Unless the Lord returns, we will all experience physical death.

"Thankfully, there is more. Praise God, in fact, there is more. There are words of great hope found in the Bible. Words like those of the apostle Paul. *'We know that the same God who raised our Lord Jesus will also raise us with Jesus and present us to himself along with you, ...for the troubles we see will soon be over but the joys to come will last forever.'[iv]*

"The apostle Paul wrote this passage to the Christians in the city of Corinth, and in essence he was encouraging them that despite all their hardships, and even in expectation of death for their faith, they should not give up. They should not lose heart. For just as God raised up Jesus from the grave, so too the promise holds that God would raise believers up with Jesus, to God himself."

"Those who follow Jesus in life will not remain in the grave at death. They will be raised just as Jesus was raised, and they will have a great joy that will last forever. That's the promise. This earthly tent, this physical body that we wear around us, with all its wonderful abilities and its many limitations, will

---

[i] From Ecclesiastes 3:1-2 (NIV).
[ii] From Ecclesiastes 3:19-21 (NIV).
[iii] From Ecclesiastes 7:2b (NIV).
[iv] From 2 Corinthians 4:14-5: 5 (NLT).

one day fold and be exchanged for an eternal home, an eternal body fashioned by God himself. You want good news? That's good news!"

"I believe Aletha expressed a deep desire to be clothed with her heavenly body as she saw her earthly tent begin to fold. I recall Glenn sitting down with J.J. in the hospital as Aletha was near death and in that soft and gentle voice, told his grandson, 'Grandma did not want to live like this. She much rather wanted to live with Jesus, with a new body and a place where she won't suffer.'

"You see Aletha recognized that her body could only go so far. It could only endure so long. And then she would have to leave it behind. Aletha's hope wasn't in her body's strength and it wasn't in the doctor's skills, and it wasn't in the many medicines she was given. Aletha's hope was in Jesus, who said, *'I am the resurrection and the life and whoever believes in me will live even though he dies.'*[v]

"How is it with us? Are we prepared for the time when our earthly tent will fold? Death is not the end for those who trust in Jesus. It's just the beginning. For followers of Jesus, death does not take us away from home, it brings us home. Aletha Mary Joice is home, and in this we rejoice. We will miss her very much. Aletha lived in such a way that her life became a beacon for others, a beacon pointing to the light of the world, Jesus."

From his concluding prayer: "Our heavenly Father, we give you unending thanks for welcoming Aletha home. We thank you that there is hope when our earthly tent folds. And we thank you, Lord, for the testimony that Aletha gave, the confidence and the trust she had in you despite the shadow of death. And Lord, as we remember her life, we give you thanks for it. And we pray that we would have the courage she had to be beacons for the Light of the world, too. Lord, thank you for allowing us to have this celebration together. May your grace abound... this day and in the days to follow. We ask all these things in Jesus' wonderful name. Amen."

—*Pastor Phil Gunther, minister, from the sermon.*

---

[v] From John 11:25 (NIV).

APPENDIX FOUR
LASTING IMPRESSIONS

In Ecclesiastes 7:1, the Bible talks about a good reputation, or a good name, being better than perfume or costly ointment. What people remember about a person with a good reputation are the characteristics the person possessed. The characteristics, or the perfume, of a good reputation are not portrayed without cost. They are worked at over a lifetime.

The memories people have of the first time they met Aletha and the words they used to describe her in the years that followed are filled with adjectives, words describing her appearance, her personality, her character traits, and her love for the Lord and those around her.

These impressions of who Aletha Joice was are the result of her life's work, striving to reflect the character of God.

IMPRESSIONS

"I clearly remember my first contact with her. She was open and friendly and very cooperative and encouraging. There was a sweetness of spirit about her, and I enjoyed her ready laugh—or perhaps I should call it a chuckle. There was a peaceful gentleness about her as well. I thought she was very pretty. My first impression of her did not change, only deepened. She was consistent through all the years I knew her. I got to enjoy that chuckle more and more. She got such a charge out of things, certainly an endearing quality. She was never combative or out for her own interests."

–BETTY ANDERSON, *friend*

"When we watched the relationship Aletha and Glenn had with each other we saw... a loving relationship, a mutual respect. We saw that she served him and he served her, it wasn't just Aletha serving him. Her friendliness, pleasant disposition. Her desire to serve the Lord in every aspect of her life created a sense of her being a Godly woman. She seemed to be in touch with the heart of God. She could draw things out of Scriptures that were meaningful."

—GARRY AND RITA MAE BRAUN, missionaries to Mali

"She always encouraged, always had the time, made you feel she was genuinely happy to see you. She seemed to sense when someone needed something. I was a new Christian... She never made an assumption about what I knew, like did I know there were two books of John? I didn't, but she never made me feel inadequate because I didn't. She encouraged me specifically to memorize Scripture. She would ask me to recite the verse she gave me the week before. She was loving. She made me feel part of the church family because she invited me to something with her circle of friends, like Glenn's birthday party with their closest friends."

—DOREEN BUTTERFIELD, friend

"I have tried to learn from her. It is not my natural characteristic to want to show an interest in people, stay in contact, show them you care what they are up to. I want to follow her example."

—JOSH BEKKER, puppeteer God Squad alumni and friend

"She was very thorough, at Bible study in particular. She carried herself in a gentle way—you knew she wouldn't be abrasive. I remember her as soft-hearted, generous. She was empathetic. At mission committee meetings, when it was her turn to do the devotional, she couldn't get through it without breaking down. If I ever would want to emulate someone—it would be her. She knew her Bible. It was full of notes in the margin."

—MARILYN DYCK, fellow Missions Committee member

"Aletha was a beautiful person! ... She has impacted my life, particularly in how I view people and the value of the church.

"Aletha was always there during crisis moments in my life... She never gave me advice, but would just smile and touch my shoulder or give me a quick hug. It says much about her lovely spirit, that those few moments each week conveyed to me immense sincerity and compassion and caring. She helped to teach me the value of the church body during those times.

"After my miscarriage, she sent notes that again demonstrated her care. I learned that things done with a genuine love matter and I found her genuineness was transparent.

"I attended a Bible study she led one year... In particular I remember her insights about how God uses difficult times to strengthen and expand our faith.

"When I prayed for Aletha these past months, I prayed for her joy. When I talked to her and received a letter from her, she always continued to affirm and encourage me. She said that she too had felt that God wanted her to have joy in her circumstances."

−VICKI CLARKE, from a sympathy card sent to Glenn

"Finally, please know that I have been praying daily for you and your family to know God's peace and joy. It seems strange to me at times that I sense God wanting me to pray that you will know more than His presence and His rest and His peace, but that in all you find yourself, I'm to pray for you to know His joy. May it be so.

"I was looking for a verse to pray through as I prayed for you and I felt God gave me Romans 15:13, 'May the God of hope fill you (and your family) with all joy and peace as you trust in him so that you may over flow with hope by the power of the Holy Spirit.'"

−VICKI CLARKE, from a letter she sent to Aletha with the Mother of the Year nomination

"Her gentle nature, soft spoken. She never put herself forward—drew attention to herself."

−KATHLEEN FISHER, fellow library worker

"She was a kind, loving person and a good example of Godliness."

−TIM FRIESEN, puppeteer God Squad alumni from the last troupe

"Aletha impressed me as very caring, concerned for others. Dedicated."

− JANEY GOERTZEN, fellow library committee member

"She showed she cared about your answer when she asked how your week or weekend had been."

−JARED GOERTZEN, reader for the performance of "Martha's Folly"

"Kind, hard working, for example in God Squad. She cared about people—especially what was going on in their lives. She was supportive. She and Glenn

helped me out a number of times—the Mexico missions trip, camp—both financial and prayer support."

—ANDREW REDDEKOPP, *puppeteer God Squad alumni*

"Aletha, you were and are a woman of prayer. I remember you showing me
long ago your prayer journal. What a blessing and challenge that was for me.

"Oswald Chambers said, 'It is impossible to live the life of a disciple
without definite times of secret prayer. You will find that the place to enter in is
in your business, as you walk along the streets, in the ordinary ways of life,
when no one dreams you are praying and the reward comes openly, a revival
here, a blessing there.'

"Aletha, I believe this to be true in your journey—you prayed for many and
my name was often lifted to God by you. Thank you so very much! God has
given me a ministry of prayer since that has happened. I often think of you as
the seed that was planted so long ago by you. Thank your Aletha for being God's
child and being such an example for me and many others.

"With prayers for your safe journey to our Father. Aletha, enjoy the trip.
God is saying, 'Well done Aletha, enter!'"

—LAVERNA GRANDFIELD, *from a letter she sent Aletha on May 25, 2001*

"She was strict, upright—prim would be the word—and proper, everything
just so. As an adult, I still saw the stately 'aura', but she was a person you could
relate to. I appreciated her more."

—HEATHER MILLER, *puppeteer God Squad alumni and family friend*

"A dedicated Christian. Aletha was always the same.
She was a 'bright light,' a spiritual example.
Efficient, well-organized, very friendly, always positive.
She treated everything like a ministry.
She always put a lot of effort into what she did.
She was a pleasant, pleasant person to be with.
She was a great reader, often the librarian."

—VIVIAN NORBRATEN, *friend and fellow Christian Women's Club member*

"Those days together in CWC are my happiest memories. We always spoke
of our families and were genuinely interested and concerned. When we got
together for lunch or coffee during these later years, we talked about our homes,

families, and our faith. I think of her positive, gentle, and enthusiastic attitude. She was an example to me and such a support in her own quiet way."

—VIVIAN NORBRATEN, *from a sympathy letter to Glenn and family*

"We loved being with her. You could confide in her wisdom, understanding, and Godliness. Her consistency—no wavering in her faith and her standards. Her faithful steadfastness, no matter what happened in her life. It was wonderful to have her as a friend.

"She had the ability to relate to all ages. She had a young spirit, which didn't change. That was evidenced by the number of young people at her funeral.

"She always had a strong faith, was gracious, kind, warm (sincere), fun-loving (sense of humor, laughed easily), had high standards, was well-organized, and prepared for the things she did. She felt there was no reason to do a poor job—not for her own glory but for the Lord's. She didn't do something unless she could do her best."

—DOUG AND EILEEN REIMCHE, *family friends*

"Aletha was an example of how, even though people in the churches you attend change, the community continues. The people in the churches are responsible for missionaries. God gave me special people in each church, holding me accountable to them. God gave continuity to me through her.

"It's interesting how important she was to me, even though I only saw her one or two times in three years. I never had a picture of her except the church directory. We were not 'buddies,' but she was an important connection to the church for me."

—LYNN SCHELLENBERG, *missionary to Liberia*

"Wise, a good advisor for a personal or family problem. She impressed me with her skill. She was authentic, a mature Christian, solid in her faith. A 'real' person. She was consistent—in her faith, her attitude, her friendship. I am sure she had her ups and downs like all the rest of us, but... yeah, consistent is a good word. The word consistent is also part of responsible, dependable, and being able to count on her. She radiated Christ.

"She was a good singer (sang contralto). One time, the four of us friends[i] sang together as a quartet. We did it once—a once in a lifetime experience.

---

[i] Irene was referring to Betty, Vivian, Aletha, and herself.

"When I was ill, this was before Aletha was ill, she supported me. She sent me a note every week for several weeks, letting me know she cared."

—IRENE SOTROPA, *friend and fellow Christian Women's Club member*

"The day we found out that Bobby Jo had kidney failure, Mom needed something dropped off at Aletha's. I went there for Mom and Aletha was so kind, she stopped at that moment and prayed with me for Bobby Jo and our family. It meant so much to me at that time. I thought of her as someone who really cared. Very sensitive to the needs of others. She was very efficient, her walk with the Lord was very important to her. She was always concerned about how she affected others to spur them on in their walk."

—DONNA STENZIL, *former library committee worker and missionary in San Diego*

"She was a hard worker—consistent, a good student. Everyone knew of her love for books and learning. She had determination. She thought through a project and then persevered. For example with God Squad."

—ELAINE WALRATH, *friend*

"Very sincere, genuine, serious about her relationship with God. It always amazed me when she told stories about her childhood and her brothers, that there was a mischievous side to her which didn't come out when you first met her. She had a strong faith. I remember the most momentous time at Bible Study when she told us that cancer had recurred and that she wasn't praying for healing. She was so at peace with it."

—ELAINE WIENS, *Women's Bible study group member*

"She was busy in lots of things. She had a deep commitment to missionaries, had a lot to do with her whole family. Always happy—happy to be alive, an optimistic attitude. Godly. She wanted to do what God wanted her to do."

—JULIE SIEMENS, *Mennonite Central Committee worker in Kentucky*

"She provided an excellent role model for me to follow; one that could be applied to everyday life. I knew that her willingness to serve Jesus was a daily, hourly, and by the minute endeavor not only through God's work that we did through puppetry, but through all the other groups she was involved with and her extreme commitment to prayer. I also appreciated the way she corrected and taught us. She was always positive, and when she told us to do things differently it was always with patience."

—JARED WIENS, *puppeteer God Squad Alumni*

"Dedicated is a good word to describe her. She was dedicated to the Lord and any cause she was working on. She was a special person all right. She was perceptive. When she was no longer able to work with Friendship Bible Coffees, she gave her archived records to a woman who Aletha felt would keep it and pass it on if ever the time came that someone wanted to use it."

—SONJA WEIR, *fellow Friendship Bible Coffee Coordinator*

"She showed a warm hospitality, genuine (knew it was from the heart, because she cared). She laughed a lot, was so happy. Had a good sense of humor. She felt that if, with some effort, you could do an average job, why not put out a bit more effort and do a professional job? She said it was not done for your own glory, but for the benefit of serving. She made it fun to do."

— GAVIN AND AUDREY WOOD, *family friends*

"Devoted. She made detailed charts of the scenario, countless pages of notes. The puppet uniforms were a lot of work. She knew what was going on."

—TYLER WOOD, *puppeteer God Squad Alumni*

GLOSSARY

Term	Meaning/Explanation
anti-anti-over	A game played by two teams or two individuals. A ball was thrown over the roof of a building while one player called out, "Anti-anti-over" (or, as it would often come out, "Annie-annie-over"). The players on the opposite side caught it and ran around the building to try and tag their opponents, before they got back around to their own side. Tagging was accomplished through the unpredictability of which direction the players would come around the building, and how long it would take until it happened.
doctor sticks	Tongue depressors.
email cafe	Cubicles where people can pay to use computers to access the Internet.
ghetto blaster	A portable stereo, which was a combination of radio and audio cassette player.
mince/mincing	To mince is to walk in an elegant (very upright and regal) way, taking short steps.
pointer	White-tipped, retractable lecture tool, usually made of metal.
popcorn feast	Popcorn made from homegrown popping corn, eaten along with homemade ice cream.
riser	Small bench, on which a puppeteers knelt to be high enough to show puppets over the top of the stage curtain. They were required on account of the puppeteers being too tall when standing and too short to reach properly whilst kneeling on the floor.

roughing   Roughhousing, including rough play like wrestling.

voiceover   Person speaking lines for a character (puppet) during a recording of a video, while not visible in the scene.

BIBLIOGRAPHY

BOOKS

"Crazy Quilts"
by Penny McNorris 1984
E.P. Dutton, Inc.
2 Park Ave.
New York, NY 10016
pp. 10

"Quilts and Other Bed Coverings in the Canadian Tradition"
by Ruth McKendry
Van Norstrand Reinhold Ltd. Toronto 1979
Van Norstrand Reinhold
115—5th Ave.
New York, NY 10003
pp. 38, 39, 40, 46, 50, 95-97, 118

"An Introduction to Keeping Sheep"
by Jane Upton and Dennis Soden
Family Press Books
Miller Freeman Professional Ltd.
Warfedole Road, Ipswich IP1 4LG
United Kingdom
Second Edition 1996
p. 71

"Puppet Theatre in Performance"
by Nancy H. Cole
William Morrow and Company, Inc.
105 Madison Av.
New York, New York 10016
1978
pp. 10-22

Minister's Manual
Faith & Life Press
600 Shaftsbury Blvd.
Winnipeg, MB R3P 0M4
1983
p. 84

"A Saga of Souris Valley"
Compiled by:
Souris Valley Historical Club (Gladys McNeil)
Published by: Souris Valley No. 7 History Club, Box 22, Oungre,
Saskatchewan
Printed by: Friesen Printers, Altona, MB

"Puppets and Puppeteering"
by Robert Ten Eyck Hanford
Sterling Publishing Co. Inc.
Two Park Avenue
New York, New York 10016
1976

"Puppetry: The Ultimate Disguise
by George Latshaw
Richards Rosen Press, Inc.
29 East 21st St.
New York, N.Y. 10010
1978

"The Story Goes On"
by Helen Duff Baugh
Published by: Stonecroft Ministries
PO Box 9609
Kansas City, Missouri 64134

"A Lambing Season In Ireland—Tales of a Vet's Wife"
Coffey, Maria
McArthur & Company
322 King St. West, Suite 402
Toronto, ON M5V 1J2

MAGAZINES/ CATALOGUES

"Best Wishes"
Box 8, Postal ST. C
Toronto 3, Ont.

Puppet Productions
PO Box 1066
DeSoto, TX 75123-1066

One Way Street
P.O. Box 5077
Englewood, CO 80155-5077

UNPUBLISHED PAPERS

Aletha's Writings

- Journals—dated 1979-2001 (prayers, personal study notes).
- Notations from Aletha's Bible margins.
- God Squad records.
- Bible Study preparation notes for Women's Bible studies at Parliament.
- *My Confrontation with Death and Life*—testimony booklet.

Aletha's Presentations

- Dialogue—CWC presentation, made together with Bette-Jean.
- Granny Talk—presentation made at a ladies' Christmas function.
- Devotional at a baby shower—presented at Parliament Community Church.
- Talk about family devotions—presented at Parliament Community Church.

"Marion Larson's Family History"
Larson, Marion (provided by Gini Larson).
A 72-page, spiral-bound volume of typewritten text, photocopied for the family. Undated.

The F.I. Rogers Family
Smith (Shultz), Fleda, daughter of Franklin Irvine (F.I.) Rogers.
A four-page personal memoir of the family. Undated.

ARCHIVES
Leader Post
- An article about Aletha being the speaker at a Christian Women's club banquet. Published December 13, 1975.

Christian Women's Club Archived Files
- Unpublished organizational notes of CWC while Aletha was involved.
- Notes loaned courtesy of Vivian Norbraten.

ENDNOTES

[1] Bette-Jean Hand, daughter of Aletha; initially interviewed Mar. 16, 2002; with follow up interviews conducted by phone.

[2] Bob Joice, Aletha's son; interviewed Mar. 11, 2002, with short follow-up interviews, in person and by phone.

[3] Elaine Walrath, friend; interviewed Apr. 09, 2002 by phone.

[4] Eileen (Mrs. Doug) Reimche, family friend; interviewed Apr. 13, 2002.

[5] Dr. Wayne Hindmarsh, former student of Aletha's (Gr. 4); interviewed Feb. 11, 2002 by letter.

[6] Glenn Joice, Aletha's husband; initially interviewed Oct. 2001, with short follow-up interviews, in person and by phone.

[7] Dawna Friesen, friend; interviewed Mar. 24, 2002.

[8] Audrey (Mrs. Gavin) Wood, family friend; interviewed Aug. 30, 2002.

[9] Jason Unrah, youth pastor at Parliament Community Church; interviewed Feb. 02, and Mar. 07, 2002.

[10] Shelley Joice, Aletha's daughter-in-law; interviewed Mar. 11, 2002, and various short follow-up interviews, in person and by phone.

[11] Bobby Jo Stenzil, friend; interviewed Apr. 02, 2002.

[12] Jake Joice, Aletha's grandson, interviewed Apr. 04, 2002.

[13] Janey Goertzen, fellow library committee member; interviewed Mar. 28, 2002.

[14] Marilyn Dyck, fellow missions Committee member; interviewed Apr. 09, 2002.

[15] Helen Braun, friend; fellow Missions Committee member, interviewed Feb. 05, 2002.

[16] Doreen Butterfield, friend; interviewed May 07, 2002.

[17] Josh Bekker, puppeteer, friend of Aletha; interviewed Apr. 16, 2002.

[18] Carolyn (Tim) Gartke, missionaries to Lithuania; interviewed May 13, 2002 by phone.

[19] Julie (Mrs. Scott) Siemens, missionary with MCC; interviewed Apr. 21, 2002.

[20] Garry and Rita Mae Braun, missionaries, interviewed Apr. 10, 2002.

[21] Nancy Jo (Mrs. Cory Ziegler) Russell, missionary; interviewed Feb. 17, 2002.

[22] Sonja Weir, fellow CWC committee member; interviewed Feb. 07, 2002.

[23] Irene Sotropa, friend; interviewed Mar. 24, 2002.

[24] Vivian Norbraten, friend of Aletha; initially interviewed Mar. 25, 2002 with follow-up questions at various other times.

[25] Betty Anderson, friend of Aletha, interviewed Mar. 16, 2002 by letter.

[26] Lynn Schellenberg, missionary to Liberia; interviewed Apr. 23, 2002 by telephone.

[27] Trever and Joan Godard, missionaries to Columbia; interviewed May. 2, 2002 by letter.

[28] Walter (Wally) & Arlene Schroeder, memorial service readers; Arlene-church secretary - first phone call for information and help Apr. 2002; various other phone calls later.

[29] Heather (Campbell) Miller, puppeteer and friend, interviewed Apr. 14, 2002.

[30] Andrew Reddekopp, puppeteer; interviewed Apr. 20, 2002.

[31] Grant Sawatzky, puppeteer; interviewed Sept. 20, 2002 (Sunday School class).

[32] Tyler Wood, puppeteer, family friend: interviewed Apr. 08, 2002.

[33] Janelle Gagnon, puppeteer; interviewed Aug. 06, 2002.

[34] Mary Lou Sheppard, puppeteer; interviewed Mar. 12, 2002.

[35] Kris Gowdy, puppeteer, family friend; interviewed Mar. 16, 2002 by letter.

[36] Tina (Gowdy) Cowie, puppeteer, family friend; interviewed Mar. 15, 2002 by letter.

[37] Jayne Werry, puppeteer and friend; interviewed Mar. 24, 2002.

[38] Kathleen Fisher, fellow library committee member; interviewed Apr. 02, 2002.

[39] Jacqui Gagnon, puppeteer; interviewed Aug. 06, 2002.

[40] Krista Bekker, puppeteer; friend of Aletha, interviewed Sept. 20, 2002.

[41] Jim Slough, video recording and production of video for "Martha's Folly"; interviewed Mar. 22, 2002.

[42] Don Hand, Bette-Jean's husband, (Aletha's son-in-law); interviewed Mar. 16, 2002.

[43] Doreen Smith, friend and seamstress; interviewed May 04, 2002 , with phone calls later.

[44] Jared Goertzen, reader for video recording of "Martha's Folly"; interviewed Apr. 23, 2002.

[45] Trevor Friesen, puppeteer; interviewed Sept. 20, 2002.

[46] Ryan Friesen, puppeteer; interviewed Sept. 20, 2002.

[47] Jared Wiens, puppeteer; interviewed Sept. 20, 2002 (Sunday School class).

[48] Laura Barton, puppeteer; interviewed Jan. 21. 2003.

[49] Tim Friesen, puppeteer; interviewed Sept. 20, 2002.

[50] Elaine Wiens, friend, Women's Group; interviewed Mar. 19, 2002.

Printed in the United States
151951LV00005B/2/P